CHILDREN
of the DECREE

A Journalist's Battle to Save Romanian Orphans and Herself

A Memoir by
MARIA D. HOLDERMAN

Copyright 2024

©Maria D. Holderman

Front Cover picture: Michael Caroll, ©1998
Cover Design: Bogdan Baciu
Photo Author: C.C. Otiliu

All rights reserved. No part of this book may be reproduced in any manner whatsoever without written permission from the author except in the case of brief quotations embodied in critical articles and reviews.

This is a nonfiction book reflecting the author's perspective. Some names and locations have been changed to protect the confidentiality and privacy of some persons. Some dialog has been reconstructed to the best of the author's recollection, and some time frames have been condensed or intentionally omitted. This is not a legal work, but instead the author's personal investigations which have been published or aired in Romania between 1996 and 2001.

To D., my greatest and last love.

To Lyman and Tata, may you protect all of us from heaven.

To my children, Roger and Catherine, with all my love.

To all the countless children adopted or disappeared from Romanian orphanages: Please, forgive us!

"The author is part of a generation of heartfelt and passionate journalists who worked tirelessly in the press.

Just liberated from a totalitarian and oppressed regime, during the '90s, Romania was walking the very steps toward democracy. Many of us just started to learn the rules of a free world. True to justice and with an incorruptible mind, Dana Achim—her name during that time—worked fearlessly for finding the truth, especially for human rights. She'd fought for revealing corruption, injustice, and the mistakes of a still vulnerable justice system. I wish her good luck in her career and hope she'd keep her heartfelt passion in promoting the democratic values."
—Emil Constantinescu, Ph.D., Former Romanian President, 1996-2000

"How can we change the world to make it better? The author of this book has a simple answer: don't be indifferent to injustice. She followed her wisdom not only through words but with actions, and not only in Romania but in the United States as well."
—Valeriu Stoica, Former Minister of Justice, Romania, 1996-2000

"A former reporter and TV personality in Romania, Maria tells the story of her marriage to an American from Vermont. Soon after arriving, her life changes to one of struggle when her new husband dies, leaving her pregnant, broke, and struggling with language barriers. At the center of a family feud, her story becomes one of survival and ultimate success with the new life she carves out in America."
—Rita Marie Robinson, author of *Ordinary Women, Extraordinary Wisdom: The Feminine Face of Awakening*

"Maria's memoir drops you into a world you will never forget, from a magical childhood in Romania to a love story that unfolds in America. The path of love is not smooth, but the author's engaging spirit triumphs over all obstacles to achieve outstanding success in her new country."
—Linda Joy Myers, Ph.D., President, National Association of Memoir Writers, and author of *Don't Call Me Mother* and *The Power of Memoir*

"Maria's work as an investigative journalist has helped to change two laws in the Department of Justice—one for jailbirds, and one for the international adoptions. Who would ever believe that a petite, fragile woman would fight so intelligently to have these laws reviewed? The downside of her work was the price she assumed and had to pay. It was her destiny. A fate that meant something for the malfunctioning Romanian judicial system, and for the future of many people of Romania."
—Ana Savu, Producer, National TV, Romania

"Maria was the 2011 Vermont Teacher of the Year when we met her at the NASA International Space Camp. She has the same passion for telling her story as she does to help her students find their potential. We all encouraged her to write it."
—Marian Gilmore, CEO, Steam Powered Learning

"In this book, the fighter looks back, to heal her traumas to bring to light, for her international public, a story about never giving up. Her brand of hopeful idealism is never obsolete—she is trying to show us that we only need to find something worth fighting for."
—Liana Anderson, Scholar, University of Texas.

Acknowledgments

This book would not have been possible without the feedback of my first supporters and readers.

First, I want to thank my friends and co-workers in Romania who believed in me: Adina Mutar and Ana Savu—you inspired me. I will always be thankful to and think fondly of my boss at the National Daily, Gheorghe Voicu, for giving me the opportunity to continue my investigations. May he rest in peace.

To Kelly Rainville and Kim Hamel: you cherished my work since I first began! I am grateful and honored to have had you by my side in those days.

To Holly Hiller: your eye for details and sensitivity, coupled with your insightful questions elicited more details, helped make this book what it is. I miss you!

To all the Binders: you rock!

And, to Janis Couvreux. Since I interviewed you, you became my go-to person when I was about to give up.

To my American angels Pam Wade, Gwen Bailey-Rowe, and my Canadian friend Janet Hartley: I can't thank you enough for your kindness, love, and support when I had none.

To Jack and Joyce St Sauveur, may you rest in peace.

To my sister Livia: you always believed in me when I couldn't see the light. Your unconditional love surrounds me every day. This book is for you!

To Dale, my better half, my soul mate, and my best friend: I didn't believe you could show me that love doesn't have an age. I look forward to growing old with you.

And to my children, Roger Lyman and Catherine Victoria (Vicky): I owe you a lot. Without your love and support I couldn't find myself. I love you all.

Foreword

Sometimes, it is easier to make up a story than to tell yours—the story of your life. Many fiction writers hide little truths behind fictitious characters, but when you expose your life publicly, you are vulnerable. People will ask questions and judge you for your choices and the road you took.

When you choose to leave behind your friends, family, country, and home—practically everything that you have and are—you must have a strong reason to make this decision. An impossible decision to make, but a necessary decision to survive.

Dana was a journalist in Romania and often fought for the underprivileged with tough press campaigns. In her hope for a better world, she fought the system and was successful in forcing change. But, at one moment in her life, she chose a different path. "Why?" I will let her answer that question in her book.

Dana's story is like other peoples who were forced to leave their families and friends behind and start a new life thousands of miles away. For those who experienced this hardship or not, this meant giving up everything of value in their life.

Like every story that falls into this category, I believe that Dana's story shows us one more time that no matter how many obstacles you must overcome, there is nothing to stop you from capturing your dreams. This story shows us that hard work, perseverance, and faith in ourselves can bring us where we want to be. It shows us that we are strong—even when we don't feel we are, in peaceful times. It shows us that if we don't give up, we can adjust to a new world and can prove who we are, gaining trust and appreciation.

I congratulate Dana for the courage to tell her story and show us how she made it in America. I commend her for showing us that it is possible to achieve what you want, even in the most unbearable moments of her life. Don't get me wrong—I don't encourage you to leave everything behind and run away anywhere in this world. My message is to invite you to follow your dream wherever you are, by working hard. Only this way you can show who you are and what you can do. And no matter how hard it is, never give up your dream!

Nadia Comaneci
Romanian Gymnast
First Perfect 10, Montreal, 1976

Table of Contents

Prologue: Conditional Alien...	1
Chapter One...	9
Chapter Two...	17
Chapter Three...	25
Chapter Four..	37
Chapter Five...	43
Chapter Six...	59
Chapter Seven...	67
Chapter Eight..	81
Chapter Nine...	91
Chapter Ten..	105
Chapter Eleven..	113
Chapter Twelve...	123
Chapter Thirteen..	129
Chapter Fourteen...	137
Chapter Fifteen..	145
Chapter Sixteen...	157
Chapter Seventeen...	167
Chapter Eighteen...	179
Chapter Nineteen...	191
Chapter Twenty...	203
Chapter Twenty-One...	213
Chapter Twenty-Two...	225
Chapter Twenty-Three...	243
Chapter Twenty-Four..	255
Epilogue..	269

Maria D. Holderman

Conditional Alien
New York, April 2001

A war raged behind me. One I'd yet to escape.

Trapped in my seat as our plane was grounded on the LaGuardia Airport runway for five hours, my paranoia had nearly consumed me. I hunkered beneath my tattered navy-blue blanket every time anyone moved or even dared glance my way, for fear I might be recognized.

Despite being in America, I didn't feel safe.

Back in Bucharest, Colonel Dan Bota had warned me that he was watching as always. He'd reached out the day before my departure from Romania, his ominous voice crackling across the phone line. I could picture his front gold teeth reflecting the light on the pay phone in the prison.

"Happy marriage! Send me a card when you arrive. Enjoy the mountains. Sign it with the initials of your novel's heroine," he said before hanging up, offering no chance to question how he'd learned his information.

A chill crept down my spine as I glanced over at Lyman, my husband of only two weeks, as he slept peacefully.

We'd kept it a secret...or so I believed.

Yet, the Colonel had known. He'd known everything, from inside the maximum-security prison near Bucharest. Even that I'd changed my name. I was no longer *Dana Achim*, a Romanian investigative journalist for the *National Daily* and a show producer on a news channel.

Not even Lyman knew my real full name.

I slunk lower in my seat, desperate to disappear, to vanish. Any one of the passengers aboard the plane could be an agent of the colonel, and I wouldn't know it until it was too late.

With nowhere to go, stuck in a plane on a frozen tarmac, my blood ran colder than the frigid temperatures outside. But I didn't know that yet. Every moment crept fearfully by, every cough or shuffle of feet in the cramped plane startled me, making me think it might be my *last* moment.

Despite nearly five thousand miles between us, the Colonel still loomed over my shoulder, watching or waiting. I thought I was being paranoid because no one was paying attention to me. And while I fortified myself, believing in my safety now, the thought of danger kept me awake and keenly aware of my plight.

Then, finally, when my heart felt as though it might bruise my ribs, the plane jerked forward, and we were rolling again. The pilot's voice came across the intercom: "Welcome to New York…" The words echoed in my mind.

I cast a furtive glance around, examining my fellow passengers one by one through the crack between the seats.

I've made it, I thought optimistically as no leering eyes stared back at me.

Now, my job was to hold on the sealed yellow envelope from the American Embassy in Bucharest that I had been instructed not to open. It was my shield against the storm. It contained my documents, including the clearance from the Romanian Police, and my medical history.

People passed us, but we turned right and followed the directions to the *Immigration and Naturalization* office. My heart clenched with every step until we reached a dead end. It was dark and foreboding. The dimly lit hallway and translucent windows were meant to keep curious eyes out.

At the door, a bold, goateed officer checked my passport meticulously. He flipped through the pages to the last one—my temporary visa—then looked at my picture, and then at me, and then gave me a ticket and said to take a seat until my number was called. Lyman showed him his passport and said he was with me, which sped up the process for him. Then the guard opened the door, and I walked in, squeezing the thick envelope from the American Embassy to my chest.

My first impression was that the place looked like Bucharest First District's courtroom I'd seen three weeks earlier, when I had to testify. Cold sweat dripped under my shirt then and now, as I relived the moment when my lawyers had taken me out and had raced down city streets until we'd lost the mafia and the Colonel's secret service followers.

That evening, I accepted Lyman's marriage proposal. *Would I be here if I hadn't been under that threat? Probably*, I thought, but I was in love, and that was reason enough to cross the ocean and start over anew.

The only thing missing now was my family. Afraid I'd burst into tears, I tried not to think of my mother. Doing that wasn't easy, I'd soon figure out. My last image of her was her standing in front of the house in my own town. Her deer eyes, were wide and wet, as if she was asking, "What will I do without you?" Tata's gentle wave as we walked away, his red eyes, and then the grin he'd tried unsuccessfully. I was sure they didn't sleep that night.

But what will I do without them around?

The staleness of the room struck me, sweat and fear, mine and others', and I pulled the collar of my sweater over my nose and inhaled the floral Versace scent clinging to the fibers to clear my nose. Lyman looked around and led me to the only chair available in the front row.

"Sit, baby," he told me. I hesitated, measuring the waiting room, and estimated about a hundred people were in there already. Cold sweat dripped down my spine, and as I sat the headache cracked in my ears. There was the sound of an overheated engine. An explosion.

He stood next to me, and from my seat, I saw his pale face in the yellow light. He'd grown a five o'clock shadow, the first time I'd seen it, and I wanted to touch his face.

As if he read my mind, he took my hand and kissed it. It electrified my body, even as tired as I was. He might not have known my secret yet, but that didn't stop him from being worried. There was always a chance I could be turned back. *I'll tell him the whole story*, I promised, knowing that I would.

A short officer passed us, escorting two handcuffed blondes in their mid-twenties to seats in the back. Both girls were a foot taller than the officer behind them, and I could hear the clank of the leg chains jangling as they walked by, so I covered my ears. A few moments later, three Asian men were escorted to the back row, each one handcuffed and shackled at their legs. They walked slowly as if buying time to reach the last row. I felt Lyman's palm on my head as if he wanted to tell me he was there, and all would be fine. At least, he knew that much about how I felt. *Where am I?* I felt as if I were back in prison. If I had counted the time I'd spent there, I wouldn't be wrong saying I served a year behind bars.

When my number was called, Lyman took my hands from my ears and wanted to come with me, but at the door an officer told him, "Only her."

A somnolent man behind the glass window took the envelope and unsealed it. "Raise your hand and repeat after me, 'I solemnly affirm that the evidence that I shall give shall be the truth, the whole truth, and nothing but the truth.'"

I barely remembered the first words, my hand up, heart pounding, as he asked, "Have you ever been in prison?"

"As a reporter."

He looked at some papers, then to me. "Have you ever been sentenced?"

"No. But…"

"You answer *yes* or *no*. Have you ever been sentenced?" he repeated. His voice was harsh, demanding.

"No."

"Where were you born?"

"Dragasani, Romania."

He then took X-rays of my lungs and looked at them in the lamplight. I had no idea what he was looking for, my head spinning. *What else is there?*

While the officer sorted my papers, I recognized the form Lyman had completed at my house in Bucharest—Form I-130, Petition for Alien Relative.

"Right hand, ma'am," the officer ordered. He rolled each finger on an ink cartridge through the small window and fingerprinted me. "Left hand, ma'am."

Once he had finished, he put a stamp on my passport and gave it back to me, together with another form. Then, without another word, he looked towards the waiting room. "Next!"

The interview was over, just like that, but instead of feeling relieved, the sadness I had been keeping inside exploded.

In front of me, Lyman was holding the door for me. The door to freedom.

I looked back to the waiting room, crowded with people from all over the world waiting for their fate. *I could tell the officer I want to go back to where I belong.* His eyes narrowed, waiting for me to make the step forward, crossing the threshold between us. Seconds passed as I stood there, hesitant and mortified, my eyes reaching Lyman's, his hand over the threshold.

"Come," he waved his hand in the air, trying to reach mine. I grabbed Lyman's hand passing the officer on my right.

"When we get home, I'll tell you the truth," I said.

"The whole truth?" Lyman smiled.

"The whole truth."

Children of the Decree

Maria D. Holderman

Bucharest, Romania
March 19, 1965

Our story unfolded at the demise of one dictator and the coronation of another.

On this day, NASA sent the first two crewman mission to the Moon, while 100,000 people protested in Berkley, California against sending the first 3,500 troops to Vietnam. In Britain, a judge fined three of the Rolling Stones members for urinating on a gas station wall near London. In Romania, dictator Gheorghe Gheorghiu-Dej died. In Russia, Leonid Brezhnev, the general secretary of the Central Committee of the Communist Party since 1964, received the news of Dej's death within an hour. On the other side of the world, CIA prepared President Johnson:

Party First Secretary Gheorghe Gheorghiu-Dej is suffering from a possibly fatal illness. Premier Maurer appears to have assumed some of Dej's responsibilities in recent days and is the leading candidate to replace him if he dies. No change in Rumania's independent policies would be likely under Maurer. (CIA, TOP SECRET March 19, 1965)

The general in charge of the Romanian Secret Service, Nicolae Ceauşescu, was still debating if Dej had died of cancer, as written on his death certificate, or from radiation poisoning during his trip to Warsaw, and later, to Moscow, in 1963.

Ceauşescu believed the radiation theory after three of the four officers he'd assigned for Dej's protection had already died.

Just a year earlier, in a secret meeting, Dej had asserted to the chief of industrial espionage of Department of Foreign Intelligence (DIE) of Romania, General Ion Mihai Pacepa: "KGB radiated me." The secret meeting occurred after the Italian Minister of Justice Palmiro Togliatti's (one of Italy's Communist Party founders) mysterious death in Crimea. He was the last communist on a list of ten to die within a few years after a visit to Moscow.

Brezhnev considered Dej an insubordinate pawn. Stalin had installed Dej as the first communist leader in Romania at the end of the WWII asking him to send the last King of Romania in exile, officially abolishing the monarchy. Secretly, Stalin met with Churchill and, on a plain napkin, they decided the fate of the former Moldavian Romanian territory known as *Bessarabia*. It would be the second and last time Russia's Red Army would occupy Bessarabia.

Then Dej turned his back on Stalin.

In the spring of 1964, six months before Brezhnev was elected Chairman of the Presidium of the Supreme Soviet, Dej issued the *April Declaration*. It claimed Romania's official independence from Russia and the possible alliance with China. The declaration unnerved Brezhnev. It was a slap in the face. What kind of example would Romania be to the rest of the communist countries when the first ally preferred China over Russia?

Now, with Dej dead, Brezhnev wanted to install Nicolae Ceaușescu. He had met Ceaușescu in Ukraine, where the youngest executive member of the Romanian Communist Party was trained. Everyone knew Ceaușescu was Dej's protégé, as Dej had been Khrushchev's, his predecessor.

But he also knew one man inside the Romania Communist Party who could help Ceaușescu take over.

Three days later, the Executive Committee elected Nicolae Ceaușescu as Secretary General of the Popular Republic of Romania. CIA informed the American President:

Nicolae Ceaușescu has been elected as the new party first secretary to succeed Gheorghe Gheorghiu-Dej. Ceaușescu will probably follow the independent line of his predecessor in foreign affairs and may introduce some relaxation of hardline policies at home. The rapidity of his selection suggests the top party leadership remains strongly unified. (CIA, TOP SECRET March 22, 1965, The President's Daily Brief)

Neither CIA nor TASS could have predicted the rise of one of the most notorious dictators of all times.

This is my generation's story: The Children of the Decree.

Maria D. Holderman

Chapter One: The Jar of Milk
Dragasani, Romania
February 1975

I was the offspring of an *enemy of the people*. If I had known that then, I would have died of shame. All the men on Mama's side were labeled, sentenced, and imprisoned as saboteurs and contra revolutionaries. They were against *the people* of my country, Romania. But on that morning, when I could have died, all I knew about my role can be boiled down to two words: I represented the *New Man*, our leader, Comrade Ceaușescu, had planned for my generation. In second grade, my mission was to bring home a jar of milk.

Every day, my parents would leave the house early in the morning to get a bus to their different schools where they taught, and I was in charge of getting milk since I was in kindergarten. I was already queued in line when the milk truck made the stop that morning, as usual, at a nearby store in Dragasani, the place that Mama and most people called "between the flats." Madam Moise, a short woman with a double chin and sticky fingers, ran the store every day from early morning until late afternoon.

The store was small, on the first floor of an apartment building. I had never liked the acrid smell that permeated the air; I can't forget that scent. The shop stank of body odor, the smell of stale perspiration, either Madam Moise's or her customers' or both. The store had a limited stock of what we needed for daily living. There were two shelves sparsely stocked with daily goods: biscuits, macaroni, sardine cans, and loose candy. I could recognize the rodents' smell from the cellar where my parents used to keep corn in the winter. Mice like corn, and biscuits, too.

Mama always had to give me the exact change, knowing that Madam Moise would cheat me otherwise. That's why I nicknamed her Madam Cheater. I'd stand in line with maybe forty-to-fifty people outside, all of us waiting for the milk truck to come. Then once she opened the store, I'd get in line for my milk, and carry the jar home holding the sharp plastic bag with my sleeves.

Children of the Decree

It was still dark outside that morning, typical for that time of year in Romania. The air was cold, and the breeze from the Olt River down the hill danced between the apartment buildings. The wind hitting the cold cement of the apartments came back with more power and chilled me to the bone. I could barely feel my face, even with a scarf around my mouth. My legs were numb when I saw the gray milk truck pull in front of the store. But on that early February morning, the truck driver unexpectedly announced that the truck contained half of its regular delivery. The surging crowd clamored in dismay, and I panicked when a tense wave surged from the back of the line. Some people behind me wanted to cut the line to get in front of me.

My parents taught me to be polite, but on that morning I snapped at a woman who jostled in front of me. "I was first!" I shouted, my blood boiling.

Mama would never cut the line, I thought, and I glared at that woman as she went back to her place. Her face was swollen as if she were congested; her hands shivered from the cold as well. There was no sympathy for her from anyone in line either. Another man shouted, "The kid is right, you should go back!" I glanced at her one more time. Behind me, I saw that some people at the end of the line gave up and left, but I also realized that I was the only child there. I counted just twenty people in front of me, so I had a good chance to get my jar.

Once Madam Cheater opened the store's door to let us inside, the mob of people behind me stampeded, and there were now five lines—not just one. I tried to stand still and held the plastic bag on my chest to keep my balance, squeezed between a man wearing a long winter coat and a Russian hat, and a woman Mama's age. I prayed that people would not lose their minds and get wild in the minutes to come. But then a strong push hit me from behind, and I collapsed on the floor, gasping. As people trampled over me, I screamed at the top of my voice, "I am just a kid, people!"

Suddenly, I was the victim of great physical damage, having been trampled by this mob of adults. Since my plea didn't work, I cried out loud and the tears fell. The next push into my body felt even harder because it came directly from above. As one person stepped on my stomach another stepped on my head. My thought was to get out and protect my head with my hands. When I finally saw a spot to roll over, I pushed as hard as I could and turned to my side. I wanted to get out, though empty-handed, but the people amassed like a wolf pack on raw flesh. I screamed again like an injured baby animal, "I am hurt! Let me out!" Finally, the man with the Russian hat pushed some people aside and I escaped.

As I limped my way home carrying the empty jar, I realized that I'd lost my money in the fight. But I didn't turn back. I was three minutes away from my house as I walked up the hill between the flats. Until that morning, I used to love the path back home, feeling proud of my attainments of the day, which usually included bringing milk to feed my sister before school. But that morning I found myself crying, wiping my face with the scarf I kept over my mouth. *What should I feed Livia?* I thought, before I opened the kitchen's back door.

I found her dressed in her pre-K outfit, the blue dress barely covering the pants. At five, she was about my height at seven; Tata was always pleased when people asked if we were twins.

"Good girl. You dressed up by yourself," I said, buttoning the backflaps. "Comb your hair," I scolded, noticing the clock on top of our old radio.

Back in the kitchen, I turned on the gas stove to get breakfast ready. The flame looked blue instead of yellow, the sign of an almost empty propane tank.

Instead of milk that morning, I poured two cups of water and added some mint leaves in the pan, but the revelation of an empty gas tank caused me to cut the boiling to just heating. The sugar was gone, so I put a hard candy in each cup to sweeten it. Unfortunately, the candy didn't melt and didn't soften the tang of the mint, but I hoped the liquid would do the trick anyway. I handed Livia her cup, but she turned her nose up when she saw the candy on top of the mint leaves.

"Drink it, it's good," I lied to her, while I was spreading some margarine on stale, leftover bread. So long as it wasn't moldy, we did not throw out any rations of bread.

"But it's cold," she said. She indeed took a few sips. How could I explain to her we were almost out of propane? And that I had failed in bringing home milk? And had even lost the money in the fight?

I didn't drink my tea but pretended to and spilled the warm water into the pigs' bucket next to the stove. We never threw away food. If we couldn't eat it, the pigs would, Tata had taught us.

The room next to the kitchen was for hanging out. A terracotta wood stove occupied half of the room, while on the other half was the dinner table where Livia was drinking her tea. The radio with the clock on top was placed on the back of the table so we wouldn't slide it over against the windowsill. I was sitting on the end of the wooden bed, a relic from Tata's mother that was a wedding present for my parents. I was pleased to see Livia dipping the ancient bread in the tea. She was taking her time, but time didn't mean anything to her.

As I stood up to get ready for school, waiting for my little sister to finish the improvised breakfast, I was overwhelmed with dizziness and a headache. *The fight*, I remembered, and I placed my hand on my head as I went to check myself in the full mirror in the hallway. I removed the red hat and saw blood caked in my hair. There was blood on my scarf, too, so I found another one my mom had knitted for me. Then I changed the bloodied hat with a clean one and tended to Livia.

"Sis," she said, pointing to the bloody clothes.

"Hurry, we're late," I rushed her, holding for her the coat, white like mine, helping her put her gloves and scarf on to cut the sharp wind and cold.

I dragged my feet and Livia on that morning. My neighbor, whose father was a doctor, caught up with us. She had an orange in her hand, as usual, and told me that she forgot to do her homework.

"I'll give you *my* homework if you give me half your orange," I said, surprised by my courage. She agreed and handed me half the orange, the first one we had ever held in our hands.

I'll never forget the look of satisfaction on my little sister's face as she savored this new tropical fruit when I dropped her off at her class. In my seat, I hurriedly erased my name and wrote in my orange-trading neighbor's on the top of the page, and passed the paper to her, as if it were her own creation, glad the teacher didn't see me cheating.

Calmly, I clutched my flower-patterned handkerchief from my pocket and laid my hands on it as we began the first routine of the school day. Like a drill instructor, the teacher walked between the rows, checking our nails exposed over the handkerchief and collecting the homework at the same time. Good hygiene was a priority for the teachers, and if one of us kids had dirty nails or forgot the handkerchief, we had to go home, clean ourselves, and come back. I had my ironed handkerchief but no homework.

"Daniela, where's your homework?" my teacher asked.

"I forgot it at home," I responded, frightened she would send me back to bring it to class.

I loved my elementary teacher, Rodica Badescu. She was a tall woman with a straight walk, short colored brown hair, and no makeup, and was a few years away from retiring. But it was her imperative voice that I adored most. I'd never heard her screaming or raising her voice, and all of us, all thirty-six students, would follow her directions at once.

"Bring it tomorrow," she said, while she stroked my head, attempting to take my winter hat off. Then the teacher quietly walked away, leaving me alone with my hat on. That day her voice was softer when she addressed me. It made me feel special, but my mind was at the slice of orange I had left in the pocket of my white coat on the door's hanger.

~

Mama was still at school when I heard the phone ringing in the afternoon. We girls were in the hangout room around the wood stove that Tata loaded with firewood, the incandescent light of flames reflecting on the alphabet cards I had made from empty matchboxes, to help teach Livia the alphabet.

The phone was in the hallway, on the stand of the full mirror I used to check myself before school. I wondered, who would call at that improper time, because Tata told us we should never call anyone between two and four or even five in the afternoon.

"That's nap time, people rest after work," was his explanation. The other rule was that when a parent was at home, we kids should not answer the phone. We kept playing with the alphabet cards while Tata answered the call. I couldn't hear the conversation, and after he hung up, from his heavy footsteps, I knew he was on a mission.

"I want the truth!" he yelled. I burst into tears.

"How in the world did you forget to do the homework? And what happened to your head?"

I bent my head down and let him gently take the hat off. I had no other choice; I told him what happened, afraid that I'd get punished for failing to get the milk. Instead, Tata cleaned the blood with a wet towel and added a bandage where it hurt the most, whispering in my ears as if I was a baby, "It's okay, darling. Don't do it again." I promised him that I wouldn't, not knowing if he'd referred to my getting in a fight or forgetting my homework.

Before my bedtime, I overheard Tata whispering to Mama. They always whispered when they had a secret they wanted to keep from us. The kitchen door was left open for the heat to spread around the house, and I was holding a hot water bottle just in case anyone would see me, as an excuse for lingering and listening.

"My kids will never fight for milk and get hurt again!" Tata sobbed loudly. "I paid my dues to this country. My father paid it for me. Your father paid it for you. It's enough!" Tata continued, trying to keep his voice low.

I was petrified. Afraid I'd be found, I propped my back on the piano, keeping my mouth on my legs as I sat there, listening to things I'd never heard before.

"Vivi, I'd crawl on my knees for my girls… I want them to become educated, to make smart choices in life. I won't let the party take over their lives. That's it."

When I got in the bed that I shared with Livia, I found her shivering of cold. The water bottle I carried to bed every night was meant to warm us up. I never knew which one of us went to sleep first, as we clasped around the hot bottle, but I think I was up later most of the time, listening to the mice in the attic, or dreaming of a better life with heat and lights. But there was something else—the only good thing—I'd experienced that day. I learned that Tata was a man I could truly trust. A man who had goals for us. That night I breathed deeply, inhaling the air warmed from the wood stove longer, and exhaling it as I freed myself from that pain and humiliation, while cuddling with Livia under the wool blanket.

Before falling asleep, I realized that the humiliation of being poor and unable to rise in life—even after generations had fought battles for the chance to do so—made us stronger than being ridiculed for circumstances I had no control over. I was just a child, yet the battle for milk was my practical introduction of my loathing of the Romanian political system.

I never went back to that store to buy milk in the morning. From then on, Tata brought milk home from someone in the village who taught science at the school. Sometimes the milk spoiled before he got home, and Mama would turn it into yogurt or cheese. It didn't matter; we loved it anyway. However, overhearing Tata's talk with Mama about the dues they'd both paid—blood and flesh, as I had no grandfathers—opened my eyes about communism.

I hated it before I even knew what that communism was, but to me, it was something that took family away and gave nothing back except heartache.

I wanted to know the truth.

With my sister Livia (left) and Tata in our flower garden in Dragasani, Romania. 1976

Maria D. Holderman

Chapter Two: Lyman's America
Vermont, April 2001

"Okay, baby, we are done here. I'm going to find Jim," said Lyman as we finally exited Customs at the airport. "You stay here. Don't move!"

I was afraid that Jim, Lyman's friend who volunteered to bring us to Vermont, wouldn't find us. Hundreds of people were walking through the large airport, and we were six hours late. We had spent the past hour in long lines at Immigration, and then at Customs, but Lyman did all the talking so I wasn't worried. While those lines didn't scare me, they did trigger, however, the image of a little girl waiting in lines in Dragasani. *It was a long time ago*, I thought, as if I was trying to remember something I desperately wanted to forget. I was in a different position now—Lyman promised my family he'd take care of me, and both my parents believed him.

As I sat on one suitcase, I felt my legs shaking and my eyes blurred. All I wanted was a warm shower and a bed. I closed my eyes and thought of my king bed in Bucharest and tears trickled down my face. I calmed down just in time. Lyman returned with a man who, I assumed correctly, was Jim. Neither of them seemed in a hurry. From a distance they looked like twins in blue jeans and matching black jackets.

"Hi, Dena, I'm Jim. Nice meeting you." He hugged me, and Lyman told him my name spelled D A N A, but the Romanian pronunciation was Donna. I smiled thinking how Dana, a common name in Romania, gave them trouble. Jim, a short man who also worked at IBM with Lyman, had rented a black SUV for the drive to Vermont. The car was large and immaculate, and it comfortably held us and our three bags. I sat in the back seat.

Our first stop was a gas station next to the airport. We all wanted coffee, and I told Lyman to grab one for me, his choice. From my reporter bag I pulled a pack of cigarettes. He understood my intention and left with Jim, telling me not to go far. It was dark outside, the air sharp, and I saw what I thought was a lot of traffic for that time of day. From the gas station, the airport looked like a busy daytime town. Colorful lights displayed names of stores and hotels, lights and flashes, cars' headlights.

Behind me, I heard Lyman's laughter and turned to see him. He handed me the coffee. I took a sip, but it made me gag. It was too weak and tasted like perfume.

"This is hazelnut. The best coffee," Lyman said, and they both chuckled seeing my grimace. I bet they would have laughed harder without me there.

Back in the car, I could hear fragments of conversation. Lyman sat in the passenger seat, and I could see Jim's mesmerized profile: "Really? Oh, man, what an adventure!" I understood later Jim had never left America. "Do you know how they drink coffee?" Lyman's fingers flurried in front of Jim, "Tiny, tiny cups, like a doll house." I smiled, remembering how Lyman had first gagged on my coffee just as I did a few minutes before when I tasted his. I fell asleep, but when I woke up only ten minutes had passed.

By down, I could see what Americans called "the interstate." It surprised me that we were on a long road with green signs here and there, signs that told drivers what turn to take. In Bucharest, signs show drivers which street is which. I couldn't imagine how long someone could drive on that road without seeing a town or even a house. *Boring*, I thought. It was nothing like the places I knew and loved, but just one long, long road with cars going one way.

My watch showed 1:30 AM Romanian time. I pictured my mother in her bedroom, wide awake, thinking of me. "And Dana's grandmother Tanta, right?" He turned to me to confirm my grandmother's name. "They have cows and pigs," Lyman kept going. Broken details of my family and places Lyman mentioned seemed a distant past. Now, my husband's enthusiasm convinced me he considered himself a part of it, and I wanted sleep. *The future.* I imagined a small, cozy house in the woods, from what Lyman told me, far away from any disruptions, with a fire burning while I was taking a shower. *I could live there, no problem.*

I kept quiet, my eyes closed, dreaming of my future. "Here we are. In Vermont. Do you see the sign?" Lyman interrupted my thoughts. A large greenish sign read "Welcome to Vermont—The Green Mountain State." Then we stopped for breakfast at a diner, but I couldn't eat. My body and brain needed rest.

Lyman drove the rest of the way while Jim napped. My husband wore sunglasses, but I could see he was getting pale. He kept the window open and the fresh air kept me awake.

To this day, I don't know which way we drove to Vermont. My first guess is that we went through Albany, then Plattsburgh, and crossed the bridge at Rouses Point, and then toward I-89 North. I could see snow everywhere. Some places had more than others. I asked Lyman where the houses were. He showed me some plain-looking buildings. They had no architectural embellishments like those in Romania.

"These aren't houses, Lyman. Where are the houses?"

"These are the houses, Dana. They look nice inside," he laughed.

"They have no fences," I nodded, and Lyman and Jim couldn't stop giggling.

I had been in the U.S. for only six hours and already there were two things I didn't like about America: the coffee and the houses.

~

Just before noon we dropped off the rented SUV, and after Lyman signed some papers at the car dealer, we all got in Jim's car and drove to IBM in Essex Junction to pick up Lyman's car. We said goodbye to Jim, and Lyman and I walked to the parking lot, carrying our luggage.

"Can you guess which one is mine?" Lyman asked, passing me in a hurry. I noticed the hoarse pitch of his voice; we, reporters, call *idiolects* when speaking in front of a camera.

Maybe that black car?

He didn't need a key to open his red Toyota. The car was open, crushed on one side and full of garbage inside. My first impulse was to scream. My second was to clean out the trash from the passenger seat and floor and dump it in the garbage bin I had spotted. Shocked, I realized then that I hadn't asked Lyman any questions about his living conditions. It was too late to ask him now. For a minute I panicked, and Lyman looked like a stranger with a voice I didn't recognize and a facial expression I hadn't ever seen before. I picked up some of the trash from the seat and put it in a plastic bag I found under the passenger seat.

"You don't have to do that. We'll take it to a car wash."

The engine started on the third try. I kept my eyes closed most of the way, my thoughts elsewhere. Pretending to be asleep, I could sense Lyman was checking on me more often than I expected. He concentrated on driving with the window open and the radio on. Two hours later we were in the town of Derby Line, Vermont.

He knocked on a white house entrance, and the door opened. I saw a blond head behind, and then we walked in. An inside door slammed, and another girl showed up.

"How are my babies? Give Daddy a hug!" Lyman said pleasantly, taking a step back to watch the girls from head to toe. I stood in front of the entrance door, waiting to be introduced. Minutes later, after they'd finished covering what was new, Lyman said he was going to the farm to check the cows before we'd all spend the night there. "You, too, Jody," he said authoritatively, closing the door behind him.

So, here I am, I thought. *Welcome to America, Dana Achim.* I wished I could control the tremor of my hands and body. Exhausted, I asked for a glass of water. At that moment I could have laid down on that kitchen floor and slept on the girls' backpacks as pillows.

"Let's sit," Jody said, and I walked behind them, holding the glass with both hands, in a bedroom with a large TV. They had just returned from school that afternoon, and if I had been better rested, I could have asked them about school and their teachers. Instead, I mentioned quickly that I was a chemistry teacher, and that my sister taught high school physics. To that, they raised their eyebrows.

The girls cuddled under a green comforter watching a show they'd paused to greet us, and I sank on to the bed at the opposite end. It felt chilly in the house, but I couldn't tell if that was the case. As I walked behind them, I admired their fashionable low-cut jeans. Jody wore a plain tank top while Pearl had a black T-shirt tucked in her pants.

From my side of the bed, I could see them well. Jody, seventeen, was taller than Lyman, with long golden hair kept in a ponytail and incredibly white skin. She had Lyman's blue eyes and a soft voice. The youngest, Pearl, one year younger than Jody, was just the opposite; dark eyes, short, cinnamon brown hair above the ears, and a light complexion. She sounded more like Lyman when he'd asked me to guess which car was his.

They spoke fast, and I couldn't understand every word they'd said. "What? Could you please repeat for me?" I found myself saying a lot. I understood that house was Jody's boyfriend's, who was at work, and she'd been living with him and Pearl while Lyman was gone. But it was clear to me that she wanted to remain there. When it was my turn to talk, I had to repeat the same words before they acknowledged what I had just said.

But there was something else I understood without any spoken words: that the strong bond between sisters, as best friends, is universal, regardless of the language you speak. I imagined the younger Dana and Livia in the room we had shared as kids, each at one end of the bed. They probably saw my tears because Pearl asked, "Do you miss your sister already?"

"Very much," I said, holding my breath to keep my calm and posture. I pictured Livia checking her email for news from me, as I'd promised, so she could pass the news to my parents. *Tomorrow,* I convinced myself. *One more day.*

It was dark when Lyman returned to get us. *But dark days or nights are in the past,* I thought.

Children of the Decree

Maria D. Holderman

The silent war that would kill 10,000 documented women, and even more uncounted, had begun on a sunny day on August 2, 1966, at one of the communist party's retreats on the Black Sea. The health minister informed Ceaușescu that in 1965, the number of abortions in the country totaled 1,115,000, which was double from those counted in 1959. It was the lowest natality rate Romania ever had. The result of the census revealed less than 17 million people. The survey's causes for low birth rate listed "lack of sexual education and contraception."

One of the Comrade's right hands, Alexandru Draghici, in charge of Securitate and Militia, explained that the decline of births was as an immoral consequence of the Decree 463 of 1957, because it allowed abortion upon request. In his words, "The decree encourages free-love and is in opposition with the true family values." Ceaușescu said, "It promotes prostitution and increases the divorce rate, against our solid socialism values. We must do something to discourage this kind of behavior. My mom gave birth to ten children and look where I am now. See? We have less than seventeen million people! We need to form the new generation. In ten years, we need twenty-two million people—the first two million born starting now."

On the next day, the propaganda newspaper Scanteia published the Decree 770.

Article One: Abortion is illegal.

It followed: Abortion could be granted to women over forty-five who already gave birth to four children, all in her care; any request for an abortion in exceptional circumstances must be approved the executive committee of the town.

If the woman's life were in danger, and the doctor decided on an immediate abortion, the doctor must inform the prosecutor in writing within twenty-four hours, and the prosecutor would analyze the evidence provided by a separate doctor appointed to supervise the activity in the hospitals to establish if the abortion was necessary.

Mama remembered Tata's words when he saw the news. "This explains our training and everything. We are screwed, and we helped them."

Children of the Decree

Secret agents had monitored every drug store in the country. Condoms and birth control pills, illegal now, were on their way to be destroyed. No other communist country thought of forcing births as Ceaușescu did.

I was born one year later, among the first batch of 527,764 decretei— The Children of the Decree.

The secret security assigned to each hospital sorted us since birth, and only the perfect babies went home. The ones with birth defects were never seen again.

Our battle for survival had begun.

Maria D. Holderman
Chapter Three: Children of the Decree
Dragasani, Romania 1970s

This I remember:

There were lines for food. Lines for clothes. Lines for toilet paper. There was nothing in the grocery stores but rice, pasta, and canned fish. The desolate meat marketplace felt like a deserted ice rink. White shelves lined up empty, getting dusty, while freshly butchered and pickled pigs' feet and bags of chicken feet packed the front refrigerator. I didn't mind looking at the pig's feet, but the frozen poultry claws in clear plastic bags turned my stomach every time.

"Kids should be home," an old man said in disgust as I tried to keep my spot in line one afternoon.

He was right. No child my age should be spotted between adults waiting for supplies. But I knew the game and was prepared. No more hurting and losing money, I had promised myself after the last time. Every time I combed my hair, the scar on my scalp reminded me of that promise. My shield against people who couldn't be patient and respectful was a low wooden chair Mama used outdoors. She'd sit on it while cutting grass for the ducklings and peeling vegetables or removing corn kernels from corn for our animals.

On warm days, I'd sit on it to read while waiting in line. But once the selling started, either outside or inside the store, it became my armor against the mob. If warriors used shields in the battles, as I saw in some Western movies, why not bring my own shield with me? It worked; the complainer gave up and moved away from my armored chair.

There was that day I got home before Tata, carrying around my neck, like a precious necklace, ten pink toilet paper rolls on a string. I knew he would have preferred razor blades or aftershave, and Mama would have liked sanitary napkins and real soap, but I was proud to bring home some real stuff.

Children of the Decree

I thought Mama would be happy that she wouldn't have to boil our white underwear to remove the black ink we all carried from using newspapers. Instead, she locked the rolls in the front room—our forbidden territory—and gave me an explanation. "These are for guests only." We kept using newspapers Mama piled up in the outhouse.

As I sat there, doing my job, I couldn't help but read the only newspaper printed, *Scanteia* ("Spark" in English.) Its motto was, "Proletarians from all over the country, unite!" The first paradigm I'd question and discover on my own over the years spent in elementary school was the discrepancy between our Comrade Ceaușescu's socialist ideology and our *real* life. It sounded nice to give each citizen the same rights, and to use our resources for our country's economic independence.

As I was reading his conferences, I felt *enormously proud*, wanting to become a real model in my profession and a simple citizen, just like our Comrade.

He watched me from the magnificent pictures where he was portrayed, and as I squished them in my hands to soften the texture while I was doing my business, I blamed Mama for locking the rolls. (To be honest, when I did use real rolls, which I thought would be heaven for my bottom, I discovered they were as bad as *Scanteia*.) At school, Comrade's portrait was hanging on every classroom's wall. He was present in every textbook. Even my English textbook had his one-page portrait printed before the Table of Contents. And every single day, his agenda opened and closed the news. He was everywhere.

Saturday evening was my favorite part of the week, after the painful bath in the afternoon that I despised. We'd take turns for a full bath in a wooden pail next to the wood stove, kids first. The soap Mama made by herself from the pig lard she saved each year, even though laced with rosemary, basil, or other fragrant herbs Tata collected, couldn't take the smell away. She'd cut the grease with lye Tata called sodium hydroxide, making the lard run smoothly in shapes she'd design to give the soap a decent shape when dried. But once the soap got into my eyes from washing my short hair, they turned red, and I was crying. Mama used to give me my worn undershirt to keep it on my eyes, but even with that on, I never escaped the sting.

"One more rinse. Hold onto the shirt," she'd say, exhausted, while I was fighting to get out of the tub. The sharpest pain was washing my genitals. "Almost done," she'd try to keep me in the pail, but I was faster and jumped on the top of the bed. After supper, we all waited to watch the show "Dallas." It aired after the news that none of us cared for, except for Mama.

She taught Social Studies, and it was her job to keep the other teachers up to date on foreign policy. To make things more dramatic than they already were, she was always scared her school, in the Olt district, might get an unannounced visit from the Department of Education. The person in charge of that department was Elena Barbulescu, a name I'd hear daily, as a leitmotiv of fear coming from Ceauşescu's native county and the President's only sister of ten siblings. It was a mystery why his only sister decided to stay in the Olt County, while all of Ceauşescu's brothers took high positions in the executive branch in Bucharest. Ceauşescu's wife, Elena, named just like his sister, was number two in the administration.

"I don't want to hear this bullshit anymore," Tata said when Mama insisted that we should all watch the news, for educational purposes. Tata taught Biology in the same county as Mama, but his school was so remote that not even the bus made it to the school. "She can't walk two kilometers on foot," Tata added in defiance.

While we kids played, Mama stood in front of the TV with a notebook on her lap, taking notes just as we did in school. I remember her cursive writing on pages she divided into columns—countries, dates of visits, political leaders' names. Every teacher could get a pop quiz on daily briefings if an inspector from Education showed up in class. Then, before the show, Mama gave the three of us a shorter version of current events. Just to be sure we wouldn't get caught unguarded, she'd leave a scrap note every morning on the dinner table with those names we had to memorize and spell. I'd had no problem with Tito, Kim Ir Sen, Mao Zedong, or Hosni Mubarak.

Children of the Decree

The hardest to remember was Mobutu Sese Seko Kuku Ngbendu Wa Za Banga.

Sick of Mama's "short version briefing," Tata told her to teach her students that BS. Then, he added, whispering to her, "I don't give a damn. If they don't show the truth, I don't care. I'm going to listen to music," and walked out.

It was the first time I'd heard Tata swear. I thought he was upset and went to check on him before the show. He was singing along with a man playing on the radio while preparing his lesson plans for next week. "Let's watch Jere and Pamela," Tata said, looking at the clock. He stopped drawing what would have been his students' quiz on a plant's parts and carried me back on his shoulder.

I'd find out later all people with a TV watched the famous show, although my favorite of all times was "Rich Man, Poor Man." I even knew Nick Nolte's name. And while some believed Ceauşescu allowed airing "Dallas" to teach us how dysfunctional capitalism was, when J.R. had his whiskey straight or on the rocks, most took it as a symbol of the American Dream. The show was the most discussed topic among those waiting in lines, in commuter trains, and in busses. I wanted to see Bobby and Pamela have children, and to see Sue Ellen divorce her nasty husband. The last episode of the third season would puzzle the whole country: Who killed J.R.?

~

Tata's father, Ioan Vasile, was killed at the onset of the Second World War—that I knew already. I wanted to learn more about not having grandfathers, *the price* both my parents paid for this country, as Tata had discussed with Mama on the day when I got hurt in the fight for milk.

It was spring, I remember, and Tata was admiring the daffodils and tulips, dressed as always in his teacher's costume, white shirt with an assorted tie, his hands behind his back. Maybe he was singing that day because he always said flowers grow with love and music. He saw us coming through the gate from my piano class and Livia's French class. It was Tata's idea to pay private tutors for our education outside of school.

From the street, the flower gardens looked like a painting, and the yellow daffodils mixed among the white Narcissus with its red or orange trumpet-shaped centered corona. Between them sat blue, yellow, white, and pink hyacinths. In the middle were the colorful tulips.

Tata was excited to see the black and purple tulips ready to blossom. They always flowered last; as Tata loved to say, "Keep the best for last." His flowers were already his supreme passion, but those tulips he'd been waiting to see blossom were his pride.

The wrinkles between his eyes had disappeared, which was a sign he was enjoying his flowers. Livia went straight to do her homework, and I got closer to him and asked, "Tata, tell me about your father."

He didn't expect it. We usually talked about flowers, but at that moment, Tata pressed his fingers on his eyelids to hold back his tears.

"No, Tata. If you don't want to talk, that's fine."

I'd never been so afraid to ask Tata a question. I gritted my teeth, not knowing what to do with my hands. Tata wrapped his arm on my shoulder, and we walked to the well on the cement patio. We sat at the table on the covered porch. The air smelled like honey, and the mild breath of the wind carried the petals of the cherry tree flowers everywhere, while the hard-working bees ignored us.

I don't remember how Tata's story began, but I learned that he had one memory of his father. Just *one*.

It was about the morning when his father left for the war, in 1941, as Tata watched him go, a blur through the window. When my grandfather passed by on his way out, he knocked on the pane where Tata sat. His father smiled and he made a funny face, waved, and turned his back.

"That's all," Tata said. I calculated Tata's age to myself. Born in '38, so he was about four years old on that day. Tata's sister, Aunt Pusa, now an OB/GYN nurse practitioner, was one.

I felt sad for Tata, imagining what it had been like growing up without a father. I couldn't picture my life without him. I was still young but realized it's human nature to have a male figure that holds a family together.

"Let me show you something. Wait here," he said, and walked away to the back entrance of the house. I could hear his steady steps inside; then, he opened the front room Mama kept locked. If I stood up, I could see him through the window above the bench where he'd left me waiting. I was curious what he'd get from there, hoping one day I'd find the key to open that sanctuary and get to satisfy my nosiness. (I'd find the key later, hidden between the strings of my piano.)

He unlocked the front entrance we always kept locked, just the front stairs between us. Standing in front of the house, between the flowerpots on both sides of the stairs, he looked taller. In his hand he held a blue album I'd never seen before. *A-ha! The secret place,* I muttered, admiring his elegant walk down the stairs.

Tata placed the album on the table, and immediately I recognized his calligraphic penmanship, "Nelu." That was his nickname since childhood and carried on by everyone in our family. For the rest, students and adults not related to us, he was *Dom' Professor.*

As he turned the first file, he ran over the page his long fingers I admired, fingers that Livia inherited. "Here's Maita with my father, after they got married," he said, with eyes of admiration and regret. "My father designed and tailored their suits. He had a tailor shop downtown, where he'd met Maita." I was mesmerized. At first, I didn't recognize my grandmother in the picture, and Tata knew I was confused.

"See? She's happy here," Tata said. I admitted they both looked elegant, but serious for a wedding picture.

How could my grandmother be that charming woman in the photograph? That wasn't the person I knew. Was Tata trying to justify why she was so mean to us? Or was it an explanation why every time Livia and I complained to Tata, he never took us seriously?

"She's a single, upset woman," he'd respond. So, we stopped complaining, fully aware Tata knew his mother well; he lived with her until he married Mama.

The Maita *I knew* lived in Dragasani with Aunt Pusa and her daughter, my cousin Mariana, two weeks younger than I, in a three-room house with a large backyard that had several walnut trees in it. It was a ten-minute walk from us, and Tata had to bribe me and Livia to pay them a visit. The only reason we went there was to see our cousin Mariana. She was like a sister to us, and my parents treated her the same when she came over. Aunt Pusa and Mariana moved in with Maita after my aunt's divorce, but I'd never figured out what went wrong in her marriage.

Tata knew how I felt. He'd heard our stories, and we wanted him to know why we'd come home in tears.

In the spring, Maita had raspberry bushes but didn't let us eat any. Instead, she took them to the farmer's market and sold them. One time, she asked me to help her wash some glass bottles to recycle at a store in town. I pulled them in a wagon that was double my size, and when I returned, she took all the coins from me and gave me none.

Nothing, however, made me dislike her more than the day she checked my pockets to see if I'd taken any walnuts. It was fall and all of us girls helped her in the garden picking up the corn. After we finished the job, we saw walnuts on the ground. We ate as many as we could, and I put some in my pocket for later, but Maita found them and took them away before we left for home.

Tata probably saw my rage. He said, "I know you're upset. But here's why she's this way if you can understand. It's not easy for a woman to become a widow at 29, and with two kids. You'll understand how these things work when you are a mother one day."

"But was she a good mother to you?" I asked.

"She was strict with everyone, including herself. I remember her walking with Pusa and me, beautifully dressed, holding us by the hand, one on each side. I can tell you many men looked at her. But she kept walking with her head high. Do you know why? Because she loved her husband, and she still does to this day. And in her mind, she doesn't believe he's dead."

"But, Tata, she is a veteran's widow, she told me," I said.

"Yes, in papers. But she believes he got deported and was a prisoner of war, somewhere in Siberia. And that he would come home one day. Some prisoners did return."

Maita's denial of my grandfather's death didn't sound right to me.

"How's that? She's a widow."

Tata tried to find his words. I remember how he looked around before he finally said, "But she never saw his body or received a written confirmation of his death. They couldn't tell how he died," he ended the conversation.

That evening Tata was the quietest I could remember.

~

As much as I disliked Maita during my childhood, there is one valuable lesson I learned from her and I still believe it's true: If you *really* want something, no one can stop you from getting it. I wanted a watch, but when I asked for it, Tata said I'd have to wait a few more years until he'd pay off the mortgage on the house. "We don't live like rats in apartments, between four walls. You can't even pass gas in peace in those places; someone will hear you!"

I was confused. Some of my classmates lived in apartments, but when I went over to one of my friend's house to play, I didn't see rats. She had fancy furniture and china cabinets, Persian carpets on the floor, and a bathroom with hot water. I loved to wash my hands there. I was confused why Tata said they lived like rats. We had a piano, took private lessons for English and French, but still used an outhouse.

When I asked him why he hated those apartments, he said, "We have the liberty to do what we want here. You can jump, scream, laugh, and no one can hear you! It's called freedom!"

I decided to buy the watch myself by selling flowers at the farmer's market where Maita had paid the fee for a corner on the third table. She'd be there in the morning, selling her vegetables and fruits, and I took over the table after school.

Selling flowers wasn't an easy job. First, I had to make sure Tata wouldn't see the missing flowers. He hated cutting flowers. If someone asked for some, he said it was like cutting his fingers. The ones I handpicked were from plants in the back row where the missing stems would be hard to see. Then I was afraid someone Tata knew would see me carrying the flowers, so I walked to the market hiding the bouquets in a plastic bag. At the farmer's market, I had to hide from my classmates, their parents, and even my teachers. If I saw a person I knew, I'd hide and let someone else sell my flowers. As much as I wanted my watch, I didn't want anyone in my class to know I was a *flower girl*.

The day came when my music teacher saw me, but I didn't see him. The next day he mentioned my name in class, giving us a speech about being responsible and hard workers. My face turned red. The classmates looked at me with approval. Then he said he saw me selling flowers the other day. Embarrassed, I put my head down, and wanted to hide in a hole so no one could find me again. I pressed my eyelids, and only then did he stop talking about me and turned to his music.

One of the boys who had a crush on me, the dentist's son, laughed at me during recess. "Can I buy some flowers?" he asked.

I answered, "My flowers are not for you, spoiled kid! First, learn to wipe your butt!" I was referring to the day in first grade when he couldn't do that job, and the teacher had to send him home after his pants stunk up the classroom. He told my classroom teacher what I'd said. She was the same teacher who called Tata when I went to school bloodied after the fight over the jar of milk.

"Don't say that word again," she said softly, and I knew she referred to the *butt* word. And that was all.

That day, I didn't go back to the farmer's market. Instead, I picked some flowers and went on the train tracks with Livia. We jumped over the back fence to the cemetery, and walked around, reading the epitaphs on the gravestones. We stopped at the Hero's Monument. The chestnut trees blossomed, and there, on a tiny bench, I told Livia our grandfather's story. We agreed to lay down the flowers together, performing a little ceremony, and we sang "Wake up Romanian, from the deadly sleep." We cried a little, and both of us agreed that our grandfather was a hero. If he had lived, our lives would've been much better.

The whistle of the 5:00 PM train sent us on a dead run. It meant there were only ten minutes before Tata would be home. Jumping over the cemetery fence, then back on the train tracks, and jumping again over our backyard fence, we got home and waited for our father as if nothing had happened.

Two years later, I had sold enough flowers to buy the watch, and asked Tata to get the best one he could find, on the day before he left for a teacher's training in Bucharest. I wanted a watch like no one else had in my class. "So much from selling flowers?" Tata looked up to me, counting the money. It felt as if the ceiling had dropped on my head, afraid of punishment. Then he raised his arms, and I stepped back. I saw his chin trembling, tears in his eyes as if he was talking about his dad. "I saw the missing flowers. Maita told me what you were doing. She learned from people at the market," he added. "But don't do it again!"

He bought me a unique Zaria with a blue background. It was beautiful.

Maita Maria and my grandfather, Ionel Vasile, on their wedding day (1933)

Maita Maria with my father in Dragasani (1942)

Chapter Four: The Mouse
April 2001

When I saw the sign "Coventry 3," I knew we were getting closer. But instead of following the road to the town where I used to mail him postcards, Lyman took a different turn. *What now?* I wondered, reaching the point at which I could easily collapse from fatigue. I was sure I would, having been on the road for two days.

In the parking lot of a Shaw's grocery store, Lyman maneuvered between two cars and parked close to the one on my side. I thought he'd hit it. Maybe that's how he damaged his Toyota.

"Let's grab something for dinner," he said and opened his door and exited. Then he pulled the seat in front and the girls got out. It was my turn. "This way." He pointed to his seat, and I climbed over it. I was pissed and refused to tell him what I'd like from that supermarket. We returned with a full cart of bags the girls stored between seats, but this time, I got in first.

No, I can't tell Livia that. She won't understand how things work here. My boot got stuck on a pile of trash under Lyman's seat.

For the next ten minutes, I only heard the engine, its muscles straining on the hills of the dirt roads. There were large areas with no houses, only farms. Lyman stopped the car at a three-way intersection. On my right, a little farther down, I spotted a tiny blue house with smoke coming from the chimney lit by outdoor lamps. I thought it was the house Lyman had prepared for our first night in America.

"We can't drive on the road," he said. "We'll walk." His voice quavered and I sensed danger. He lit a large flashlight, pulled a yellow plastic sled from the trunk, and he put my luggage on it. On the road ahead, the dim light lit his early steps. Then he tugged the sled. The road was narrow, so I walked behind him. *That's not the house. Where am I going?*

I could hear giggling from behind as I tried to step with my high-heeled boots in Lyman's footsteps but missed. I would have laughed too in better circumstances. On my left, along the path, there was a forest with signs hanging on the trees: "Private Property." And a picture of a gun. It scared me. On the right, waist-tall snow. I'd find out later that we had walked a quarter mile that evening, but it felt longer because I didn't know where I was going.

Once in a while, Lyman would turn back and ask, "Are you ready?" His glassy eyes, like wolves preying at night, frightened me. A flashback. "The Death's Taxi Driver"—the lifer I had interviewed in prison. He had killed five college students and other girls he'd picked up in the taxi from the train station in Bucharest. When I'd asked him about the last one, he said she did him wrong, stole a ring from him, and tried to escape. I couldn't sleep for weeks after that interview.

On that road I didn't recognize the charming man I'd married. But it was his voice that scared me to death. *If I die, no one will know,* I thought. Just like the missing girls' families. A sharp sting clouded my vision. Afraid I'd collapse, I switched my mind to Livia.

The last time he asked me the same rhetorical question, we came to a wider area on the right. A dead-end in front of us. Barbed wire fence on the left. I followed him a few steps ahead, then more to the right, and tried to spot smoke from a chimney. I saw none. Way back from the road, the flashlight lit up a flat gray trailer.

"Home, sweet home," he said, leading my way with the flashlight, as I tried to avoid stepping in the cow manure. He opened the door, no key needed, and then I knew it was real. As I entered, a narrow hallway going to the left, sprinkled with crumbs of snow and ice from Lyman's boots, guided the way to a no-door area he called the living room. The tiny candle he lit fogged my glasses. Without glasses, I saw my first suitcase already on the floor and Lyman placed the second one he carried on the sled next to it.

"Dana, make yourself comfortable," he said. He lit a second candle and moved some clothes from a two-person sofa, inviting me to sit. The girls brought the grocery bags and went to the back. I sank on the sofa, stretching my legs, and wanted to take my boots off, but I was cold and kept the jacket on. Lyman lit a fire in the woodstove. The discreet light and warmth reminded me of Mama Tanta's place. I probably smiled melancholically.

Dancing shapes on the wall. Livia cuddling near the terracotta stove, an apple, or a quince on the stove for smell and snack.

"We'll make dinner," he ordered the girls on their way to their room. From my seat, I couldn't see the kitchen; it was in the back of the living room. They talked and kept busy, moving things around. Lyman told them to set the table and bring the hamburger packet to the stove. I turned to see them. He got a pan, fried some meat, and put it between two slices of bread with ketchup. Jody invited me to dinner. When I got closer and saw the floor and everything around, my appetite disappeared.

"I'm not hungry," I murmured, as they were sitting down at the dinner table. Instead, I opened a can of Coca-Cola and grabbed a few chips. As I passed Lyman on my way to the sofa, I felt weak. My body ached; my brain was dead. Two feet and an ocean away, Lyman was my mistake.

After the girls went to their bedroom next to the living room, I changed into my Romanian sports pants Lyman bought me at the mall in Bucharest. It was too cold to wear pajamas, and there was no water to take a shower. I asked Lyman if I could at least brush my teeth. He ran outside, put some snow in a pan, and placed it on the woodstove to melt.

He said we'd sleep on a mattress on the floor and brought some pillows and a blanket. He hugged and kissed me good night, but I didn't respond. Nothing I had dreamt of was there. Holding back my tears, I kept asking, *What did I do?* I fell asleep hoping to wake up from a nightmare—*my first night in America.*

~

When I woke up, the daylight illuminated the trailer, but it was cold. It was real, I realized. I was in America in Lyman's house. Still on the mattress, I peeked around the room—newspapers, old receipts, and clothes on the dirty floor. I saw a new shirt and two white bed sheets. The kitchen's walls and cabinets looked like they were falling apart. I got up and walked to the woodstove. A dead mouse in a rusty metal pan had been cooked by the previous night's fire. Sick, I ran outside. Lyman came after me, as I tried to cover up the puddle of the Coca-Cola from last night.

"Why didn't you tell me?" I screamed. I was in tears. "I can't live here. I just simply can't. I can't even tell my mother where you brought me. You lied to me, Lyman. I want to go back home now!" I said one more time, "Now," and the girls showed up to see what was going on. I guessed Lyman expected my reaction. He put his hands on my shoulders and looked into my eyes, his face pale.

"I didn't lie. Listen, I couldn't tell you *everything*. We don't have to live here, I promise. We'll get a decent place in town. We'll look for one now, okay? We'll build our life step by step but give me a chance to show you how much I love you. Please, don't get upset."

I wasn't sure about that. He tried to hug me, but I pushed him away. I ran inside, my face on fire, and instinctively, I swallowed a birth control pill without water.

That I knew, for sure.

Maria D. Holderman

"The Romanian regime was acutely concerned that US attention to human rights could impede renewal of its most-favored-nation status. More importantly, Bucharest was worried that this might set back its "special relationship" with Washington that had been of major political use in fending off the Soviets. As a consequence, the Romanians—except for a brief crackdown in the spring of 1977, when they apparently feared that there would be a dramatic increase in dissidence—have encouraged dissidents to emigrate. The Ceaușescu regime has not shown, however, an inclination to adopt more enlightened domestic policies, and remains perhaps the most privately played down agitation for increased cultural and linguistic rights by the Hungarian minority, calling it Moscow-inspired, Budapest-engineered tactic to tar Romania's image." (CIA, September 1, 1978)

"Romania faces a bleak winter and Ceaușescu recently made some panic moves, ordering a centralized meal distribution program and sending in the military to oversee power generation plants. He also purchased some grains abroad this fall—after his ambitious grain export drive drew down reserves during the early drought. A repeat of last year's hardships is likely and worse privations could accompany another harsh winter." (CIA, Secret, December 3, 1985, Assistant National Intelligence Officer for Europe; page 3.)

Children of the Decree

Chapter Five: Mama's Secrets

"Don't tell anyone what we discuss or do at home," Mama had warned us. She was the best at keeping secrets, every word weighted. But I was an inquisitive child and wanted answers. Who were her *real* parents? And what had they done that would mean Mama had to remind me every day to not mention or talk at school about them? If she trusted me to take care of the house, and cross the street holding my little sister's hand since I was five, what else could I do to prove I was trustworthy? I'd be in my thirties when I truly understood her demons that she spewed on us in bits of whispers.

My favorite story to hear was about her meeting Tata.

"Mama, tell me again how you met Tata," I begged on a night after I was done with my homework. Propped up by a pillow on the bed, her legs crossed, Mama knitted a sweater for one of us. She loved making us colorful sweaters since all of the yarn that was usually available in stores was dark or gray.

"Why don't you take care of your schoolwork?" She wanted to change the subject again, as she'd done every time I tried to find out about her father's death. Most of the time her face turned red, and her voice grew sharp. "He died when I was in college. That's all you need to know," she'd answer. Talking about herself was not in her blood.

"Please, Mama," said Livia, peeking her round head from the iron crib where she still used to play with the dolls. "Tell us again!"

"I told you. He said he was a poet. What else do you want to know?" When she'd say "what else" I knew it was the end of the conversation.

It took me years to learn their story, but even today I'm not sure I know more than when I was a child. They met at a census training, in the early spring of 1965. All teachers in the country were required to attend the training at their regional centers. Dragasani was the second largest town in the area, and Mama, in her first year of teaching, packed for two weeks and went to Dragasani. During the first week, they had training classes, and in the evening, had dances or excursions around the town. Tata lived in

Dragasani, so he went home every night. But he attended the dances and everything else on the schedule.

"Your father was very handsome, tall and sharp, with a little mustache shaved just below his upper lip," she explained, pointing at her lip, her face lighting up. "And he was a very good dancer."

It was funny hearing Mama discuss Tata this way since they never displayed affection in front of us. In the second week of training, my parents were assigned to the same censor group. I guessed they spent even more time together doing the job Ceaușescu wanted.

They didn't know it then, but I found out much later what the scope was of that census where my parents met. Secretly, Ceaușescu had summoned his Executive Committee while vacationing at his protocol villa in Neptun, a beautiful seashore on the Black Sea. He was concerned about the previous year's low birth rate and ordered a detailed report about the population's age, especially of the women and children. He couldn't understand why women didn't want to have more children. In his words, "We were ten children, living with the parents in two rooms. What's wrong with women?" He was talking about his birthplace in Scornicesti, in the Olt district, just over the Olt River where my parents met and bought their house in 1969. He wanted numbers and reasons.

~

When I asked Tata about meeting Mama, he said she had a beautiful body, a little curved, "and had the nicest legs around." After I stopped laughing, he added there was something special about her, the allure of her nose and face, and the hair, and he knew right away that she came from a noble family. "You can't miss that," he said. He went on, telling me about how he invited her to dance, and how he was afraid she'd say no. But she accepted the invitation.

That day, Mama was doing laundry by hand outside; it was summer, and she had on a loose summer dress. I watched her bending over the wooden water pail and saw that, indeed, she had perfect legs, with her bones running in a straight line, the ones I wished I'd inherited. It is strange how

DNA works. I have Mama's nose and hair and Tata's dark eyes, and the same expression as Tata whenever he smiled. I remember he often smiled. But Mama never laughed. In fact, I have no memory of her ever laughing during my childhood.

That was the time Tata started his lifelong passion for flowers, or *herbs,* as Mama's family sarcastically loved to say. When he acclimated Passiflora—the Flower of Passion—many of Tata's friends came to see it. Dressed in his school suit and tie, he'd talk about this flower to anyone wanting to listen. The first year when it blossomed, he told me its story. I remember him standing by the balustrade near the front door, where Passiflora hung on the wall. I learned that each flower would live for twenty-four hours only, which made me think of it as something magical.

"This is the most beautiful flower I have ever seen," Tata said. "See how the white petals, the blue, and the red create different flowers within this one?" He looked deep into my eyes. "You can see in this one flower in the other flowers of the world. Every flower you could imagine is here, in this little, gracious thing. Here is the first flower, so white and pure," he continued. "Then it's a set of orange and purple petals, like the colors of the fall. And then look at this beautiful blue—this astonishing blue. You wouldn't think we could find it in nature." He showed me what he was seeing. "But this beauty stays here only for a few more hours; one by one, all of the petals will fade, and all that will be left is this image in your mind, the beauty you could see maybe once in a lifetime."

Tata took my pointer finger and gently touched it to the petals. I was scared I would rip one. "Don't worry, you can touch them," he said. Keeping my hand close to his heart, he looked over my head. "Passiflora is a wildflower. It survives in the cold and the drought." I still remember his words as if it was yesterday.

~

It was Mama Tanta, my grandmother on Mama's side, who gave Tata his nickname. On one of her overnight visits, probably in the late spring, in the time when the Passiflora still had some of its flowers, she patiently listened to Tata's lesson about his favorite plant. I didn't witness it, but I believe

Tata told her the full Latin name: Passiflora Elegans. The next day, while Tata was outside, she couldn't remember the name of the flower and called it *Passy*. She'd say, "Flowers come and go, and what's in the pantry is important." I remember her walking from the pantry, and we probably didn't have much in it. "Where's Passy?" she asked.

~

Perhaps the reason I despised all the waiting queues in Dragasani was that at Obogeni I felt freedom. It was Mama's birthplace, and Mama Tanta lived there. I couldn't wait for vacations so I could go there.

There were three villages around Obogeni. First, Ursi (or Bears) was about twelve miles down the hill from Obogeni, the place here the bus made the last stop when I was very young. Second, there was Geamana (Twin), a remote village where my great-grandfather Ion Marinescu lived and taught. To get there one had to walk the trails in the forests and many hills for six miles. The third was Balcescu, over the Topolog River, where Mama Tanta lived before she married. This last route was the scariest. To cross the river there was a suspended walking bridge so narrow and unbalanced that I had to close my eyes when Tata was carrying me under his arm. Mama never brought us there by this route.

The only safe road for me was from Ursi to Obogeni. Before the discovery of the oil in the forests we had to walk six miles or stop a car to give us a lift. But the oil discovery brought in workers and a direct bus to bring us to Obogeni.

People living in Obogeni didn't find it attractive, but I did. It was a rural village of twenty-six houses spread over hills and curved roads, with forests and fruit trees, and everything was wild. I knew everyone by name and played with the kids my age from sunrise to sunset. At the edge of the village, the dirt road ended in a forest, and because no one lived there, I'd assumed it was the end of the world.

It was also the place where I first heard about America. I had no idea where it was. But I got the feeling it was a perfect place since my grandmother mentioned it several times. She said that during the war against the Germans, Romanians had waited for the Americans to come to the country and save them. If they had come on time, she said, the communists wouldn't have taken over Romania.

The closest I got to America was chewing gum. It was my wedding present when I first *got married* at age six in an early summer as I watched the cows on the hills. The groom, Eugen, also six, a little taller than I, but with very dark eyes and hair, braided a wreath of wild daisies he found in the forest and asked me to marry him. I'm not sure if it was his idea or my cousin Nae's, who was five years older than I.

Eugen's uncle lived in the United States and would mail him presents that included chewing gum. So, in exchange for that gum, I accepted his proposal, and Nae married us under a tree, pretending to be Father Buga. He tried singing like the priest of our little church, but he was better than the Father. I tried not to laugh. We were distracted by the ceremony, and the cows disappeared into the cornfield.

I loved the smell and taste of the gum. For days, I kept the gum with me, taking tiny bits and put it back in the pack at night after chewing it. Curious about where the peppermint gum came from, I asked Nae where America was. He was, just like me, on vacation, but had a pile of math exercises he had to complete for school, and I'd promised his father, my Uncle Nicolae, he'd do that. I think his father had a planned trip to Obogeni to bring us some supplies and check on Nae.

"This is the world. We are here," he said, spinning a globe my uncle Tica had in a spare room. "This is America, the third largest country on Earth." And then he went back to his studies.

With the globe in my hand, I measured the sizes. Romania was my pinky fingertip. America —my palm.

~

Mama Tanta was frugal with words but was much better than Mama. I wanted to know our family story, and the more they both pushed me away, the more inquisitive I became. With Mama Tanta, I learned to wait for the right moment—watching the cows. Her favorite stories were about her mother, who died young, probably from an abortion, leaving five children in the care of my great-grandfather Ion Obogeanu. Coming from a well-off family, and even with a handful of siblings, Mama Tanta studied at an etiquette school, where she learned how to cook, talk, and behave. I always laughed when she showed me how to peel a potato in one cut. She never broke the peel.

When she was ready to apply her skills, she had an arranged marriage to a man twelve years her senior—my grandfather, Ionel Marinescu. She was only sixteen years old. "Did you love him?" I asked her one day.

Mama Tanta said that love was not in the cards for her. I found it strange when she told me and thought that I would never marry someone I wouldn't love. She described how they first met. "He came on a horse to see me, twenty kilometers away, in Balcescu. It was a Sunday and raining, and the tree buds were popping. When I saw your grandfather and his father on the horses, I hid under a table. They came to see me and arrange the wedding with my dad. My sister called me, 'Tanta, they are here!' I was shy and didn't look up, not once, until we sat down to eat."

The following autumn she moved to Obogeni as Ionel's wife. She left the house with the bride's trousseau—several horses, cows, and boxes full of handmade bedsheets, dresses, and gowns. I tried to find out what she thought about my grandfather, but all she said was, "I was a kid." I didn't push her for more. Later, I *translated* and discussed her response with my cousins, and we all agreed she didn't love my grandfather at the beginning but grew to respect him.

My grandfather owned properties in Obogeni and surrounding areas, as well as farms, horses, and cows. He came from a renowned family of teachers from Geamana (Twin.) That's how Mama Tanta ended up in Obogeni. Their firstborn child was Nicolae, my cousins Nae and Gabriela's dad, then my mother Vivi, and last, Uncle Tica.

The homestead had several houses and barns. There was the Big House, where Uncle Tica and his wife Nina lived. Its high walls and large fireplaces, and the old furniture occupying the six large rooms, were all a mystery to me. I used to look at a black-and-white picture of my grandparents hung on a yellow wall in the main hall. Mama Tanta bitterly told me how the communists occupied the Big House for several years, after the war and under Dej's reign, but Mama's memory—I think I was in high school when I fully understood this episode—provided me with more details.

Mama told me she remembered the summer night when she was seven, and the sound of cars and gendarmes surrounding their house. Her father had grabbed her from the bed and locked her in a cubicle cut in the floor.

"You don't move. Keep your ears covered, and don't make any sound until I get you," he warned, fear and desperation in his voice.

She'd wanted to ask who the people outside screaming were.

"Come out! Hands on your head!" she heard, shouted over and over.

The last thing she remembered was the scratching sound of a dresser being dragged across the floor to conceal her hiding place.

She woke up next to her younger brother, Tica, on a wooden bed in the small house they used as a summer kitchen, her older brother, Nicolae, wiping her face with a wet towel. How she had gotten there, she couldn't recall. Her mother started a fire to warm them, but there was no sign of her dad.

"Where's Pa?" she asked Nicolae.

"They arrested him," he answered, holding her hand in hopes of comforting her.

She didn't know what arrested meant but realized it was something terrible.

It was still dark outside, and she was cold despite the fire. She'd heard the engines of cars pulling in the driveway and stopping between the big and the small house, just a few feet away from where they had been hiding. Then there was a terrifying silence. It weighed upon her.

Though she couldn't say then that had happened, she knew life had changed.

At daybreak, she spied the red flag fluttering on the roof of the big house where they'd gone to sleep the night before. The gendarmes were moving her bed and other furniture from their home, placing it haphazardly in carts pulled by her family's horses. The sheep, pigs, chicken, and her horse were already gone. By noon, several trucks had carried away their supplies, vegetables, and all the grains they needed to plant in the spring.

Their home was no longer theirs.

The big house became the new residence of the communist leaders in the area, while forty feet away, the spare, one-bedroom shack, formerly used for summer days, would become her family's residence and solace.

They had lost nearly everything overnight, yet life went on and, after a time, it seemed once more to fall into routine, as though the one great upheaval had been the whole of the change.

It had, however, simply been the calm before the coming storm.

Two years later, the news that she was to go live with her aunt in a village about fifty miles away, came as a total surprise. More surprising still was that she was going to be adopted and forced to change her surname, to gain a chance to attend a day school and eventually go to college.

The day she left the courtroom with a new identity, and before Mama Tanta brought her to a photoshop to take a picture together before dropping her off at the bus station with her adoptive parents, Mama understood that her childhood was long gone. That day, she buried her past, her memories, and the few walnuts she'd grabbed before the trip to Olanesti, her new residence. It would take some time to remember her new name, Olanescu, changed from Marinescu. Her new family—Mama Tanta's sister and her husband, would protect her and hide her identity.

Later, as a history student, two hundred miles west in a city called Timisoara, she learned the way communism took over the country during the first years of Dej's reign. She memorized the Stalinist history of Romania in the way that the party dictated. Besides her college trips to visit monuments and learn the history of the country, she mentioned how the guy she fell for had complimented her, and how she had broken up with him over a refused kiss, just a few months before her graduation.

The other memory—when she felt revenge over Dej's death. She was twenty-one years old. Her short, dark-chocolate hair contrasted with her light skin, the bangs over the top of the head, the prominent cheekbones I inherited. Deer eyes, I called them.

I can picture her how, at 10:30 AM sharp, on March 24, 1965, Mama stood in silence at the university while the sirens rang. All the church bells and the sirens of naval vessels and factories sounded at once, and everything and everyone stopped what they were doing for three minutes—buses and trains, people on the street, students in school, doctors in hospitals, factory workers—every single soul.

While Dej was laid to rest with the salvos of tanks and artillery firing, just like Stalin, Mama's mind was somewhere else—what had happened on that night when the gendarmes arrested her father and took everything away. This was her past that she couldn't talk about. Her identity. Her true family and siblings.

How, on the night of the arrest, with Dej's signature, her family became the capitalist enemy of the proletariat. I learned later in life about this war against the middle class and anyone who owned land and animals. This war had a name: Decree 83, issued on March 2, 1949, and applied on the same day. Right then, all the productive land became the property of the Romanian government, like the kolkhoz in Russia.

"The poor peasants support our actions for collectivization, and we'll start the callous war against the rich peasants," the decree read. They were the enemy of the hard-working class.

When Mama graduated, she naively believed that no one could surpass Dej's tyranny, that Ceaușescu would bring about a positive change in their nation, a defiance of the Soviets' influence and the return of Romania to its people.

Little did she know how wrong she was.

Her hope for better times grew as the new leader, Comrade Ceaușescu, condemned his mentor Dej's personality cult and actions and promised, in exchange, a new era with new people. "We intend to create the most noble product of nature: *The New Man*—the creator of everything that exists in our society. The New Man will be pure and honest and raised with healthy morals," he said at the following Communist Party's Congress. "As a social innovator, the New Man thinks and acts upon a revolutionary spirit and hates the old ruling."

He immediately changed the name of the country from the Popular Republic to the Socialist Republic of Romania and promised sovereignty from the Soviets.

Like many other people at the time, my mother believed him and accepted a teaching position at a school closer to Obogeni, but far enough to keep her away from home during the week. She waited for the day when she could go to Obogeni without taking hidden trails in the forests and walking miles in the dark.

The first thing she was required to do as a new teacher was to enroll in the Communist Party. The local government announced a meeting with all new teachers and handed them the form. Those who refused to enlist in the party were considered the enemy of the Comrade and the party.

The application to join the growing list of Ceaușescu's party, whose motto was, "Proletarians from all countries, unite," listed the objectives: the ruling class were the proletarians, and it was based on Marxism and against any western influences.

To her, the petition sounded just like Dej's pure definition of nationalism when he ordered the arrest of the opposition party leaders and sent them to terrifying prisons. Some died immediately. Others, like her real father, would begin the digging of the Danube-Black Sea Canal, meant to shorten the traveling on the water by 100 km. His death in 1962 was still a mystery to her.

The discrimination didn't end with her father. She saw how much her brothers had struggled to finish high school because of their upbringing, and how the name they held onto weighed them down like an anchor. They had to keep a day job and attend night classes, while she could go to high school because she appeared to come from a different family. If she stumbled across her brothers on the streets of Ramnicu Valcea, the capital of the county, where all three continued their education, she would willfully pass by, avoiding each other's eyes until they were safe to talk.

This was the world Ceaușescu was building around them, formed on the ashes of Dej's rule.

She thought about all that when the form was laid before her. Then, without an option, she signed the promise and paid her first dues.

~

A year had passed, and Mama's hope for a real change faded. As a teacher in 1965 she was made to use the new history manuals regarding Ceaușescu and communism, making sure she didn't bring any real heroes from old times into her teaching. "No one was greater than the young boy who sacrificed his life for the country, Comrade Nicolae Ceaușescu."

Monitored day in and day out by the local government, Mama received a *satisfactory* evaluation at the end of the school year. Just before school ended, at the last party meeting, she learned that all *untainted* teachers in the country were required to attend an important two-week training at their regional centers to further their education. Mama was one of them.

The nearest town was Dragasani, about fifty miles away from Dragoesti. It was also the second largest town in the county, after Ramnicu Valcea where she went to high school.

Her first time in Dragasani, she loved the surrounding hills covered in vineyards and the Olt River she could see from the second floor of a high school dorm she shared with twenty women, crowded together. She didn't need to guess which ones were infiltrated by Ceaușescu's Securitate—she could tell through their language and behavior, but especially the Soviet doctrines she had memorized in college helped her identify those people without a second guess.

But Mama had prepared since she was a child to live her life in dorms. She had a *pure* family, and when she was pressed to talk about those who had a bad influence on the country's communist future, she condemned the *enemy*, as was expected of her. Most of the time, she read or played chess with a colleague she knew from college, avoiding placing herself in situations where the Securitate might approach her. And then she met Tata. I'm not sure when she'd told him about her true identity.

~

Finding out how my grandfather died was not an easy task. Over the years, while I heard stories about different events, Mama Tanta referred to that time frame, "When Ionel was in prison at..."

It occurred to me he spent many years in different prisons to reeducate him and clear his mind of faith in God and his political beliefs. I can't imagine what life was like for him there, although I have read testimonies from those who survived these long sentences for political purification. I refused to imagine my own blood spilling at the hands of incarceration officers. But I could picture the difficulties he and other political prisoners encountered while digging with a shovel the largest canal from the Danube River to the Black Sea.

The last time my grandfather was released from prison was January 1962; by that time Mama was already attending college in Timisoara. He wrote her a letter that Mama saved, and I found it in her secret room. He complained about some back pain and a headache and questioned himself if his heart was all right. Waiting for her to come home in the summer, Mama Tanta told me this story when we watched the cows one day. I didn't see her shed any tears, but her voice was softer than usual.

One day in February, my grandfather went to visit his father in Geamana. He had to walk there on those hills and forests he knew very well. But he never came back. It was a harsh winter that year, she remembered, and she waited and waited for Ionel all night. The next morning, worried, she sent someone to check with her father-in-law about Ionel's whereabouts and got word that Ionel had left the previous day. For the next few weeks, some people and even Mama Tanta walked the trail back from Geamana to Obogeni but couldn't find any sign of Ionel. At one point, Mama Tanta thought he probably got arrested again and waited to receive a notification or hear from her husband. When the snow began melting in March, someone found his body on the side of the trail.

"I couldn't tell your mother; it was a long distance from Timisoara, and very expensive. Nicolae and Tica thought not to let her know," she told me, her voice stern. "She *had* to finish college."

Mama told me she'd found out her father was dead while waiting for the bus in Ramnicu Valcea at the end of the semester. Her plan was to go to Obogeni for a few weeks and later, to Olanesti. Someone she knew from her native place asked her how she was feeling. "Feeling about what? That Tata is home?" She remembered the confusion when the person realized Mama didn't know. The world crashed then. She said the shock almost killed her. When she got home, walking all the way from Ursi to Obogeni, she didn't feel the weight of her luggage. Her heart did.

~

I thought about this story for a long time. Mama Tanta waiting for Mama at the front gate, walking the dirt road to greet her. Mama, seeing the black fabric posted on the front of the house and on both sides of the wooden gate—the Romanian sign of mourning someone who died. Only then did she believe it was true. "Tata? Why didn't you tell me?" Mama asked, pointing to the black fabric. "If I had told you, what could you have done?"

Perhaps this was the reason Mama never laughed during my childhood. She'd probably buried her emotions in the place where my grandfather was laid to rest. But one thing never changed over the years—Mama's sobbing every time we went to Obogeni. Only then did I understand why Mama cried on one side of my grandfather's grave, while Mama Tanta—on the other, each hiding their tears. And I knew, without any of them saying it, that Mama blamed all of them—Mama Tanta and her brothers—for not telling her the truth. The tears that fell were those of regret on one side and those of blame on the other. But, because of their pride, none of them would admit it.

Mama Tanta and Mama, on the day of the adoption

Mama in college

Mama (left) with my aunt Tuti, Nae's mother, in Olanesti. Probably Mama was in college.

Chapter Six: Immigrant Lesson

Derby Line, April 2001

The girls were ready for school and waiting for Lyman to come back from feeding the cows. Instead, they found me grabbing some clothes from my luggage. Not knowing where we were going that day, except for dropping off the girls at the school, I hoped to find a bathroom somewhere to wash and change the clothes I'd been wearing since leaving Romania.

"Did you sleep well, Dana?" Pearl asked while grabbing her backpack. I nodded, "Yes," hiding my underwear, socks, and bra in my briefcase, on top of my pants and a blouse.

"Ready?" Lyman hurried, leaving the plastic pail next to the entrance door. His face was red, with icicles on his eyebrows, and the snow on his pants reached above his knees.

"I found the dead cow," he told the girls. "On the other side. On Perkins' Road. "We need to remove it before he sees it," Jody muttered.

Outside, the irradiant light felt too strong; even protected by photosensitive lenses, I had to dim my eyes. Except for our tracks and the sled's, no other foot had stepped here. I walked behind everyone this time, clenching my fists in the gloves, looking around as if I had landed on foreign land in outer space. The truth was unbearable to me. Thoroughly irritated, I couldn't forgive myself for missing the clues Lyman brought with him to Bucharest.

To that point, I had thought I was good at reading people. I did it for a living, and my instincts of fear or trust always worked. I wasn't mad at Lyman. His response, "Don't ask, don't tell," was sufficient to understand that it was my fault that I hadn't asked a lot of questions before coming to America. Suddenly, a memory of me at five or six years old struck me, the first time I remembered it: it was the day I didn't recognize Mama's voice. It was winter, Livia bundled up to the head with a scarf and white hat, her legs on the sled trail, and me, pushing her uphill on the same road I'd walk to get milk. But the outside phone bell was ringing so loud that I could hear it from the top of the hill. I wasn't supposed to answer the phone and I ignored it, wanting to slide a little longer. The bell stopped but then rang again and again. *Someone wanted to talk,* I thought.

"Daniela?" I heard my name from the other end.

"Yes. Who's that?"

"You don't recognize me?" a lady was questioning me.

"No."

"I'm your mother," the woman said.

"You're not my mom. Mama is at school."

"But who do you think I am?"

"I don't know, but I need to hang up. I'm not supposed to talk to strangers."

"Wait!" the woman snapped. "Ask me anything if you don't believe I'm your mother."

I asked her everything I thought only Mama knew: her name, nickname, where she worked, Livia's name and age, Mama Tanta's village. Indeed, she answered everything correctly, but still, I didn't believe it was her.

"I'm at the hospital," she said. "*That* hospital where Aunt Pusa works."

"Are you sick?"

"A little, but I'll be fine."

I wasn't sure why that memory popped up about thirty years later, but I couldn't take my mind off it. Indeed, Mama was fine after she'd gotten back from the hospital, but why she was there in the first place I'd never know or understand. That morning, protecting my face with a scarf, the answer came with sudden pain, a truth I had avoided for so long.

She had an induced abortion, I was certain, and I planned to ask her the first time I'd have a chance to call her. *Strange,* I thought, *I had to come to America to find out about Mama.*

But the memory of Mama's secret intrigued me on that morning: not knowing my own parent, the one I had trusted the most. How was I supposed to read Lyman's mind if I had failed with my own blood? And how did the man I thought I knew and loved become such a stranger, one I would have avoided in other circumstances? The simple way was to call my sister and tell her that I needed money for a ticket. I needed to get to the airport by bus. But first, I needed documents to leave the country and access the Internet to talk to my sister. By then, the court case would have clear me. As for my Romanian friends, I'd take the blame and move on.

I needed to know the truth about him before leaving America, and if I was blinded by love or plain stupid. Or both.

~

After we dropped the girls off in front of the high school, we went for breakfast at a diner on the road closer to the farm. With the smell of bacon and fresh coffee came an inviting warmness from a fireplace. I was ready to cry out with happiness. Next to the window—I always love window's seats, probably to see everything going on behind my back—Lyman pulled the chair up for me and helped with my coat. He removed his hat and coat also and unfolded the menu for me to look.

I asked Lyman to order the same for me and hurried to the bathroom, grabbing my briefcase. Relieved the green *vacant* light was on, I locked the door. A few minutes later, I saw my face projected into the mirror. If there had been more room, I would have taken a step back. The raccoon-like eyes were dimmed by circles I never had before. Only the pea freckle on my left cheek showed the old me. In a hurry, I washed and changed, dumping the worn clothes in the garbage can. On top, I rolled paper towels. Lastly, I combed my tangled hair and applied pink lipstick. Still, my eyes were worn out, and my heart seemed heavy.

I found Lyman talking to the waitress. He introduced me to her. "My beautiful wife, Donna." He still couldn't pronounce my name as I expected, but hearing my name mispronounced wasn't my worry. The look of that woman was. She was a middle-aged woman with long colored blonde hair and an athletic figure, and Lyman said she was the owner of the place. She didn't say much of anything to me, and before she returned with the coffee, Lyman gave me my first immigrant lesson.

"Women here don't like it when their available men go outside the country to get a wife. There are plenty of single women looking for a smart man like me!" He laughed, and his face turned red. Pondering if I should say something or not, I watched his hands grabbing mine, kissing each of them. "I love you. I would come for you to end of the world. Soon we'll get wedding bands. I promise I'll take care of you."

I wasn't sure who was more nervous, Lyman or me, but I knew the more he talked, the less believable he was becoming.

I wanted to say that he'd lied to me, but the truth was he hadn't. *I* hadn't asked. *He* hadn't told.

The lady returned with our orders on four large plates: enormous French crepes, eggs, bacon, and toast.

"It's called a pancake." Lyman invited me to try it while I stared at the plate. It was buttery with a lot of syrup and Lyman said it was the best— Vermont maple syrup trademark. I took a bite and didn't like it, so I had an egg and tried the coffee again. This time, I didn't detect any perfume. The coffee was so weak, even without milk. I closed my eyes and drank some as if it were good poison to give me a kick. It made Lyman laugh. "You'll get used to it," he said. "Now, can you understand my take on your coffee? How I felt about it?" He made a grimace as if he were collapsing from too much caffeine. I smiled. "That's my girl!" Lyman exclaimed. It had been so long since either of us displayed any sign of excitement.

He ate slowly, talking about the eggs and bacon from organic farms, cows and manure, and Vermont mountains. "Everyone wants a piece of Vermont. I have ten acres." But my mind was somewhere else.

~

Half an hour later, we were in a parking lot to fill the car with gas, Lyman said. In the Romanian language, gas means *fart*. I smiled, thinking of how hilarious the translation sounded in my native language. Then I saw him removing the nozzle and pumping, but I wasn't sure what. My guess was the American cars run on something special, some secret gasoline made to solve the oil crisis and become energy independent. I thought I'd give Livia a hysterical laugh in my first email, "Dear Sis, Americans save their farts in a canister to run their cars!" It felt good laughing, and I pulled the passenger's mirror to see the latest transformation. The little food and coffee helped me get some of my strength back as the dullness disappeared. It took an egg and a weak coffee to clear my thoughts.

Lyman returned with a couple of newspapers and parked on the side of the store next to a pay phone. He circled some phone numbers and made calls, every time returning disappointed. I wanted to ask him why he didn't have a cell phone, especially having children in school, but he'd anticipated my question. "I don't want to be disturbed. If I need someone, I'll call." He sounded convincing but I didn't buy it.

"Give me a kiss for good luck," he said. "We'll find a place, I promise. We won't go back to the farm tonight."

I felt his cold lips pressing on mine, but the butterflies in my stomach were frozen.

"Let's go for a ride, to show you Vermont. We'll get your ID card today. It's your first step living in America."

I couldn't believe he read my mind—the ID to get out.

Children of the Decree

Maria D. Holderman
Romania: Popular Hatred of Ceauşescu Grows

"Popular hatred of Romanian President Ceauşescu, which has been building for several years, has taken on a harder edge in recent weeks, [redacted] a recent series of minor and unconnected protests directed against the President and his even less popular wife. [redacted] increased grumbling that the time has come for someone to kill the Ceauşescus.

Still other Romanians reportedly amuse themselves by speculating openly about painful ways for them to die.

The reemergence of grim humor and bitter grumbling undoubtedly reflects intense concern about the approaching winter. Many Romanians believe they face record food, heat, and energy shortages as well as crumbling social services and punitive wage cuts and layoffs. As in late 1985, when memories of the previous severe winter produced similar fears, exaggerated rumors of further draconian restrictions might trigger spontaneous protests such as the recent riot in Brasov. The situation is likely to be most tense in late winter when privately stored supplies are depleted, and economic production slows in the face of energy cutbacks and transportation bottlenecks." (CIA, Top Secret, 28 November 1987, page 6)

Children of the Decree

Chapter Seven: Enemies

Proud of the watch Tata bought with my money, I couldn't wait for the next vacation, to go to Obogeni and show it to Mama Tanta. I remember how I dressed for the trip. That year, I participated in the school dance, and each of us had to wear a white shirt with some material attached to the arms, like a butterfly. I loved to hold my arms and pretend that I was flying. That's how I arrived at Obogeni, Mama Tanta waiting for us at the bus stop in front of the church. She didn't like my shirt, she said, right after she kissed me.

"Too colorful, and it looks like you have wings."

Later, I changed and put the shirt in a bag, along with a blanket to sit on the grass while watching the cows. Then I grabbed my stick to turn the cows around and gave Livia the bag with clothes to bring with us.

We were both excited to start our summer in the hills with no parents to tell us what to do. So, as always, we played tag and climbed in the trees, ate berries, and lay down in the grass. We couldn't have been happier listening to our laughter coming back as an echo from the other side of the hill. I guess those were the happiest days of our childhood.

But that summer I also found out why Mama's youngest brother, Uncle Tica, who lived with Mama Tanta, disliked Tata. Too young to understand the cues prior to that summer—although I had the feeling something wasn't right between the two men I loved so much—he asked me directly why Tata didn't work in the garden. Then, without waiting for an answer, he told me that Tata was a dandy and left everything around the house on Mama's shoulders while he spent his time *watching flowers grow and die.*

His voice grew sharper when he complained that he found Mama working in the garden whenever he came to Dragasani to visit. If he wanted to listen, I could have told him that Mama's habits with the garden included exclusive attention. No one was allowed to weed or water anything without her input.

"When Passy doesn't watch his flowers, in his suit and tie, he sleeps," my uncle said. "Why doesn't he help my sister?"

Mama Tanta overheard the conversation and asked me to follow her into the house. She observed that I was sad and explained that Uncle Tica had a few shots of *tzuica*, a vodka-like drink.

Still, it didn't justify his attitude toward me.

While I was seething about what my uncle said about Tata that summer, I learned that "Passy," Tata's nickname, was not the only way to pick on him. This time, it referred to Tata's obsession with the plants' Latin names. I was cleaning my room, keeping the window opened, the chore of the moment, and I heard him telling my aunt, "Go get some *Stellaria Media* for the chickens," imitating Tata's voice unsuccessfully. He could have said chickweed as before. But, instead, I laughed, lip-synching my uncle. Since that day, he and I had used the Latin names for all the weeds. It became my game, a way to soften the relationship between my uncle and Tata.

When one of us got a cut or an open wound, I'd say, "Per Passy, some *Plantago Lanceolata* would stop the bleeding." That was the ribgrass. When I really wanted to be sarcastic, I referred to parsley as *Petroselinum Crispum*. He had a hard time pronouncing this name. Exactly what I wanted.

But the truth about Tata and my uncle's feud, however, included a dowry. It happened before my parents got married, on one of Tata's first visits to Obogeni. It turned out that Uncle Tica promised Tata a fat piglet to serve at their wedding but gave him the runt of the litter. When Tata asked Uncle Tica why he changed his mind and switched the thriving piglet, my uncle said that the promised pig didn't grow much because it didn't like oak leaves, like the rest of them. Tata never got over that.

"He lied, and I don't like people who say something and do the opposite."

For a child, I handled their affairs by keeping quiet. I never told one what the other said, and in time my strategy proved to be successful. They never fought again.

~

However, my biggest enemy was my cousin Nae. He was the son of my Uncle Nicolae, Mama's oldest brother who lived in Olanesti. Just like Livia and me, he and his older sister, Gabriela, spent many summer vacations at my grandmother's, and he would tease us incessantly. But that summer, when I was twelve, I paid him back.

A great drought gripped Romania. Not a drop of rain had fallen all summer. Vegetables died on the vines. Even the weeds died of thirst. The heatwave killed any breath of wind and dried the wells and cracked the soil. You could step into a hole and lose your shoe if you had any on. So, of course, I only wore shoes on Sunday mornings when my grandmother forced me to put some on before going to church, as if God cared if I had shoes on or not.

Early one morning, Mama Tanta woke Nae and me. She wanted us to bring a bull to a farmer living in another village about ten miles away, who wanted to buy it. We had to walk. She sent us on our way, giving Nae a bag with food.

"You have some tomatoes, onion, and bread. Here is the water." The water was in an *ulcior*, a pottery jug. Once on the road, we crossed the forest to shorten our journey. I walked behind the bull, and when it slowed down, I had to say *hais* to make the bull go to the left or *cea* to make him turn right. Nae was in front, holding the rope looped around the bull's neck.

The morning was fresh, the sky dark blue, and the birds were waking up. I was still sleepy, but the cold air snapped me awake. I heard something move in the bushes and then a strange noise. I paused, my heart jumping in my chest.

"A bear!" Nae yelled.

"Where?" I screamed, but Nae started laughing. It was clear he'd planned to scare me. Then Nae asked me all sorts of stupid questions, but I didn't answer. Soon the sun rose, and I stopped listening to him altogether, so he finally gave up. We took a break and ate some food and drank some water.

We went up a hill, and at the top, we saw the Olt River just a mile away. The water was sparkling in the sun. I felt as if we'd been traversing a desert and had found a spring.

"Do you see the river?" Nae asked.

"I am not blind," I said, staring at the distant river.

We stopped for some time to look at the river from a distance. I just wanted to stand with my feet in the cold water and wash my face.

"Passy, do you know that it's still early? We saved a lot of time going the short way. Let's go to the river for a few minutes, and then we'll hurry to make up the time. Ah?"

We picked up our pace and made it to the river quickly.

"You can take a bath here, where the water isn't deep, and I'll go ahead. Hurrah!"

I couldn't swim, and the only way to take a bath there was to be naked.

He ran off, leaving me to tie the animal up. Meanwhile, I saw Nae's bare back in the shallower water as he jumped into the river. I called his name but heard only his laughter and the splash of water.

I thought of all the mean things he'd said to me at different times—that I was "dark in the mouth," which spelled I was mean. Or another time, while I set up the dinner table, he asked me, "Passy, has your forest blossomed?" That indelicate question embarrassed me the most.

It was time for payback. I followed his tracks and found all his clothes. I picked them up, one by one, except for his shoes—I had too many things in my hands already to be able to grab them. I buried his clothes in the mud under a big rock in the water, and then I ran away. I left the bull tied to a tree but took the bag with the water and food.

I strolled, taking the time to study the trees and flowers—I had nothing else to do. I picked leaves, hay, and moss. But as the hours went by, I felt guilty, and I knew I was in trouble.

When I got closer to home, I waited in a nearby forest until almost sunset, watching for Nae. I lay down on the grass and spied a deer nibbling on the green carpet. It turned its head in my direction and returned my gaze. It was the most beautiful creature I'd ever seen. So gentle, yet wild. I tried to remain still, afraid it would leave, and that the beauty of the forest would disappear with it. Eventually, however, my leg tingled, and when I moved it, the deer fled.

I walked up the hill, back to the dirt road. It wasn't yet dark, but the last remains of the day faded away. Since I saw no sign of Nae, I decided to wait for him instead of going into the house. So, I climbed the tallest apple tree in front of the house, next to the fence, and waited for his arrival. But the dog, tied to another tree, wouldn't stop barking. Finally, my grandmother opened the door and looked to see if someone was at the gate. As she peered out, Uncle Tica appeared at the next door.

"What happened to them?" my grandmother said. "They should have been home by late afternoon, and they're still not back. You need to go look for them."

Just then, I heard Nae opening the gate behind me. My heart jumped from my chest, and I was afraid I'd fall off the branch—my bottom hurt from sitting for so long. I was curious what he would be wearing if he'd found the spot where I buried his clothes.

"Where is she?" Nae asked.

I kept quiet, but the dog kept barking, and I stifled my laughter as the interrogation began.

"What did you do to her?" my grandmother asked.

"Why is the bull back?" Uncle Tica asked.

"She left me with the bull – and without clothes. I'm going to kill her!"

"How did she get your clothes?" my uncle asked.

The moment I saw Nae, by the light of a gas lamp my grandmother had brought outside, I could not help but giggle. He'd made a skirt from wild rhubarb leaves. I wanted to scream, "You, Tarzan, I, Jane!" But I kept my mouth shut. There was no way for me to get out of the tree without fighting Nae.

"What if someone killed her? What if she got lost? Oh, Virgin Mary, bring her home!" Mama Tanta cried.

I could hear her praying for my salvation from the devil. But the *devil* was still quiet, her sore bottom perched on the tree's branches. I waited patiently, listening as they sorted out what I'd done. Finally, Mama Tanta called my name, shouting no one would hurt me, and it would be better to get in the house. Still, I waited until they went inside before I climbed down from the tree and opened Mama Tanta's front door.

"Are you alright?" Mama Tanta asked.

"Yes, I am," I said and closed the room door behind me.

The following day, afraid I'd be in trouble, I heard Mama Tanta scolding Nae. "If you don't mess with her, she'll leave you alone."

He promised her he'd leave me alone, but I knew I had to watch my back.

Dynamite comes in small packages, I thought.

~

For the next two weeks, all was well. We played Hide and Seek, and Uncle Tica joined in, but he didn't like it when we found him buried in the haystack. My uncle wanted to win, and so did Nae. I had fun playing with them and didn't mind when they tricked me; it was part of the game. I felt as if I belonged there, and I wanted to stop time right then, with all of them around.

I knew Nae was a senior in high school, and that he'd soon take on new challenges. So, one night, watching the lightning bugs, he brought me some and said, "I hope they'll help you find your way."

I knew what he was talking about.

On a hot day, my grandmother sent Nae and me to fetch some water. The Obogeni well was one mile away, on Father Buga's property.

"Do you wear a bra?" my cousin asked me, smirking, as we walked on the dirt road, carrying our pails. He gazed curiously at where a bra should have been, and I felt ashamed, which was just the reaction he wanted, as when he'd asked about me growing a forest. *He didn't learn his lesson.*

Since the day was hot, Nae wore a tight swimsuit, and I could see something engulfed in the shape of two eggs—part of a man's anatomy.

When we got back home, I pulled Luiza aside, Uncle Tica's four-year-old daughter, and told her Nae was stealing eggs from the chicken coop and had hid them in his shorts. It was a lie.

"Guess where the eggs are?" I asked Luiza. Then I planted the seed, "In his Speedo! If you don't get the eggs from Nae, you won't have any to eat. And you'll be sick. You'll die!"

Luiza believed me and ran after Nae in the yard, screaming, "Nae has eggs in his panties! Give me the eggs!"

Nae ran fast, trying to get away from her and into Uncle Tica's house. He caught his foot as he jumped over the pigs' trough and fell to the ground. Luiza got on top of him, trying to find the "eggs." He was hurt, and his legs were bleeding, but Luiza was still screaming and clawing at his private parts, "My eggs! My eggs! Give me the eggs!"

I watched the battle from the top of my grandmother's stairs. Nae held onto his Speedo while Luiza tried to pull it down to *find* the eggs.

"There are no eggs!" Nae yelled.

He heard me laughing and glared at me. I slammed and locked the doors on him and stayed inside the house until it was time to take the cows to the pasture.

Nae never tried to mess with me again. A time began when we both silently agreed we were equal.

~

After the harvest, Mama Tanta came to visit us. She brought us some walnuts, pears, cheese, and eggs in a bag filled with corn meal so they wouldn't break, and *tzuica*. She had visited Nae and his family a few weeks before. Sometimes, Livia and I got jealous when she talked about Nae and his sister, Gabriela. We thought she loved them more but later found out that our older cousins felt the same way when she spoke about us.

She said Nae was busy studying for college, and that Uncle Nicolae had hired private tutors to keep him focused on his studies. That was a big deal. Spots at universities were limited, the exams were difficult, and only the top students were accepted. I knew why the selection was strict. Ceaușescu didn't want to create many intellectual people, as the country's emphasis was and was to stay on industrialization and farming.

Children of the Decree

Mama Tanta had a soft spot for Uncle Nicolae and Nae, her first grandson. I found out how my uncle lost his right arm during that visit, a taboo subject we couldn't talk or ask about.

It was in the early fall, she remembered, when my grandfather still in prison. Mama Tanta had hired a combine to cut the grains on holiday, which was the only time she could get help. This was even after the communists took most of my family's land for collectivization, part of the Russian agriculture plan to unite all the land into one large farm. There was only grain left on the hills where no machinery could reach. Then they carried the sheaves of hay or grains by hand.

That day, Uncle Nicolae untied the grain bundles and threw them in the combine. A young *patriot* walking by saw him and pushed him into the machine's claws. Mama Tanta heard Uncle Nicolae screaming, pulled him from the claws, and wrapped a blouse around his arm to stop the bleeding. She carried him in a horse cart to the hospital in Ramnicu Valcea, about thirty miles away. Uncle Nicolae cried all the way, she said, and I guessed she did, too. He lost his right arm, from under the shoulder, at twelve years old.

I saw the pain in her aged hazel eyes, and perhaps a tiny tear dropping, and I understood right then why my grandfather swore at the communists and resisted them. Mama Tanta and her children were the collateral damage, the indirect victims. I knew by then I didn't want to become the next victim. In fact, I wanted none of us to continue to suffer, and I prayed for my cousin Nae's success. I concluded that we were blood, and that we all had to succeed.

The following summer Nae was accepted at the Polytechnic Institute in Bucharest. I was thrilled. It meant my older cousins, Nae and Gabriela, were on their way to achieve their dreams in the world. I was right behind them, waiting for my turn.

~

"Nae is getting married" was the buzz in the family. It was fall, school had started, and I was in twelfth grade.

We prepared for the wedding with new dresses for the girls and a new suit for Tata. Since we couldn't find any quality clothes in stores, my mom bought some fabric, and we kept our dressmaker busy. I was the fussiest one. Because I was skinny, I wanted something that would show my tiny waist but would also cover my small shoulders and my chicken legs. I designed the dress myself and loved how the folds ended above the knees; when I twirled around, it unfolded like a parachute. I was one happy young woman.

On Nae's wedding day we packed early, all of us scurrying from one room to another. When Tata said we needed to leave, we found the car's trunk too small for all our boxes and luggage. It was the first time the four of us would spend a night away from home.

First, Tata praised his car, which he named Maricica. I've never understood why men give their cars and vehicles women's names, but in Romania it seems it's a tradition. When Maricica would stop on hills, or needed new cylinders or coils, Tata would call it Mar'shica—slang for low-class woman—as punishment.

Livia and I stopped annoying Tata when we saw the hills and then the mountains. We passed the roads to monasteries, hidden among the trees, in fortresses hard to conquer in old times. The sun was mild, the air was fresh, and my mind was wandering.

The most spectacular road was from Ramnicu Valcea to Olanesti, which went up into the mountains. The trees were green there, the rivers held plenty of water, and Maricica was still chugging along. It was beautiful.

Tata said that Maricica, the Trabant's name, was a good girl on that day, starting on the first try every time. Maricica was an '81 blue Rambler with two doors, the only vehicle Tata ever owned. He bought it brand new six years prior; it was imported from communist Germany and was a little cheaper than the Romanian Dacia cars.

We parked Maricica on my uncle's street, behind a big hotel and near the police station, in an area that contained the nicest two-story villas. I jumped from the car as soon as we stopped and was embarrassed when I saw the other cars parked there for the wedding. Maricica was the trigger; I could already see the others laughing at it.

We arrived at the town hall and saw Mama Tanta with Uncle Tica and his wife Nina, talking to people outside. When I spotted Nae, he looked sharp and content. We hugged and kissed.

"Come with me. I don't want Tata to see me smoking," he said. We walked behind the town hall, and he lit a cigarette.

"Uncle Nicolae still doesn't know you smoke?"

"No."

The sun was hiding behind the clouds and the mountain peaks. It was a little cold for me, while I waited for Nae to finish his cigarette.

"What time does the "show" start? I asked.

"11:00."

"Hurry. It's 10:45 AM," I said, looking at my Zaria watch.

"Passy," he said, stepping on his cigarette, "you look beautiful."

I asked him if he was happy getting married.

"I am, don't you see it on my face? Look, I am smiling!" and he made a funny face.

It was time for the official ceremony. From my spot, I could see Nae's parents and all my relatives. Next to Nae stood a tall blonde with short hair and thick, full lips, wearing a gray suit with a white blouse, her eyes glowing. I observed Uncle Nicolae's tears. Mama Tanta wept, too. Finally, she whispered, "He looks handsome," and I agreed.

My eyes were on Nae, and I observed that he couldn't rest his hands. For a moment, I forgave all the things Nae did to me when I was younger. One flashback from our childhood sparked in me just then: we watched the cows and ate prunes together. In another, we played Hide and Seek in the dark. Then, I heard a deep sob behind me; I turned and saw my Aunt Tuti, Nae's mom, crying. She had wanted a neighbor's daughter as her daughter-in-law. She was the only person who didn't look happy, and she didn't hide it.

Nae and Cristina signed the marriage license and kissed each other. I saw in his hazel eyes he was happy and heard him saying, "I love you" to his wife.

The reception took place at the most famous hotel in Olanesti, behind my uncle's villa. I was amazed when I saw the lobby. At dinner, the tables were full. This was my first meal in a restaurant. The best part of Nae's wedding was seeing Mama Tanta dance with Uncle Nicolae. I don't remember the name of the song, but I know it was a blues song. We all watched, mesmerized, because Mama Tanta had never danced since her wedding day.

Nae was busy visiting with people, but he came to me several times to ensure I felt all right. He handed me a short glass with a brownish liquid and told me it was whiskey.

"Passy, do you want some? It's American, Johnnie Walker. It's excellent." I didn't know what whiskey was. No, I didn't want any, but I smelled it. It smelled sweeter than the *tzuica* Uncle Tica made from plums, and it didn't stink. When Nae left, I tasted the whiskey with my tongue. *Too hard*, I decided and went back to dancing. When I returned the glass was empty.

On that day I wore makeup and felt beautiful in my black and yellow dress. I could feel some eyes on me. *Not the right time!* I roared in my head when a sharp-looking guy invited me to talk outside on the balcony. Instead, I stayed in and danced my heart out. Some of Nae's friends gave me a lot of attention. Ignoring those eyes, I knew I needed to concentrate on the international baccalaureate program that summer and, after that, on the exams for admission to undergrad school. I felt determined to finish high school with no distractions.

We spent the night with one of our relatives in the village, but I couldn't sleep. I was thinking about my future and how I wanted to be loved.

Tata's Trabant.

My cousin Nae, in his first year as an engineer.

Mama Tanta and my grandfather Ion Marinescu.

Children of the Decree

Chapter Eight: On the Border

Lyman kept quiet, watching my reaction as we drove into the mountains toward Montpelier, Vermont's capital. I could hear Enrique Iglesias playing "Hero" on the radio station known as 95 Triple X. Lyman sang as if he had written the lyrics himself when he married me. When the song faded, he said the lyrics were his true thoughts. "The day we went with George to the mountains…" he said, contemplating the view. "I was speechless. I knew you were the one and I wanted you to be mine. But I was afraid you'd reject me," he added.

I could've told him he was wrong: I was already in love the day my friend George brought us to Bran Castle, known being the home of Dracula, which was the place Lyman most wanted to visit in Romania. A historian and architect, George was born and raised in Bucharest. We met in November of 1996, while waiting for the results of the presidential election at the Social Democrat Party's headquarters. He was the chair of the infrastructure department.

George took the routed through the Rucar-Bran corridor, one of the most spectacular European racing routes through the Carpathians mountains. I could hear George and Lyman's laughter from the back seat while talking about cars and racing, and I watched how Lyman pretended to faint when he saw the narrow road snaking up the mountain without a parapet. That sight alone would have made any adventurous spirit reconsider the risks; one could not help but think of rolling over and sinking into the 2000-meter depression below. Finally, we stopped at the highest point of the mountain.

I flashed back—Lyman was taking pictures and George was smoking a cigarette. I got closer to George and asked for a lighter. We sat on some stones and watched Lyman. "He's all into you," George said. I couldn't believe he just said that. "You're so lucky, Dana. He'll do anything for you."

I remembered asking him how he came up with that idea. "Oh, it's a man thing, you know."

Children of the Decree

At first, I thought Lyman wanted to scare me, as a payback from that Dracula trip. Still, when I saw the turquoise icicles on the side of the majestic mountains covered in snow, I remembered his words, "Our mountains are not high, but they are beautiful."

I had never seen such a blue-green natural color before. But then I remembered the color of my birthstone, the turquoise of Sagittarius, and I thought if I were to choose my preferred stone, it would have been that one. It felt chimerical, shining in the cold weather, and I knew they would disappear soon. I wanted to get out and touch them, wondering how they would feel in my hand.

"Iron ores," Lyman explained, surprised by my spirit of observation. "I told you you'd like it here, remember? I wish George could be here. Vermont is one of the smallest states but has the greenest mountains in the country. And in fall, people come from all over the world to see the foliage. It's breathtaking."

I peeked at Lyman, his profile covered by eyeglasses, the same as during the trip with George when they argued which band was more famous. Now, as I watched him patting the wheel and singing, I relaxed for a second and it felt good. There wasn't anything wrong with this picture: both of us learning how to adjust again.

"I miss George," I said.

He touched my face and moved it closer to his lips. I waited for a kiss with my eyes closed. Instead, his warm breath awoke the sleeping butterflies in my stomach. My lungs filled with air, and I exhaled a long sigh.

"Da, da, da." *Yes, yes, yes.* He smiled.

My memory fell back as if we were with George in his tiny car, crossing the highest Carpathians and spending our lives together, talking about the Rolling Stones, racing cars, and destiny. I remembered flashes of how I first fell in love and how scared I had been, and I wondered if it was possible to love someone I had just met not so long before. I knew he was the one I had been waiting for through all of my life; how I had tried to resist the temptation to let my soul speak, opposing every possibility of being in love with Lyman; how, in my most sincere moments, I understood that *freedom* meant not the cliché of what we hear all the time, but a state of mind one could believe with every cell and nerve.

On that day I thought of every angle of freedom, but ultimately, I could only think of its price.

And then I wanted to remember everything.

~

The plan, Lyman said, was to book a hotel room until we'd be able to rent a proper place. "I'm so sorry I didn't think to stay at a hotel the other night. I should have known we needed a good sleep in a decent place. But, tonight, I'll give you a massage and we'll have room service."

I believed him. He sounded again like the man I had married in Bucharest. He didn't have to say anything else—my heart lightened as if he lifted the weight of the world from my shoulders.

On the way back to Coventry, we stopped at the post office to get Lyman's mail from the past month. He opened his mailbox, grabbed a handful of envelopes, and quickly sorted the *junk* from his paychecks. He was almost done when a childish voice arose behind us, "Goodness, you're back!" A lady almost jumped in the air to hug him. About Lyman's height, she had short, amber brown hair with citrine highlights and a milky tan. Lyman introduced us and said that they were friends. "Best friends," she corrected Lyman.

Juanita P. worked for the state of Vermont and had recently moved to Derby Line. She kept the same post office box in Coventry and was picking up her mail as well. She and Lyman spoke about Lyman's trip and our marriage, and both appeared excited and happy. I loved watching Lyman's hands gesturing in the air. Juanita suggested we have a late lunch in Newport and Lyman agreed immediately. They had so much to talk about. Back in Newport, I thought he had forgotten about our plan when he suggested a tidy restaurant on the lake. Once Juanita learned that most rentals wouldn't be available until the beginning of the month, and that we planned to stay at a hotel, she offered us a room in her rented apartment in Derby Line.

Children of the Decree

I wasn't sure at first if that was a good idea but considering there was about three weeks until the first of the month, I couldn't see why not. In fact, I would have done the same for George, if he had found himself in my situation. And then I understood something else: why I considered George to be one of my best friends. With him, I could talk about everything, and I guessed I meant more to him than just a man's vanity of platonic bonding with the opposite sex. The same was true for Lyman and Juanita and their genuine friendship, which extended back decades. When one was breaking apart the other picked him or her up, became a shoulder to cry on and an ear willing to listen. They seemed good enough for each other.

Juanita lived with her cat in a well-maintained two-story apartment. The spare room was small and empty, facing the street that connected the American and the Canadian border. While Lyman went back to the farm to feed the cows and bring my suitcase, I took a shower and wrapped up in a pink bathrobe Juanita never used.

That evening we went to the mall and bought a mattress, sheets, some towels, food, and things we needed for the bathroom. Lyman knew what we needed. It was clear to me that he had a plan in mind. I didn't want anything for me, I told Lyman. Somehow, my mind was far away, and I couldn't stand the pain of missing everything I loved. The word *Romania* sounded now like a song, coming in syllables, and I wasn't sure how or if I could take it.

We came home late and the lights in the house were dimmed. We tiptoed upstairs with the mattress. The room held nothing but my luggage and the mattress, and I felt like I was in a dwarf's house. The night light across the street glared through the window. Once we made the bed, I grabbed my Romanian body wash and filled the bathtub. It was my real first time alone since I had arrived in America, and I locked the door and soaked in the water. The musky smell transported me to my large bathroom in Bucharest. It wasn't melancholy but the unanticipated torment of a new life suddenly weighed on me. With my hands clamped around my knees, I let the tears run until I choked. I got out of the bathtub when my body and teeth shivered in the cold water.

I found Lyman asleep on the top of the green-brown comforter. He had passed out while waiting for me. Holding my breath, I opened my suitcase in slow motion, concerned not to wake Lyman and face his desire to get intimate. My ironed clothes emanated a familiar scent that impregnated in my brain. The streetlight gave enough light for me to find my pajamas. The scent of my clothes melted me again. I wasn't *home*. I was far away. *Too far away.*

~

Wednesday, the third day after my arrival in America, Lyman went back to work. I learned his ritual quickly: he'd leave the house at 4:00 PM sharp and went to one of the two coworkers' homes he carpooled with. IBM was in Essex Junction, about 80 miles away, and it made sense to carpool and save money on fuel. Lyman was always happy to take a nap in the car when he wasn't driving, and that day he was a passenger.

Once Lyman left, I felt an inner happiness, as I had longed for solitude. Alone for the first time, I grabbed the novel I had stopped writing before Lyman's arrival in Bucharest and read a few pages. The once profound and meaningful words sounded hollow, as if someone else wrote them, and I questioned my wellbeing over the past three days: how could I have changed so fast in so short a time, and how extremely? I knew then I couldn't write to anyone until I gained a balance within my spirit.

~

Through the first week I slept day and night. Trapped between borders I was afraid to explore my surroundings on foot and alone. But I was more afraid to write to Livia and tell her my real situation—where I was living and why, and how much I wanted to return. Instead of writing to my sister from a local library, I spent the time with Juanita's cat. That *girl* was my shadow since I first arrived, and when Juanita said she was wild and attacked people, I was completely surprised. That cat snuggled on my lap and purred whenever I moved my hand to pat her. She became my shadow and followed me around the house.

The first signs of hope arrived at the end of the month. Juanita heard about a rental that would be coming available across the street from her apartment, and she wanted me to see it. It was in a white three-story building I could see through the window while I was lying down on the mattress in my room. We walked over and knocked on the first door on the left. She introduced me to Jack, the manager of the building. Juanita told him I was from Romania and that I had just married a man who worked for IBM. Juanita said we needed the space to start a new life. Jack said a couple had just moved out, and that he had an apartment available on the second floor. I observed Jack, who was over eighty years old, summing me up. He grabbed the key and walked up the stairs slowly and asked for my name.

"Dana or Daniela."

The apartment on the second floor contained French doors, wooden floors, three bedrooms, and a large kitchen. It had a European flavor and my heart lightened. The spacious living room had a China cabinet built in the wall. Daylight came through the windows, conveying a mysterious atmosphere. The back porch looked out to the river, which cascaded beneath a bridge. Jack watched my reaction and smiled.

"Do you like it, *Danielle*?"

"Yes, I do! Moving here?"

He wanted to meet Lyman first and talk to him. He mentioned he would want some letters of recommendations.

"I am one!" Juanita said. "I've known Lyman for many years. He'll make the payments on time; don't you worry about that. He'll be here in the morning to speak with you."

I couldn't wait for Lyman to come home in the morning. When he opened the door, shortly after seven, I jumped from the sofa and told him about the apartment.

"Let's go then!" he smiled. We walked to the building and found Jack waiting for us on the stairway. His living room's large window faced the parking lot in front of the building. He asked Lyman about his job and his whereabouts, and then Lyman followed him upstairs. I stopped in front of the apartment, taking deep breaths of what I felt like was a European smell. The stairs and the doors looked so familiar to me. Until that moment I didn't understand how much I missed everything I left behind.

A sudden pain grew in me as if I were mourning someone. That pain imploded in my brain and heart in a way I couldn't endure. A crack on the stairs, and then the smell of fresh coffee coming somewhere from the third floor transported me back in time. I sighed deeply, a sigh of either of regret or longing; I couldn't figure out which feeling was stronger. *At least*, I convinced myself, *I'll feel home every day.* I wanted to hold onto that moment a little longer, and then Lyman checked on me.

"I know this is the place," he said.

Jack wanted Lyman to bring him a paystub from IBM to prove his employment along with two more references. It was fair, I thought, and Lyman gave him the names and the phone numbers of the colleagues with which he carpooled every day.

"They live around here. Everyone knows them," Lyman added, and indeed, Jack knew one of them.

The next day, Juanita said we could move in. Jack called her at work, and she couldn't wait to tell me the news.

"Really?" I jumped. I wanted to see Jack right away, but the time showed a little past 5:00 PM. The Romanian custom is not to call or visit someone until 6:00 PM. It's called "rest time." So, I waited, pacing around and looking at the building from my dwarf room, and prayed Jack wouldn't change his mind.

He didn't. I guessed Jack saw me coming because he waited with the key in his hand. He handed it to me.

"Danielle, I'll wait here. See if you can unlock the door."

"Thank you," I said, and rushed up to the apartment, skipping two stairs at a time. The door opened and I waved to Jack who stood at the bottom of the stairs. "I feel Romania here," I said, and he shook his head as he saw me doing a silly dance.

Lyman was at work, so I moved everything from Juanita's to the new place myself except the mattress. In the bedroom next to the bathroom, I opened my suitcases and took out some memories that I had brought with me. I placed them in the China cabinet in the wall in the living room. As I walked back and forth between Juanita's and my new place, Jack introduced me to his wife, Joyce. Joyce was seventy-eight and was Jack's second wife. She was from England and had kept to her English upbringing. I loved her short white hair, which was like Mama's, and I told her about my parents.

It is a Romanian tradition to bring something to someone you appreciate, and in my little world out there, I handed Joyce some Romanian embroideries made from macramé. Jack and Joyce then invited me to dinner, and we talked more, and by the time we finished eating the crème of tomato soup with grilled cheese they had prepared, they said to consider them my grandparents. I also learned their stories.

Jack said he was eighty-six years old and had been born American but had changed his citizenship after his first marriage to a Canadian woman. He was an active man—the director of the chorus at the church in Derby Line, the security officer at the library when they had a show, and the manager of the apartment building. I loved his permanent smile and posture; he looked tall and sharp, with silver hair and green eyes.

Joyce served me tea and we all talked on the sun porch, a place I would grow to love. They wanted to know about my family, and we spent the evening talking about Romania. I tried not to cry but I couldn't hide the tears. They both understood that I wasn't happy.

"I saw your desperation in your eyes," Jack said. "I convinced the landlord to accept your application as soon as I met you."

I wanted to thank him again, but Joyce wanted to know more about me. "Now, as our granddaughter, we want to get to know you."

That night I slept under a blanket with the cat for the last time. The streetlight from Jack's building projected the shadows of the passing cars onto the walls of the room. The faint sound of the river pushed its way downhill and through the night. My last thoughts before sleep were about Jack and Joyce, and my wondering when I should start telling them my story. The *whole* story.

Jack and Joyce St Sauveur.

Children of the Decree

Chapter Nine: Wanted

Bucharest, 1997

It was summer in Bucharest and the second day of a heatwave that sent people to hospitals and kids splashing into water fountains. I had to pull my high heels from the hot asphalt as I walked to the taxi station, three blocks away from the apartment I had been renting since the beginning of the summer. I had taken a reporter job at a daily newspaper. I remember the humidity of that late morning, and the notebook I carried with me on that day, and how people walked through their daily routines around me, getting what they needed. I remember all of this because my life would change that day, and I am still not sure if the change was for the better or the worse.

As a chemistry teacher on a three-month vacation, I was waiting for school to start. On that day I planned to meet the Ambassador of Palestine for an interview. My photographer Otiliu had promised to be on time so that we could enter the embassy together, and I worried whether he'd dressed appropriately or not. That was part of the etiquette I'd learned: dress one step behind the black tie, let the ambassador shine, don't bring too much stuff with you and, if possible, carry your notebook in your hand. This way, the security doesn't have to watch your every move when you open your purse for what you need.

"It's so hot," the taxi driver complained when I told him where I was going. "Are you going to the embassy?"

"Yes."

I could see him checking me out in the mirror, but I pretended I didn't notice. Instead, I concentrated my attention on the streets and intersections, which were still crowded, as if the heat simply didn't bother any of the 2.3 million people living in Bucharest. Yet, I'd learned that fresh air, space, and trees were a luxury to those living in the country's capital; this made me long for my hometown.

We passed the People's House, now the new Palace of Parliament Ceauşescu had left us as a legacy and a remembrance of his persona, as if he was screaming from his grave, "Look at what I did for you!" I took a deep breath and calmed my stomach. I wasn't sure if I despised him or the monstrousness he left behind more, and I couldn't care less if you could see the building from the moon or not. People paid with their lives to dig secret tunnels during the construction, just to accommodate his paranoia.

For about a mile or so down the hill from the People's House to the Unirii Square, a new generation of children stuck in Bucharest during the summer found their heaven in the water fountains. I listened to their laughter and loved to hear the splashing and their jumping in the water. My smile grew as I thought *if I were the same age as the children, that was the best place to find me.*

I exited the taxi, giving myself one more self-check—no running makeup, the line of lipstick straight, my teeth clean, no dust on my shoes. I always had my secret notes on the last page of my notebook—the *just in case* dates and details if I needed them. One had to be prepared. It would be best if one knew what mattered most for each country and had an understanding of the conflicts and interests involved. It was important to anticipate questions on sensitive issues that I didn't want to bring up, such as Gaza or the West Bank.

Otiliu appeared from under a shade across the street as sharp as ever.

"You know, don't get in his face, and wait until I bring up the photographs," I reminded him.

"Of course." He buttoned up his light summer suit and opened the metal gate for me. We checked in with security and entered the embassy at five minutes to the hour. I could hear some distant voices and then a handful of diplomats came and greeted us.

In an instant the smell made me dizzy. I could have gone into a hypnotic state right there if I had wanted. The smell was suave but distinctive, a mixture of some biblical incenses I tried to identify but couldn't—the Middle East's smell of coffees and ancient secret plants that even Cleopatra had used to seduce and conquer. To this day, the scent of jasmines, bergamot, santal, amber, and frankincense, and other mystical plants, put me into a euphoric mood.

Maria D. Holderman

I didn't find this ambassador's office different from the others where I had conducted interviews. Before starting, I made sure I wrote down his title and name correctly: Ambassador Extraordinary and Plenipotentiary, H.E. Fouad Al-Bitar.

The interview went well but two things shocked me: I was the first reporter he had accepted to give an interview to since Yasser Arafat appointed him to the embassy in Bucharest in 1990. I also didn't know about the high Palestinian population in Romania. And then the ambassador asked, "What studies do you have?"

Shocked, I look at Otiliu getting ready for pictures, somehow asking him, "What do I do now? Should I answer?" We talked with our eyes and body language, and I understood, *Tell him, what the heck!* It was the first time in my career when I became the interviewee.

The ambassador had other questions for me. He wanted to know how I saw the world and the country, and my take on politics and life in general. I could hear Mama's words ringing in my ear: "white gloves and party manners, and don't say one word more than you need." After about half an hour I was still answering his questions; I realized I had to change the subject and end the meeting. I pointed directly to Yasser Arafat's picture on the front wall and asked about their interactions. The diplomat said Arafat was his brother-in-law.

That answer shocked me. I realized then how my life had changed over the summer. I had become close to people responsible for the world's peace or its wars, the two extreme situations, and all I wanted was to promote peace. I wanted to remember the colors of Yasser's keffiyeh, a detail I wanted for my interview. They were black and white, just like the extreme of deepest sentiments, as when too much of each, of either love or hate, can implode or explode.

"Thank you very much for your time, Your Excellency," I said, ready to leave.

"Ms. Achim," he said on my way out, "it's a sin people like you need to survive day by day in this society."

Outside, I pushed Otiliu to keep moving, afraid he'd say something. After we passed the white fence and turned the street corner, I stormed, "What was that? No other ambassador asked me questions for half an hour!"

"You're charming, smart, and take everything seriously. You just intrigued him. You'll intrigue others. It's your personality, that's all." I didn't believe a word of what he said.

The wind shifted and the humid air and dust carried pieces of garbage, big or small, that swirled around in our faces. A storm was coming, and the traffic was insanely jammed. We hurried to the newspaper office, taking the subway. The trip gave me time to think about writing up this, my last interview for the summer. It was a bittersweet feeling.

"You'll do fine, Dana, no matter what you'll decide to do," Otiliu scattered my melancholy. But I wasn't ready to find the answer.

~

As a freelance reporter, I didn't have an office or an assigned place. We were everywhere where we could find space in which to sit and write. This time, Adina Mutar, the editor for political affairs, offered me a place in her office. She had just come from our editor-in-chief and she saw me looking lost.

"Hey, Dana, come here! We just made coffee. Do you want some?"

I told her all about the interview as we sipped coffee together and she asked me questions. I gave her all the details and she listened to me as if she would write it for me.

"That's exactly how you'll write it. In this order. With these great details."

Two hours later, I handed Voicu the material and waited to hear his comments. He said it was good.

"It's my last; I tried to make it the best," I said to him. On my way out of the office for the last time, I thanked him for the chance to work there, and tried to take in the ambience and the smell of fresh ink one last time.

"Wait," he stopped me. "What are you talking about?"

"Next week I start school. You know I'm a full-time teacher."

A few seconds later I was leaving his office thinking it was the last time. I didn't look back and tried to suppress the choking in my throat. I hid in the bathroom on the second floor. When I finally entered Adina's office again, she handed me the phone.

"Mr. Voicu wants to see you now," I recognized his secretary's voice.

I walked one floor up and found his door open.

"Come," he invited me in. He didn't say I could sit. "What do you teach?"

"Chemistry. High school."

"What's that?" I sensed sarcasm. "How much do they pay you per month?"

I exaggerated a bit, upset that my salary was small after five years of intense studies and having scored ten out of ten on my teaching tenure. I said 400 instead of 325 lei.

"If I offer you 700 now, and 900 next month, and 1,250 every month starting in January, would you work for me full time?"

"I can't! I'm the fourth generation of teachers in my family. But I can work on weekends and during vacations."

I could see his eye pulsing as he lit a Marlboro red.

"You know, there are many teachers out there doing a good job. But not many journalists could write as you do. I see your talent. Think about it and let me know."

Now, I had a problem I had to solve on my own.

~

After dinner at Adina's, while she spent some time with her son, I found myself worrying. I was alone in the living room, thinking of Voicu's offer and if my friendship with Adina would continue if I didn't stay at the newspaper. It wasn't easy to assess the situation. As Tata loved to say, teaching was in my blood, and I enjoyed being around my high school students. But in every public institution, the old communists were still in charge, and it appeared that my generation couldn't do much to change old-school mentalities.

Children of the Decree

It didn't take long for me to understand how things worked behind the scenes. When I learned that the principal used school students to work on his farm, I wrote a piece denouncing the practice. I sent it to a magazine owned by Nadia Comaneci's brother, Adrian. My article, considered a fresh voice, was so well received I became a part-time reporter for the magazine, and very soon I took on another assignment for a second magazine while working full time as a teacher. There was so much to explore and learn that I thought I'd need a second life to fulfill this, my new mission.

The second magazine's name was Super VIP—Very Important People. Just like the name implied, my job was to interview and keep in touch with Bucharest's elite. Everyone wanted to be portrayed in the magazine—politicians, actors, sportsmen, and ambassadors. It became easier for me to schedule interviews.

How could I give up teaching? Less than one per cent of us, the Children of the Decree, were accepted into higher education. All universities were free, based upon one's score after a three-day entrance exam, but the University of Bucharest was the toughest of all to be admitted to, and even tougher to graduate from. Difficult exams took place after sleepless nights, and most of them were delivered as oral examinations. One would grab a ticket with a number from a pile, read the topics aloud that would be addressed, and wait for the next available place at the board, before the examining committee. My specialty was organic chemistry, which required one extra year and an additional thesis; I took two comprehensive written exams on everything I'd studied during five years. Those alone were terrifying.

Adina found me daydreaming. "You're quiet. What's up?" she asked.

I told her my dilemma, but she didn't hint at her feelings one way or another. "That's a big decision. I'm sure you'll think of which job would give you more satisfaction and where you could make a difference."

That was a hard response to analyze, but she was willing to listen to my arguments and I saw her face heating up when I told her about my parents' struggle under Ceaușescu's sister. "I think you need to find these answers," she said, sucking on a cigarette. "You should start finding out what happened to that woman after December '89 and what has changed in education since then."

A surge of past emotions I thought I had buried deep in my mind resurfaced. I saw myself as a child and student, and then I pictured my classroom where I was teaching. I saw shy children opening up, one chapter at the time they gained confidence as I gained their trust. And then I saw a bigger picture, of a society rising in the shadow of a new democracy but still retaining the terror of its past principles. My job would be to understand *why*.

"I could live with the idea of giving it a try," I told Adina next morning.

And just as I expected, the engineer in her snapped smartly. "QED," she said, grabbing her purse. It meant, *quod erat demonstrandum*", the Latin quote of "What was to be shown" we used in school when we proved a theorem.

~

"You know what I like about you?" Voicu told me the day I signed my new contract. "You see things differently. So, I won't assign you to any department because I don't want to limit you. Bring me stories no one has thought of."

The *National* journalism team emerged like Eve from Adam's rib when *Evenimentul Zilei* (EVZ), the most popular and the best-selling newspaper, split. Voicu left with his people, and the rest of us remained with the brand. On his Noah's Ark, I felt alone and wanted answers.

It was the fall of 1997, and one of the best times for print media in the country, eight years after the Iron Curtain fell along with communism in Eastern Europe, including Romania. People wanted to understand where the country was going. I was interested in finding out how Ceaușescu's executives in the education system at the elementary school level had fooled us into believing their propaganda.

Ceaușescu had only completed elementary school, and his Minister of *Securitate* and Internal Affairs, Tudor Postelnicu, had only reached grade six. I still remember part of Postelnicu's televised testimony during his trial: "Your honor, I was an idiot."

With corruption growing like weeds after the rain, we kept busy. The Internet was still a luxury to much of the world including in Romania, so magazines and newspapers were the best ways for people to stay engaged with the news. People would line up in the early hours to buy newspapers. Suddenly everyone was reading.

The free press was in the hands of a new generation of journalists, who pushed aside the older generation that was trained to write odes and raise the communist's leaders to the rank of Gods.

Over that summer, just a few months after the inauguration in June, *the National* daily reached the top three in national daily sales. We attributed this success to Voicu's brain and vision and were proud to be a part of his team.

I was the only outsider with no real experience at a daily.

"Hey, don't be remorseful," Adina said one day when I told her my concern about what my parents would say about my giving up teaching.

"I'm an engineer. Do you know how Ion Cristoiu hired us at EVZ?"

I nodded, all ears. Of all the press legends, Cristoiu, the visionary of EVZ, was number one.

"First question: Did you work in the press? He wanted and hired only those who didn't. But for the department chiefs, he wanted some experience. Voicu was Cristoiu's right hand because of his talent. Plus, he could do all the work while Cristoiu was gone. The stakeholders were making money, and Cristoiu let Voicu run the show while he was gone studying at the National Library, and Voicu didn't dare to ask for more money. Win-win. Pac! Boom!" Adina snapped her fingers and said, "I have one page-and-a-half today. But the point here, Dana, is simple. You either have the talent or you don't. Experience comes later. That's it. And Voicu told you to stay. That should tell you a lot."

Her body language—her click of the mouse and her grab of a pen—meant, "Let me work." I would have to catch her after she had outlined that day's news. Only then would she reward herself a coffee with milk from Voicu's coffee pot. Yet still, I wasn't sure why Voicu hired me for such a salary.

My friend was searching online with a cigarette in one hand. She was a little heavier than I, and taller, with short dark hair and a peal of contagious laughter. Her husband, Adrian Mutar, was the editor's private driver and confidante. Adrian was slender, with a darker complexion and a beautiful voice; he looked like a Native American, as Adina liked to say, and he played the guitar. They had met in college and got married, and they had met Voicu at EVZ. Over time, I had learned about their highs and lows, but one thing never changed: that Voicu and Adrian were deeply bonded to one another and kept their old-time secrets from others and even from their spouses.

She watched me staring at a blank sheet of paper and said with an air of authority, "If you want, you can come home with us. I think we have a lot to talk about."

From that day on, I assigned myself a chair in Adina's Foreign Affairs department and, later, the dark blue sofa in her living room as my bed. (Two decades later, while talking to Adina about this episode to clarify how our friendship started, she said: "I asked Voicu what to do with you, 'cause you weren't in my foreign affairs team."

He said, "Whatever you want!" with a laughing emoji. I wished I could have witnessed this dialog.)

Adina came into my life with a complete package—a husband, a 10-year-old son, a dog Intzi, and her half-and-half Algerian-Romanian friend Sadee, just six months older. Suddenly, my life was enriched and moved faster. I had to keep up with so many names, starting with my new colleagues and Adina's extended family. Adina's words about her time at EVZ became intoxicating to me. I couldn't wait to get invited over again. From her stories, I came to realize how much I had to work, but the *actual* fact of working couldn't scare me. What scared me was the idea of finding a subject or a topic for a piece. Adina's stories from EVZ's times were now legends in journalism schools and included names I was afraid to write on a piece of paper because of their popularity and success, and because of my being a relative novice at journalism.

In all these stories, Adina mentioned important people who would change the face of journalism and manage to sell three quarter of a million newspapers each day, in two editions, serving a population of seventeen million. The scope could leave anyone mesmerized and jealous.

In my role I knew I had to prove myself.

One morning while at Adina's, Voicu's secretary called me in to his office for the first time. Voicu wanted to talk to me as soon as I arrived. I panicked and asked Adina what it was about. "I think he has something in mind for you. That's his modus operandi." My jaw dropped while I was spreading butter on toasted bread. "But be happy because he wouldn't give you his ideas if he didn't believe in you." I was sure she was as curious as I was.

One hour later, I stood in his office. Voicu wasn't a fan of pleasantries. He got right to the point.

"I want you to do me a favor. I know you are a smart girl. And I believe you could also be discreet." My eyebrows rose.

"Do you know who SRS is?"

"Of course…the *Ziua*'s (Day) director." I didn't tell him Adina had mentioned his name just the night before.

"Okay. One of our girls wrote a piece about him, and before we could talk, his lawyer sued us. We worked together at EVZ. I want you to go to his office, talk to him, and see what we can do to solve the problem. Maybe he wants us to write something. Whatever he wants… He's waiting for you."

I couldn't believe what I was hearing. I wondered if Voicu could see the expression on my face, and I wondered what I looked like. I decided to not give him any more time.

I dashed to Adina's office to grab my purse and saw her busy writing. She had on her "Don't Disturb Me" face, but her dark eyes took a moment to acknowledge me. I left the office without a word, knowing that she had to prepare for the morning summary brief. I needed air. Skipping two stairs at the time, I couldn't stop saying to myself the mantra of that day—holy, holy shit. I was going to meet the secret agent and informant, SRS. His real name was Sorin Rosca Stanescu, but his acronym was more popular than his full name. Everyone knew who he was. He was like JFK in America.

SRS's secretary opened the soundproof door. He was sitting at his desk reading, of course, and he stood and shook my hand politely, inviting me to have a seat. He looked elegant and came across as very smart.

"I'm glad Voicu sent you."

I wanted to know if he was the one who had asked for me, or if it had been Voicu's idea. Instead, I waited and didn't blink my eyes.

"Look. I can't control what my lawyer does. He sues everyone who writes about me. Last month he sued someone who wrote something nice, but what I can do is for him to ask to dismiss the case. I invited my best reporter, Horia Tabacu, to participate in this meeting. You'll work with him on this subject."

There was a short knock on the door and a tall man with a buzz cut appeared.

"Horia Tabacu," he said, as if he wanted to apologize that the stars had aligned the on night before and had made us meet. He took my hand and kissed it.

"Dana Achim."

There were two names in the press nobody wanted to mess with: SRS and his buddy, Horia Tabacu. Adina told me this on the previous night. In the press world, SRS was called The Godfather, and Horia, The Godson. In fact, they addressed each other like that, as if their names had been written by Mario Puzo in his famous novel. I was scared of the experience ahead of me.

I took solace that I knew them ahead of time. The hardest part for me was to stop thinking about what Adina had just told me—their pranks on others, how they faxed materials from one office to another, intentionally fooling everyone. I couldn't contain myself thinking how those two men had alerted the police by faking a terrorist attack on the House of Press where every newspaper had their headquarters. Looking at them, I could picture Adina's face and I could hear us laughing the night before. I probably smiled.

"I'll let you two talk. Okay?" SRS excused himself and left the office.

I wanted to stand, but SRS waved at me to not bother. After a few minutes of observing Horia trying to find some words, I broke the silence. "Mr. Tabacu, what do I have to do exactly? I believe you know what it's all about, but I don't know."

He giggled discreetly. "You can call me Horia. May I call you Dana?"

"Sure."

"Okay. Let's talk somewhere else. Too many ears around."

I followed Horia down to the first floor and then we went outside. I let him lead the way, thinking we may stop to talk in a library or at least on a bench. I knew very well the street parallel to *Ziua*'s office, as it was the backside of Bucharest's university, my alma mater.

"I graduated from here. Romanian Literature and French. I was a teacher after."

"Really? I graduated from here too, as an organic chemist. I was a teacher until last week."

He stopped, measuring me from head to toe, and asked where I had been born. Then he laughed. "Dragasani. So, you're Olteanca!" (The Oltenia region, where Dragasani is located, is known for its peoples' noticeable regional dialect called *Olteanca*).

We walked on Ene Curch's street and Horia pointed to an apartment building, and said he once lived there. We crossed the street and entered a tiny restaurant at the first floor of an apartment building. Immediately I sensed that he felt at home. The waitress came with a bottle of white wine and two glasses. I turned down the drink. After his second glass my fear vanished. Surprisingly, in this environment, Horia turned out to be soft-spoken and calm.

He wanted, he said, a promise from Voicu that if they needed a backup story, *National* would be on guard.

"I need your phone number to keep in touch because I think you are the best to conciliate."

I wanted to write his number down, but Horia asked for my phone. He called me from his cell and stored our numbers.

I left him there, rushed to the bus station, still puzzled what that experience was even all about.

~

Voicu's secretary announced me at the door, and he gestured to go in. He didn't take a seat, and his left eye throbbed—the nervous sign. His face relaxed by the end, his eye in his place. "Okay, call Tabacu and tell him we are on the same page. Good job."

On my way to Adina's office, my cell phone rang. The caller ID read, "Horia Tabacu *ZIUA*." I answered it and transmitted Voicu's message.

"Good," he said. "It was very nice meeting you."

"Same."

"Oh, I didn't call you for that. What are you doing this evening?"

"Mmmm, I'm going to my friend's place." I paused and waited for a response, but he didn't speak. "Have a good day, Mr. Tabacu," I ended the conversation.

Adina covered her ears pretending she didn't hear. "Tabacu? *Horia?*" Her tone sounded more like "Jesus? *That* Jesus?" I nodded.

"Voicu sent me there… some stuff, you know."

She dimmed her eyes and said, "Be careful."

Unsure why I was the chosen one, I felt good at succeeding in my first negotiation, not knowing where I might land one day because of my experience. But at that moment, I wanted to know more about Horia's stories, and so I waited for Adina to edit her newspaper's page, for the chance to talk with her into the night.

It was a sleepless night.

During my time at the "National" daily.

Chapter Ten: Double Standards

Bucharest, 1997

By mid-fall the *National* skyrocketed in both national sales and popularity. We were mentioned by other news outlets and press conferences, which started to fill my heart with an audacious pride every time I heard its name. I loved seeing our newspaper on stands in town or in people's hands while riding public transportation. Its red square title—sometimes on the left side, or center, or anywhere on the first half of the front page—attracted the eyes, inviting one to pick it up and read it. The headline on front page was always above the newspaper's name. Several intriguing pictures or titles provided ideas about the edition, which had something for every taste.

Many attributed the success of *National* to Ion Cristoiu, the guru of the modern media, who was the first founder of EZV. He was the one who saw in Voicu the geniality of a new voice and chose to mentor him in journalism. When Voicu's team migrated to form *National*, with Cristoiu on board as the editorialist, many believed Ion Cristoiu was not only the brain of this newly created team—his visions were still featured in the editorial on the first page—but he was behind *National* as the main shareholder. Despite the rumors, I never saw him at the office or anywhere else. People said he could overturn governments and societies so, to me, Cristoiu was more like a ghost and not human.

The rumors about Cristoiu's demands for more money or more shares in the newspaper escalated. Even Adina knew something went wrong. Her husband, Adrian, would often come home late, sweating and swearing because Cristoiu had given Voicu a hard time by not sending in an editorial, which meant he had to personally retrieve the text from Cristoiu's house and bring it to the newspaper at the last minute before printing.

On one of those days, Voicu called for me and demanded a second favor. "I know you're resourceful and can open any door. Bring me the filed documents for the newspaper from the Chamber of Commerce. Have Adrian bring you there and back." He didn't ask if I would be able to get the papers, but he assumed I would succeed again because he knew I could.

Children of the Decree

Adrian was Voicu's chauffeur and Adina's husband. He was a quiet guy, and that day we were on a mission together for the first time. I thought the stars had aligned well for me. Two hours later, I paid for the photocopies and left the Chamber of Commerce with the requested documents in a manila folder. It was still daylight, and the clouds predicted a steady rain. From the backseat I could hear the music on the radio station, but my mind was on the documents. I could have looked at them while the clerk made the copies, but I wanted to be perceived as well-mannered and to not be caught peeking into other people's business. Still, at the last stop, I pulled out the first page and read it. All the shareholders were listed but Cristoiu was not one of them. Interestingly, the list included Voicu's name as well as known figures in the media, and some business owners I wouldn't have guessed would have had anything in common with the press.

We found Voicu pacing in the hallway. "You're back," was all he said, and I handed him the folder. He opened it on the spot and flipped through the pages as he walked to his office and closed the door. He didn't signal me to follow him, so I waited in the hallway in case he had questions for me. Minutes later he opened the door and saw me.

"You're amazing," he said, passing me on the way to the pre-press room. Then I knew I had to keep his secret and had never confirmed or denied any rumors. I guessed Voicu just expected that from me. To my relief, he never brought up the subject again and I never asked for the money I paid for the photocopies. It was a closed subject, and it remained that way.

~

Around that time, a person I had never seen before at the office gained my interest—a slim brunette about my age with large eyes and short curly hair. She was dressed in designer's clothes and had a smoky voice. I saw her pacing around in the third-floor hallway, from one end to the other, as if she had something on her mind that prevented her from standing still. A newbie or not, I remembered how I felt when I started working and had no office or desk assigned. I was watching her while I waited for Adina's fresh brewed pot of coffee. Once she stopped moving for a few seconds, I approached her and introduced myself. "Irina Prosan," she said.

"Prosan? I know this name."

She smiled immediately and we took a seat on the hallway.

She asked me what I wrote about and then she told me her story. She reminded me why I was familiar with her name. Every textbook coming from the *Didactic and Pedagogic Publisher* had her mother's name listed as the techno-redactor. And, of course, her father's name was so familiar. Traian Prosan was Ceaușescu's personal photographer and the head of the *Agerpres* Photo department, the Romanian Press Agency. I was shocked to meet someone who really had a direct connection to the past, to Ceaușescu's family, and to the propaganda I grew up with.

Why in the world was I surrounded by the past?

Irina was a brand with her own studio, a select clientele, and her father's talent. During communism, she was a photo reporter for the *Free Youth*, a propaganda newspaper dedicated to the young generation. Now her name was on music album covers, press releases, photographs for media, and pamphlets of actors and musicians in the modern world.

My interest in Irina extended far beyond musicians and famous actors. She was an encyclopedia of Ceaușescu's private life as told to her by her father, and through the life she experienced growing up. She intrigued me enough to go visit her the next day to see her work, which was the real reason Voicu wanted her on the team.

~

I found her living with her mother in a spacious three-bedroom apartment. Her father had passed away just six months before and the pain of her loss was still present. It haunted her. For six months she didn't want to talk to anyone except her boyfriend, a renowned musician.

She waited for me with coffee and cookies and a table covered with pictures. I removed my farsighted glasses to see the mostly black and white pictures Irina had selected to share with me. Several portrayed the dictator and his son, Nicu, playing chess at the Neptun Villa on the Black Sea. "I think this one was taken at the villa in Olanesti," she said, as she showed me a picture of Elena Ceaușescu dressed casually.

I wanted to say that Mama's brother had lived in Olanesti, not far from the closed road going to the protocol villa, but she quickly changed the pictures and I felt lightheaded. She handed me a few colored shots of both Ceaușescu and their dog. She didn't know where that one was taken. "I guess it's at the villa in Sinaia." Irina explained how her father was able to save those pictures. "My father had a secondary camera. He used it when he felt safe. Some of the pictures were discarded, but my father saved them. They counted the films rolls and every negative." I didn't ask who *they* were—the director of the news agency and the Securitate.

As the only child she learned to adjust her life around her mother's doctor appointments and the photo sessions at her studio; inflation motivated her to get a job at *National*. She needed a fixed income to pay bills, but the increased prices of utilities and food were a burden for everyone in the country. The new government imposed closing the unproductive factories and directed the workforce toward enrollment in infrastructure and technology.

I was mesmerized while listening to the stories from her childhood and adolescence. Her neighbors on the Dorobanti Avenue were children of diplomats and attachés, and they'd play together and dance together at a membership club that I didn't know existed. One day, she said, when her father was overseas with Ceaușescu, she invited a friend over and went to the club.

It was very late, she remembered, and the moment she entered the club, a strong hand belonging to an undercover agent stopped her and said, "you go home now." Now in front of me she was laughing about the episode, but I could sense that she was still suffering from her father's loss. "If Elena Ceaușescu didn't ask for him as their photographer, maybe things would have been different," Irina believed. "Elena was the hardest to take a decent picture of. During the lengthy congress conferences, she would nod or stay with her mouth open. It was a pain to get her in the right position, so my father had to work the pictures until they were good."

Irina's favorite memory was of the candies her father would bring back from China. He would hide the candy in his socks, afraid the security would find them. I almost envied her, thinking about the taste of the Chinese chocolate my uncle from Olanesti brought to us once. I remembered how I saved the pieces to last longer and that I saved the wrapping paper in a book. I didn't have Irina's benefits, but I was able to roam free in countryside at my grandmother's. I had to be cautious and keep my family's secrets, but Irina's phone was wired, the security followed them, and their correspondence was intercepted. Her life was nothing to envy, really.

~

Later on that same evening, I decided to go to Ceaușescu's native village to meet his sister, the one that terrorized all teachers in Olt county during my childhood until the last day of communism.

I envisioned that day since I was a child, screaming at her to leave my parents alone. I wanted to tell her that Mama used to get up at night in cold sweats talking in her sleep, saying "Nicolae Ceaușescu, the General Secretary," and repeating all his functions and titles. I wanted to see her face as I told her that we all hated her and all Ceaușescus from dawn to dusk.

The sting in my heart from this not-so-distant memory claimed its territory, and I knew I had to kill the beast inside me, forgive myself, and free myself from it before accepting the present around me. Only then I could feel liberated from the humiliation that my generation never signed up for.

I would come to learn that I would have to return to my roots to be able to move forward.

Nicolae and Elena Ceausescu at their villa at Snagov. (Traian Prosan'archive)

Traian Prosan and Nicolae Ceausescu. (Traian Prosan's personal archive)

Children of the Decree

Maria D. Holderman
Chapter Eleven: With Ceaușescu's Sister

The taxi driver slowed down at an intersection, about three kilometers away from Scornicesti. My heart pounded and an internal fire that I recognized from earlier times burned in my face. It was a Saturday before noon, a mild fall day, and the traffic was slow.

Eight years previous one could see cars lined up for kilometers at the entrance in Scornicesti. People from all over the country would park and sleep in their vehicles for a chance to buy food the next day. They believed, as my parents did, that Comrade's native village stores would have some produce, since all of the other stores were empty.

I couldn't recognize anything from when I went there with Tata in seventh grade. We spent the night in Tata's *Maricica*, his tiny Trabant with its automatic gears. I remembered Mama's face, and how she appeared mesmerized when she first saw two packs of real butter. That episode remains so vivid to me because at the time we, the children of the sleeping-in-car food hunters, had made a campfire at the edge of a cornfield and had found some late half-ear corn that we had cooked over the embers together. The ten of us played the telephone game, where one whispers a word into the next person's ear, and so on, and the whole group waits to hear the last person's version of the original. Of course, we selected funny words that would be passed along as phonetically wrong, something intentional to make us laugh. The whole point of the game played well.

If we had arrived two weeks earlier, the cornfield would have been protected both day and night by military forces. Not even a corn cob would have gone uncounted. As we found it, it was all for us to search within with our flashlights, so our parents could always see us from a distance. We were not afraid of anything, not even the dark.

I can't remember if we were cold that night or any of my playmates' names, but some of the jokes about Comrade are still fresh to me. The laughter, the joy of being outdoors at night, of taking turns around the fire, and of the happiness of being a child—nothing meant more at that moment. We even forgot about our mission, about why we were there. But most importantly, how we trusted each other. If one of us was an informant, we all could land in prison. Maybe we were too young to carry on the burden of communism on our shoulders.

I wanted to revisit the cornfield—my generation's legacy of a night well spent.

"Take it easy, please," I told the driver. The man sensed my internal turmoil. I checked him out. His cheeks looked sunburned, and he had a short mustache that was recently trimmed, and he wore a red tee-shirt that was in stark contrast to his green silk pants. The scent of his laundry softener reminded me of the fresh smell of clothes Mama lined up outside. I was about one hour away from Dragasani.

"Lookin' for something, miss?"

"Nothing special. Were you born here, sir?"

"Of course."

"Where were you at the Revolution?" I asked this to help determine his age.

"Just out of school, miss. Working."

So, we were in the same boat, both Decreed Children.

"Bring me to the town's cemetery."

"Town? Miss, look around. You can put lipstick on a pig, but it's still a pig," he sarcastically said. "Here, they've built an enormous stadium for thirty thousand people. This village, or town, or pigpen, has only eleven thousand. Ceauşescu condensed seven villages to make a town, and now, all young people left for cities. But you know what's really sad? All the factories around are closed. See? They are abandoned. They weren't productive, they said. So, now, we have nowhere to work. I'm lucky to have a car and do taxi on the side, but all I do since the buds break in March until the first frost is work the damn land."

He lowered his shoulders, opened the window, and said, "We have an agriculture high school now, but we don't have students," as he pointed to the left. "And here is the central area." Several four story-apartment building hosted stores on the ground floor.

I recognized the store on the right and recalled how Tata had kept me on the side until he got closer to the counter, and had protected me with his body, to not get pushed aside or hurt. For one person (a kid or an adult), one stick of butter was the rule. But when I reached the counter, a boy I had played with the night before pushed me to the right of the line. Again, I felt Tata's arm supporting me. It was a shield no one could break, I remembered. We both got a stick of butter, but Tata wasn't happy. While driving home, I could see red veins in Tata's eyes. Then, he avoided talking to me for days after. When our eyes met, he looked the other way. Probably he felt ashamed we had to fight for a darn stick of butter.

"Do you have family here?" the man said, disturbing my daydreaming.

"No. Just visiting."

"Left side, Ceauşescu's museum. Now, it's nothing. No one comes anymore. And here's his sister's house. Her husband passed, and she's here alone. Here's her store." He pointed to the right to a small boutique. An awful feeling I couldn't define made me choke. I held the scream inside me, but my eyes blurred.

"Miss, what are you looking for?"

"I'm not sure."

He became suspicious and turned on a dirt road on a hill. A deep sigh emerged from my lungs when I saw the cemetery's iron gates a hundred feet away. I grabbed my purse, handed him a large bill, and didn't wait for change.

The first tombs on the right side from the central alley belonged to Ceauşescu's parents and grandparents. Next to these was a large modern stone of Ceauşescu's brother-in-law, Vasile Barbulescu. Those were, indeed, the most imposing and well-cared resting places in that cemetery.

I walked around the graves and discovered I felt at peace as I read names and epitaphs just as I used to do at the cemetery behind the train tracks in Dragasani. I recognized the same solemnity, love, and sorrow as I looked at people's graves. Just like in Dragasani, the graves concealed children, parents, anyone, everyone.

Children of the Decree

To the right, the metal roof of a newly remodeled church shone in the daylight. I walked in, surprised to have found it open, and crossed myself. I breathed in the air. It smelled like every other church—the scent of myrtle and natural pine incense burnt earlier that day. I felt like I was in the church at Mama Tanta's as I scoured the iconostasis, looking for anything out of place. Everything there respected the old tradition of the oldest religion in the world: Virgin Mary's icon appeared on the left and Jesus Christ's on the right. The orthodox holy door and the two angel's doors separated perfectly.

Looking to the entrance door, right at the feet of St. John the Baptist, a painting of two people in old traditional Romanian costumes that I couldn't figure out attracted my attention. I walked closer, expecting it to find it was a new version of the Saints Constantin and Elena. But that couple's names, inscribed on the wall as if they belonged to the mystical personages and episodes of the Bible, were Alexandra and Andruta Ceaușescu. Comrade's parents. On the other side of the door, two feet apart, was another displaced painting: Maria and Andrei Ceaușu. These were his grandparents.

Holy Mother of Jesus! Communism and religion were two words we couldn't use in the same sentence. I knew Ceaușescu was more than an atheist. He hated church and religion because he wanted people to listen to him instead of God's words. He demolished churches and prohibited access to any party members inside. I was baptized at home; I knew for certain. My parents had never stepped into a church. During my high school years, certain teachers watched the entrances at our churches in Dragasani during Easter and Christmas. We could be turned in at school and get expelled for being seen attending services. So, *Christmas* became an abolished word. Our Santa Claus was Mos Gerila (from ger—freeze), the proletarian version of the old magic knight. But Mos Gerila was young, athletic, and somehow resembled Ceaușescu, and December 25 and 26 were working days.

I couldn't believe I found a church in the least expected place in Romania.

As I was following the dirt road down the hill to the main street, I heard someone walking behind me. My pulse grew faster, and a droplet of sweat formed on my temples. I estimated I had about three hundred meters to the asphalt and tried to hurry. I always traveled light, with just a purse and a jacket over my shoulders. I could always run fast if I sensed the danger. I peeked behind and saw an old woman pulling a noisy cart. Down the hill, the cart rolled faster than her legs, and she hardly could manage it. I stopped to help her.

Her name was Ioana and was in charge of the church. She said they had no priest because all of the old people were gone. In the past year, they had a funeral every week.

"Do you miss the old times?" I asked her.

"We all do. We had a good life here, jobs, food... Now, it's nothing."

Once we reached the asphalt, she posed herself straight and grabbed the wagon's handle. Her voice grew harsher before she turned in the opposite direction. "I just wished *he* did more for us than *she* did in her village. *He* deserved a fair death."

In her bitterness, I understood that the woman was jealous because Elena Ceaușescu helped her native place more than Nicolae Ceaușescu did for his. It was a pity argument, which may have been the morale of communism.

I reached Elena Barbulescu's residence with a desire to confront her. I had been repeating what I had wanted to say to her in my head, and I was ready to deliver, if she were home and was willing to come to the gate. I called once, "Mrs. Barbulescu," and I heard a weak yes coming from the back of the wooden villa. A few seconds later, a woman with a headscarf and in house clothing appeared at the gate. I could tell she was immediately trying to figure me out.

I introduced myself as Dana Vasile, the daughter of two teachers from Dragasani, and told her I was in the area and wanted to stop by to see how she was doing.

Then, I added, "My mother wanted me to send her regards."

"That's very nice to hear that. Come in."

She invited me to sit on a bench under some dark blue and deep ruby grapes that were hanging from vine arches, just like the ones at my parents'.

For a moment, I saw myself having a coffee on the bench in Dragasani, and the sweet smell of fall made me feel at home. The scenery impregnated in my mind as if the fall was part of me. I loved its smell and colors and the buzzing bees around the grapes and wildflowers, and my mind transported me to Dragasani, on the bench with my parents.

Who would have believed that this woman that I had hated with every cell in my being since I was a child would come to show me her family's intimate past? Was she *really* the way my parents and others had portrayed her?

I had hoped to have an answer for myself before leaving.

As if she read my mind, she asked if I wanted some coffee.

"If it's not too much of a disruption, I would love one."

The woman disappeared into the house, and I was left to worry about what I was doing there. Where were the words that I had repeatedly said in my mind? Was that all I could say?

She returned with a tray with two cups of coffee.

"So, your mother was a history teacher? Where?"

I told her the name of the village and she said she knew the school.

"They said I was strict. Of course, I had to be severe. It was my job to make sure the women dress like women. No pants and boots. School was school, not like now."

That was the moment when I could tell her why I was there. There was my part of the story to be told. Instead, I told her about the church I had just seen and asked about the situation in the village. A church without a priest was an issue.

"People said I was an atheist, but that's not true. I supported churches. I still do."

She wanted to appear as a pious woman, and I almost believed her. But then, she talked about the way her brother, Comrade Ceaușescu, had been executed. "I was surprised they didn't make it. He was betrayed by his Security, the ones supposed to protect him. Where were they? They will cry for their mistake. They will cry for him, miserable people," she stormed.

She didn't say her brother's name. I wasn't sure how to react. I held my coffee cup with both hands as I listened.

"Do you want to see the museum?"

"Of course, if it's not too much trouble."

"Finish your coffee, and then we go."

She grabbed the keys, and I followed her on a path that traversed a young orchard to the left of her property. We ended up at the back of the museum. In front of me, painted in white, was a two-bedroom house that had a wooden porch decorated with geranium flowers. From the main entrance, I recognized the porch; I had seen it before, many times, in pictures. One picture showed Comrade with his children and wife and his parents on that porch. I remembered that picture then because he looked more human in that image than in any other I had seen, or ever would see. I stepped up the stairs, and from that porch, I looked around, just as he had, years before me.

"It's so peaceful here," I said.

"I agree. Too bad, no one comes here to visit."

She unlocked the door. I stepped over the threshold and the odor of fresh paint emanated from the wall. I saw an oil painting by a renowned artist. In tones of blue and white, the former presidential couple smiled while flying with angels. I told her the painter's uncle, a priest, lived on my street. She didn't know that.

"We used to sleep here, in this room, four of us, and the rest, in the other room." She pointed to the other side. "I was ten years younger than Nicu, and by the time I went to school, most of my older sisters and brothers were on their own. My oldest sister helped all of them with housing and jobs in Bucharest." I wasn't sure if she sounded melancholic or not.

An orange handmade blanket covered the bed; next to this was a tiny round wooden table. On the wall, a framed picture of him and the parents, the mother in the middle. Elena explained that her brother loved his mother very much. In her later years she lived with him in Bucharest, and he made sure she had everything someone her age would ever need. I felt compassion. On another wall, a portrait of Comrade from his early years.

He looked handsome in that one, I thought. The second room had a stove for cooking with some pans on a base and two beds. My guide said they all ate and slept there.

"How was it possible, with ten children and two parents in three beds?" I asked. She explained that not all of them were ever home at the same time. The eldest child went to Bucharest to live with their older sister, Niculina, a textile factory worker, who was pictured smiling on the wall. Nicolae Ceaușescu was eleven when he left his village to work in Bucharest, right after he completed elementary school. Initially, he was a cobbler's apprentice.

Then I recognized the grandparents from the painting at the church—the same attire, a long white scarf for the woman and a hat for the man.

A rug covered the dirt floor, although I could see the mud between the bricks around the woodstove. In each room, two old-style Romanian beds with hay mattresses adorned with handmade dark orange coverlets sat opposite each other.

I asked if she'd made any changes since the Revolution. "No, everything is the same." I avoided saying her brother's name as she did. Her brother, the dictator, was executed by a firing squad on the holiest Christian holiday, Christmas, in 1989. Ironically, the soldiers who shot both him and his wife were my age at the time of the execution; the soldiers who did the shooting were the generation Ceaușescu had envisioned and trained to fight and die for our liberty. *The first battalion of the decreed children of Romania, all 57,000 of us,* The New Man experiment of the Golden Era, that ended the epoch of torture and hunger and freezing homes. I wasn't on the streets when Ceaușescu fled; I was afraid of more protests, and anyway we were forced to evacuate the dorms to clear the Capital. But that never stopped us from building momentum.

I wondered what she thought of seeing her brother and sister-in-law executed on television. Or what she thought of what Elena Ceaușescu had said before the execution: "Hey, children, we are your parents. Don't tie us." I wondered if she cried when Ceaușescu dropped dead.

I knew I couldn't ask any of those questions.

"Do you get sympathizers here?" I asked instead.

"Rarely." With that, she locked the front door.

I left the museum on the front gate of Ceauşescu's home still wondering how a man with only four elementary classes ever became the country's president, and how an uneducated woman became the education secretary over people who studied and sacrificed for years to become educators. How people like her could pretend to care for God. I knew she couldn't have both God and evil in her.

She stopped a couple of times to pick up ripe apples and handed me one, just like Mama Tanta used to do.

We went back out on the street to walk, and she invited me to visit her store. "I'm making a bit of money because the idiots took over my protocol house in Slatina. My husband's dead, my son, in Bucharest, and I'm here by myself."

She sounded humanized and I felt pity for her. From the chair of a goddess, she had sunk to the space of a mundane latrine. I could see the family resemblance and turned my head away. I decided I was looking to get out of there.

"Call my son, Dana. He's so lonely. I'm sure he'd love to talk to you. You are the daughter of teachers. Pretty lady. How old are you?"

I said I was twenty-seven.

From that point all she could talk about was her and her son. I grabbed the note with the phone number and called a taxi and didn't look back.

But something else confused me: the woman I considered a demon was, in fact, a mother who loved her child.

Children of the Decree

Maria D. Holderman
Chapter Twelve: Michael Jackson's Orphans

Bucharest, Fall, 1997

It was a beautiful evening with frayed clouds that stretched over Bucharest. It had not been long since my outing to Scornicesti, to attend a black-tie reception at the Latin America House. The Romanian Diplomatic Institute, situated on the Primaverii (Spring) Boulevard, was only a few blocks away from Comrade Ceaușescu's Palace, which had been converted into a museum.

Every fall, the Latino American ambassadors invited native artists to perform and celebrate with traditional music, art, and food. This was my second year attending this event. I believed the true intention of the event was more a discovery of folklore and culinary habits on the upbeats of the Mexican mariachi, which seemed to raise everyone's spirits, than was the public mission. My favorite was the Peruvian song *El Condor Pasa* as played on panpipes by a folklore group of Inca descendants that lived on Machu Picchu, the Old Mountain.

I was ready to leave and thank the ambassadors for the invite and tried to remember each of their names and their home country as they stood at the exit. The tallest was from Mexico; the shortest, Peru; the heaviest, Columbia. My favorite was the Chilean ambassador, who was an authentic replica of the Araucanian people—aquiline nose, olive tan, slim, and athletic. Only the Mexican spoke English, however, so at every event I relied on Alin Bogdan, a Romanian-Spanish interpreter I knew.

Between the ambassadors, Bogdan looked like one of them and not only because of his expensive suit. Medium-sized and slim, Bogdan was in his late forties, and his darker complexion contrasted with his salt-and-pepper hair. He had a gray mustache trimmed over his full lips, and he had dark-brown eyes. He had worked for Romania International Radio, in the Spanish section, as a journalist—his favorite job, he'd mention, whenever asked. But I had always heard that he was much more than that: an accredited interpreter of the minister of external affairs, an author, a translator of Spanish literature, a chess coach and player for the Romanian Chess Association.

It was protocol to wait for several others to leave an event before I did. I couldn't wait to enjoy a quiet walk on that day for as long as possible before taking a cab. In that part of Bucharest, seeing a woman walking in high heels and a long black dress was part of the scenery and not an extravagance.

"Wait for me," Bogdan said in Romanian with a Spanish accent, after translating for the last ambassador. The timber of his radio voice sounded too sensual to not wait for him. A few minutes later, he stood in front of me and opened the gate.

"What do you know about international adoptions?" he asked as we crossed the street.

"Not much," I responded, thinking he would start giving me a lesson I wanted to avoid.

"Here's the phone number of a friend, an English interpreter I've known for a long time. Give him a call. It's a long story."

"What's the short version?" I snapped, losing a shoe in a bank of leaves as I tried to open my purse. My face turned red when I saw him smiling.

"Let me help you," he said, grabbing my arm so I could fix myself.

"Short version," he repeated my words. "Romania's adoption agencies refuse to honor contracts. How's that?"

I wasn't sure if he referred to the short version, which sounded more like a headline or the gravity of our country's situation.

"Why me?" I asked after a pause.

I studied his face. His eyes perforated mine, and I sensed intelligence and honesty. He picked a chestnut from the ground and handed it to me. I checked his hand. His fingers stood on my palm a second longer.

"I trust you," he said, as he opened the cab's door and waited for me to get in.

He dropped me off, holding the door for me and kissing my hand as a goodbye. I could hear him whistling *El Condor Pasa* as he got back in the taxi.

The song stayed with me all night, and pieces from my past came to me as though through a movie projector. I was flying with my childhood wings from a dance T-shirt Mama Tanta had said was too colorful to wear. In hindsight, the thought of Romania's unwanted children seven years after the fall of communism kept me awake.

At daybreak, I knew what I had to do and dialed the number Bogdan had given me.

~

By noon, no one at *National* could answer the question the Spanish interpreter had asked me. "International adoptions? That was in the past. We don't have kids up for adoption, dummy," Adina said.

"All I know about is the orphanage Michael Jackson visited twice," Irina responded. "And he donated some money for a playground." She tried to be helpful.

Unbelievable. Michael Jackson was one of Mama's favorite singers. I remembered her laughter as she saw women fainting at his concert in 1996. "Michael! Michael!" Mama laughed, imitating some girls. I didn't care much for his music, but she always enjoyed it, asking us to turn the volume up every time he was on television. Mama's favorite Michael Jackson song was *Billy Jean*. She loved how the beat and the video told a story that transcended any language barrier. "You just listen and watch," she'd say to Tata, the same response she gave him at every soccer game. She never missed watching a soccer game.

Voicu raised his eyebrow. "We wrote about him when he came here."

"What about the playground?" I asked Voicu. "Who cares," he responded.

I stepped into the Ambassador Hotel's lounge thinking that I shouldn't also care about the playground and planned a short meeting with the English interpreter. A night out with Sadee sounded more interesting than listening to a topic that no one seemed to care about. As for Michael Jackson, I loved "Earth Song," and thought about how its message got to me.

~

I knew the Ambassador Hotel very well, having spent a week there with Mama during the summer of the entrance exams at the university. A cold sweat dropped on my spine as I thought of that time. We had been competing for a place in higher education, and we knew that only the top 0.35 percent among us would be admitted. We, the children of Ceaușescu's New Man experiment, had trained for these exams since we were born. We knew very well the party wouldn't increase the available positions in the universities for many years to come, if ever.

Upon my first time in the lobby since the admission exams, I pictured Mama holding a suitcase full of books in front of the elevator. That memory stung me. During that time, staying in an upscale hotel required a good word from someone in the party. I never asked Mama how she'd managed to book a week at this hotel. Now, I was there on a different mission, wondering if I'd made a mistake in giving up teaching for which I'd prepared and sweated so much. My heart ached and my throat constricted when I realized how much my parents had sacrificed for me.

A subdued yellow light welcomed me into the lounge, which was on the right side from the elevators in the lobby. I looked around, trying to identify the English interpreter, and heard someone say my name. From the direction of the call, Bogdan waved to me. I didn't at all expect to see him. Instead, he kissed my hand and introduced me to the English interpreter. Both wore suits, and I suddenly felt I was underdressed for the occasion. That made me nervous.

They already ordered drinks, so I settled for a coffee. Then the English interpreter got to business: a couple from America, now on their fourth trip to Romania, couldn't find the girl they were in the process of adopting for the past two years. So, instead, the authorities offered them a different girl for the same fee, but they needed to wait another year and spend a whole month in Bucharest.

"But if they can't adopt this last girl?" Bogdan intervened.

"What happened to the first one?" I asked.

"We think someone else adopted her," the English interpreter said.

He didn't say why, but my gut told me there was money involved. *More money,* I guessed, but said nothing.

I could see the story unfolding in front of me and wanted details.

"I can't give you names and places. If this family is exposed, who knows what happens after. But be prepared. If they can't adopt, you'll be the first to know," the English interpreter consoled me.

Then they grew quiet. I listened to the background music until I finished the coffee.

"What's your plan for tonight?" Bogdan inquired.

"I'm going out with my friends," I said, grabbing the bill for my consumption. Bogdan rested his palm over my hand. It felt good.

"I'll take care of it. Be careful out there," he said as he looked me in the eyes.

I left them to finish their drinks and I guessed that they would probably have more after I left. At home, I called Mama that evening and told her where I went. "Remember?" I asked her about the suitcase with books. "That was my favorite time with you," she said after a long pause. "You did it. Why did you give up your career?"

It hurt to hear her say that. I thought I knew the answer, but I wasn't sure anymore. Who cared about essential issues happening in Romania? How many children were there, waiting for adoption? And why were there still unwanted children after opening the borders and living in democracy?

I needed time to reflect. By daybreak, I concluded Romania wasn't ready for that kind of answer. At least, not yet. A sudden revelation conquered my spirit, and I knew I needed to wait and find out the answers right away. If not me, then who?

"Dead tired," I said to Sadee. "Super tired," I told Horia Tabacu after his third phone call. They could wait.

Children of the Decree

Chapter Thirteen: Caprice d'Enfant

At first, I thought Voicu was testing my endurance and loyalty when he invited me to talk to an attorney in his office. "You have more experience with children as a teacher," Voicu said, justifying my presence. The attorney who represented the first nonprofit autism organization wanted some public exposure. "People need to learn about these children so they would accept them in society," the man in his late thirties pleaded to us.

Until that day, I had no idea what autism was. I'd never heard that word mentioned in my studies to become a teacher. I probably looked surprised because Voicu said I should visit the placement center to get an idea and write a story.

We arranged the visit at the center, and after the meeting, I asked Irina Prosan if she had any idea what autism was. "No clue," she confessed. "The movie *Rain Man*," Adina said.

The next day I encountered well-dressed children under seven years old, who were sorted by their skills. Supervised by several adults, the nonverbal children were housed for the week, while the most skilled and potty trained among them were allowed to go home in the afternoon.

I watched the children as they were lying down for a nap or eating, playing outside or indoors, but after I was there a while, I asked myself: *What happened to the autistic children during Ceaușescu's rule? Where were they?*

That night while reading some brochures from the center I understood my aunt's whispers while I was growing up. My memory was blurry, but I remembered how Aunt Pusa, Tata's sister, had mentioned to my mother how we had been selected and handpicked at birth. Those of us with deficiencies would never see another day. Maybe that was the reason why Mama had mentioned several times to me that I had received a perfect score after birth.

I puzzled about this for several days, and even called Mama to ask her about the details of my birth. Finally, she confirmed my suspicions, telling me how women during that time were petrified because newborns had to pass the survival or vitality test almost immediately after birth. Those deemed unhealthy were declared dead the next day, and many women left the maternity hospital crying over a dead newborn. Some left the dead bodies in the hospitals, and some held funerals. Many others went mad. To my surprise, Voicu didn't promote the article on the first page, as I anticipated.

"This is not the right time," Adina concluded regarding the placement of the article. I guessed that she knew more than what she was willing to elaborate upon, from the information she had learned in their department meetings.

To me, though, it seemed the perfect time to investigate and educate those who wanted to hear and learn.

~

"Journalism is something you can't rush," he said to tame me after he'd assigned me to court to find sensational cases. "You'll get the experience, practice the writing, but no one could do your work. It's what you see and feel, the angles of the story, and how you relate it. Who is your audience, and what do you want to convey? But do you know what makes one the best storyteller? When many pass on a subject or walk around *it,* you come and give *it* life and meaning. Find the details. So many run to find that *it*, but only a few succeed. My bet is on you. Just open your eyes, feel it, and listen to your instinct."

One day he sent me to represent him at the Chamber of Commerce's party. I walked in holding his invitation, watched a show, and left with a gift for my boss. The next day, I handed him the packet.

"Open it," he said, watching my gestures.

It was an electric grill the size of a watermelon.

"Keep it," he told me. Then he went back to reading the daily newspapers.

"But it's for you." I tried to escape the unpredictable situation.

"Why? Don't you cook?" he said as he smiled. I couldn't tell him that I was one of those who merely eat to live.

"I have work to do," he said, and I understood then I was expected to leave with the grill. Once I got to the door, I could hear him smirking. "You look like Ally McBeal," he said. My face turned red. "It's a compliment. She's smart, pretty, and funny. Watch the series," he suggested, still smiling at my innocent embarrassment as I stood there, still holding the package as if it were a bomb.

~

One week after assigning me to court duty I had no material for Voicu, and he wanted answers. I told him the reality of the court system: rich people's cases got less attention than ordinary people, and that corruption and poverty were the two most significant causes of criminality, and that the divorce rates were higher than ever before.

In the hallways, however, I heard lawyers defending more corruption cases than the court could possibly handle.

He listened to me as if I were reciting a poem. "This is what I need from you. Could you write me an article about that? I want this human aspect most journalists ignore."

Later, he asked me to follow him to the computer room. "How do you like that?" he said as he pointed to the screen. "You earned it. It's your column." He smiled. He named it "What happened yesterday in the court." I was shocked.

The only startling court case I thought Voicu would like to have had covered involved a cold-blooded murder by one of the former president's counselors. One night, this man became jealous and killed his wife in front of his two minor children. On the day of his sentencing, I saw his children in the audience and sat behind them. An older woman I assumed to be their grandmother tried to comfort them.

My instinct as a journalist directed me to concentrate on the effect of the murder, the children's collateral damage of growing up without a parent. I felt no remorse for the man. My concern was for the children.

"You want sensationalism?" I asked him a few days later. "Let me go to the prisons. I think if I reiterate the human condition behind bars, we can educate at the same time."

"Go for it," he said, stepping out from behind his desk.

All I could think of was the uncertainty I heard in his voice.

~

Not long after, Voicu sent me to cover a story about someone who was found dead in an apartment. I guessed he had received a tip and wanted us to be the first journalists at the scene. By the time I arrived at the location, I realized the person had been dead for several days, based purely on the smell. The putrefaction smell extended to the parking lot, fifty meters away from the apartment building, and even with the windows closed and a chilly fall day, the scent still penetrated the car.

I walked up the stairs to the sixth floor, covering my nose with a scarf. Only the medical team was there, a sign that, indeed, I was the first reporter on the scene. I entered the apartment, holding on to my breath. With the bedroom door opened, I saw a man on the floor covered with maggots, some coming from under the rug and making their way to the living room. Again, the scarf on my nose couldn't contain the smell, and I gagged several times.

Outside, I talked to some neighbors and then with the medical examiner and found out the man was a renowned artist who had died alone at home.

"Excellent details," Voicu complimented me after I handed him the story. He had no idea I drank a beer in the car to eliminate the odor I sensed for days in my breath.

~

"Good reporting," Horia called from his office. I wasn't sure if I wanted to talk about that experience and how I put the story together.

"I want to take you out. What do you say?" I heard say as he sucked on a cigarette.

Later that afternoon, he appeared at my door holding two bottles of wine. He looked taller than usual in his long brown coat, probably made by a French designer.

Although I had prepared for the visit and cleared the table and the chairs, my living room, packed with books, still seemed small.

"I like that you have plenty of good books. What's the latest you read?" Horia inquired, surprised.

"I love reading. I bought most of them when I was in college." Then I handed him *The Book of Sand* by Borge. "Yours?" I guessed he wanted me to ask the question.

"The Fist and the Palm. Dumitru Radu Popescu."

I told him I hadn't read the book and asked him if the author was the one who carried the nickname of Popescu—God.

The author, one of Ceaușescu's right hands in culture and education and member of the executive party, had a notorious reputation for censorship while contributing to Comrade's adulation and personality cult.

"The prose is very good, I must admit. Regardless of who Popescu was, I found the book interesting enough to keep me up at night. If you want to read it, I can lend it to you."

"I think I have enough literature here to keep me busy for a while."

He asked for wine glasses. "I don't drink. I only have coffee cups."

"No problem," he said, and I tried to avoid my embarrassment. "We'll take them to go. You promised to spend some time with me."

We took a taxi downtown and went to a strip club, close to the local restaurant where we had spoken for the first time. I was shocked. Luscious women were dancing around a pole in the middle of a stage. My first impulse was to flee but he placed a hand on my shoulder. "Stay. I'll show you what life is. All the good and bad stuff."

"You're such a kid," he said after we sat down at a table. His eyes shone a candid vibe. "You are inexperienced and naive but a fast learner."

I blushed and played with my hands under the table.

"I looked at you and thought about this French song by Mireille Mathieu, *Pardonne-moi ce caprice d'enfant*. I think this is the song that suits you. But you are much younger than me and probably never heard it. I'll play it for you when you come over."

I knew the song and told him I understood the lyrics well enough after studying French for seven years. The lyrics told the story of a girl who was so much in love that she apologized for being innocent.

"Tell me more about you. Who are you?" Horia asked, sipping his wine.

Was he flirting with me?

"If you are so curious, maybe you can find out." I looked into his eyes.

"You sound like you're provoking me. Maybe I'll find out. What do you say?"

"Whatever pleases you."

"You know, if you need anyone to talk to, I'm here. Remember that."

I checked my watch, grabbed my purse, and left. I thought *we're done*.

The next day Horia called and asked to see me after work.

"Don't even think you'll escape this time. Do your job and come here. I'll wait for you. If not, I'll come after you." I knew he meant what he said when he asked me to write down his address.

Two hours later I rang the bell at Horia's apartment. He opened the door, smiling, wearing a soccer jersey. He looked younger than forty-three years old. He kissed me on the cheeks, a custom in Romania when you meet someone familiar. I smelled booze and cigarettes and a fresh aftershave.

"Come in." He invited me into the living room, taking my coat.

"This is the kilometer zero zone," he said as he opened the door to the living room.

He pointed to take a seat on the sofa while grabbing a glass from a built-in China cabinet. There were two empty wine bottles on the floor and an open one on his coffee table. The ashtray was full. He offered me some wine, but I refused.

Sitting next to me, we listened to his favorite French singer, Charles Aznavour, and then he played a recording of Mireille Mathieu. "Listen to this one," he said. It was the song he had mentioned the day before, the one whose message he wanted me to understand. He sang along, translating some of the lyrics, and I knew then he was indeed curious about me.

But I observed something else at that moment too. While he was drinking, his hands shook, and he made a grimace when I spotted these gestures.

He talked about his investigations, describing events and places, famous people, and politicians. Then he wanted to give me a lesson about journalism from his point of view. "There are two kinds of journalists. The first category sits in the office and transcribes the news agencies reports. The other is the one involved in the story, digging and finding a new way to expose or investigate one aspect or the other. This is the category I belong to. I think you can achieve this level, but you need to be able to write about everything. Put yourself in the story. Learn what the story is about before you approach it and have a secret ace to play when things don't go your way." With this he had my full interest.

As soon as he talked about *reportaje*, I understood that Horia was a mountain of surprises, and had been in search of a silent audience for his stories. He loved overseeing initial conversations but rarely waited for a dialog or overall approval. Instead, once he observed someone's fascination with his life's stories, he teased them, as if to try to take over their lives and dictate what they should do.

"I don't want you to talk," he told me. "Just listen."

By midnight, after listening to one story after another, it was as if I were living a version of Scheherazade's *1001 Nights*. I found out that he had been married, but then got divorced because he was in love with a married woman who was much older than Horia.

"I like you. Please, come back tomorrow," he said as he kissed me. My heart raced and I felt dizzy, unsure if I wanted to see him again at all. He was, as Adina said once, too experienced for a girl like me.

~

A few days later, Bogdan showed up at my office holding a large bucket of carnations. I could see him standing next to the porter and watching me coming down the stairs. I didn't believe the flowers were for me, so when he handed them to me, I became suspicious and wanted to know the reason behind his surprise visit and kindness. His smile made me uncomfortable, as if he were planning to trick me and had been caught in the act. I smelled the discreet aftershave he left, and my knees weakened. Why was he there?

"I don't have your phone number, so I thought to come here. Can we talk?" he asked. We walked down the hallway.

He probably sensed my discomfort when Voicu passed us on his way to the tech room. I invited him to Adina's office, the only place I could find appropriate. At least I had a desk there. I hid the bucket of flowers behind my back as I entered the office, afraid Adina would say something. Instead, I read the surprise in her eyes and graciously grabbed an extra chair for my guest.

"I wanted to see this place. I was always curious how a newspaoer functions," he said.

I looked around as if I were trying to find something to talk about. My eyebrows stood at their highest level, and I sensed that he understood it hadn't been a good idea to have come there. From the inside pocket of his suit, he pulled out an envelope addressed to me. I opened it slowly, taking my time. It was an invitation to the annual winter concert hosted by Radio Romania at the Romanian Athenaeum.

"I thought you'd like to come. As my guest."

"Of course, if I have time," I responded, wondering if my face looked red.

"Your phone number, please, to keep in touch."

Behind his chair, Adina turned her head so I could see her.

"She'll make time. I'll make sure," she said. I introduced them, and then Bogdan left the office with my number.

"Are you crazy?" I snapped at her.

"I'm realistic. I think it's better than going to a strip club, don't you think?"

But I knew she meant something else.

I didn't go.

Chapter Fourteen: Mad World

My life was moving fast, and I was learning quickly. I was afraid that I'd miss the chance to embrace the challenges to truly give my life meaning. I felt as though my existence mattered for the first time to the wider world, because of how I used my voice in the newspaper. The reach of my voice expanded from my chest to hundreds of thousands of people. A new world I had known only from movies appeared before me, waiting with opened gates for me to make my first move.

Was I prepared or trained to see the unseen and hear the unheard?

Everyone—Voicu, Adina, and Mama—had told me to be careful after I told them I decided to go to prisons to write stories. Careful of what? I wanted to know. Guards? Prisoners? Families? No one could have predicted what I was going to experience—not even Horia.

I told him about my plan. "In this business, Dana, you need to have experience and feel the crooks right away. Some play this game so nicely it's easy to get screwed. And then it's your reputation. Once screwed, you're out. It's not a woman's job."

I believed him.

One evening, when I thought he was in good spirits, I asked him to give me some tips on being a good reporter. He had inherited his journalistic experience from his deceased father who wrote for a newspaper called *Bucharest Information.*

But Horia beat his father's reputation. Proud to be asked such a question, his face lightened, and with a smile, he responded by asking me how I would proceed to investigate if I got a phone call about a car accident. I faced him from a chair, and I raised my hand like I was in school. Then he permitted me to talk. He loved watching me play the schoolgirl. "I like you," he said. "I think I'll marry you. So, what would you do?"

"I'd see if the cause was a DUI first. And talk to witnesses," I said. My face turned red instantly, surprised he'd pop the M-word.

"Wrong!" he snapped as he sipped his wine. "You take a white lab coat and get there as if you were the doctor. No one asks you what you're doing if you get there first. You get the story firsthand."

He had used that technique several times in his coverage of some high-profile cases.

I analyzed the way he held the glass as if the shape of the glass were a woman's hips. His lips longed for a kiss. I kept my eyes open to watch his expression and to try and memorize the moment. The wrinkles between his eyebrows disappeared and a discreet smile rose on his lips. *He is in love with me,* I thought. He guessed what was on my mind and opened his eyes, but instead of accepting the fact and saying it back, he told me, "You're a peasant. I'll have nothing to do with you." Then he pushed me aside, afraid I'd discover his love for me.

I left him drinking and let myself out. Helpless, I contained my tears in the elevator and walked to the first intersection. On my way I was followed by a stray dog. I wasn't sure which one of us was more petrified of each other. I stopped for a minute, allowing the pup to smell me and to decide I was alright. The dog circled me and paused. Then he lifted a leg, urinated on my shoe, and walked away.

It was well past midnight, but life was intense in downtown Bucharest under the lights of the streets and the tallest building, the Intercontinental Hotel. It felt as if the day had never ended, and as I walked past people and tried to stop a taxi, I thought of my short but traumatizing marriage with a prospective doctor in the army that I had tried so hard to forget. (My sister and brother-in-law kept in touch with him. I know he served in Afghanistan, and he lives a lovely military life).

My brother-in-law, Livia's husband, invited him to Dragasani one day. Friends since high school in Craiova, and both medical students, we all became close friends. It looked ideal, as Mama had said: "Two sisters married to two friends." In my last year of college, I was not sure where I would get appointed to be a teacher. Mama had insisted I should find someone while I was still in school. I guessed she wanted me to finally put my books aside and learn what real life was. All had happened fast, between my exams and time to study at Dragasani.

Even the small ceremony at the town hall was cut short because I had to take an exam on the following day. As I look back at those few short months, I think we had been best friends. Some people should be happy with small things, we both had agreed, soon after we came to realize that a forced marriage from a short friendship wouldn't solve either of our problems.

This mistake I regretted came from the old tradition of women being married as virgins. This man had been the first boyfriend I had met who was ready to settle with a pure girl, but it didn't take long for us to discover that we weren't compatible. Instead of pleasures, as I heard from others or had read about in books, I found out sex was something so painful it made me cry. I tried to resist him, but he pushed me on the bed one day, and while I kicked him, he snapped my left knee. He was a tall man, 1.90 meters tall, and I was only 1.57. Afraid I'd report him for the physical abuse, he refused to bring me to the military hospital, which was right around the corner of the military compound from where we were staying. With swelling and a bruised leg, I wasn't allowed to leave the military compound for several days. That's how Tata found me when he came by train to visit us at our one-bedroom military hotel in Bucharest. He figured out quickly that something bad had happened.

Tata found me alone, and soon after he grabbed a suitcase and packed my things. "I'll kill the bastard. He put a hand on you, I'll put mine on him. He better not show up until we leave," he said. I prayed for that, invoking a catastrophe of any kind to keep him away from coming *home* from day drinking with his friends. The timing to leave him was perfect.

"You'll teach at home, just like your mom and me. I'll take care of your divorce. You won't have to show up," Tata said. But I knew I'd want to go back to Bucharest and my teaching position. I would miss that opportunity, despite my parents' desperate speeches all that summer. The only thing I kept was his last name, Achim, which means pure in Arabic. It became my pen name.

That night, leaving Horia, I relived the emotional kind of deception that another man I had almost forgotten about had planted in me. This time, however, I knew that healing would take longer than the recovery from any physical pain. And I knew too I had to end the relationship before I'd become a worm smashed under his foot.

My phone rang as I jumped in the taxi. "Come back. I'm sorry," Horia said.

Those words were enough for me to go back and gave him one more chance. I tried to promise myself I'd stick to that promise.

~

At the court, people kept divorcing, neighbors kept fighting over fences or trees, and in some exceptional circumstances people would end up in prisons. Those convicted and sentenced either pushed their luck or didn't know when to stop. Only the naive ones got caught on the first attempt.

The breaking point of my experience as a journalist in courts emerged in the summer of 1998, as revelations broke about the most disturbing money laundering scheme in Romania's history. The laundering involved civil airplanes from Ukraine carrying untraceable loads of cigarettes. At night the aircraft would land at the military base, supervised by the Military Commander of the Airport. From there Colonel Gheorghe Bota, in charge of the country's Secret Services and protection of everything regarding air traffic, supervised officers' transferring of the cigarettes from airplanes to trucks and then to storage. It was an underground and planned scheme, one that proceeded with the knowledge and approval from the Army, Police, and Secret Service. The operation that revealed its existence was named "Cigarette Two Operation."

Just a few years prior, Horia and his friend SRS exposed the Cigarette One Operation, which was very similar in scope except that the smugglers brought in cigarettes from Greece and Turkey on ships that crossed the Black Sea. Horia never told me how he'd gotten to the bottom of that scheme.

Something probably happened between Horia and SRS because Horia never told me why SRS assigned him to the *Sport* section and took him off of his duties in *Investigation*.

With the Colonel and his trustees sentenced to seven years in prison, it was my turn to figure out the rest—where the money came from and went, and why I suspected Bota was willing to take the blame. First, I had to gain Bota's trust. I secured a pass to Rahova, a maximum security prison just outside of Bucharest.

The day I met with the general director of prisons I told him the truth: I was after an interview and information from Colonel Bota, and I wanted to proceed discreetly. We came up with a bargain and a plan. He'd give me unlimited and full access to any prison in the country if I'd first inform him about what I was going to write.

"Let's say you do an interview with a prisoner. I want the name. Plus, I can provide you with everything else—file, sentence. I don't want to read what you write—it's not ethical for me to ask you that. But I don't want surprises."

We executed the plan together successfully. My presence at the prison would look like my volunteer service, to rehabilitate prisoners. To justify my almost daily presence at the prison, Voicu agreed to give me a weekly column called "Messages from Prison." Underneath the title, the newspaper thanked the general director for his support; I knew what this really meant was, "Don't mess with me. I have protection."

"You'll get him to talk. I have faith," Voicu told me.

I knew this was the right thing to do.

~

The first time I met Colonel Florian Gheorghe, the Director of Rahova Maximum Security Prison, I found his physical appearance contradictory to what I'd expected from the man in charge of the most notorious prison in Romania. He seemed fragile, about four inches taller, slender but muscled, with light golden hair and green eyes.

I expected to meet someone that looked like Arnold Schwarzenegger, knowing the prison was home for serial killers sentenced to the death penalty under Ceaușescu. Now, these prisoners had been placed on life sentences without the chance for parole. I heard rumors about several cases that had terrified the country when I was a kid, and I learned about others years later, but I took everything under suspicion, as potential rumors meant to scare young girls to not go out alone. Even if the stories of these cases were true, the press would have never published anything so atrocious. For a long time, Romania was the country of honey and roses under the hammer and sickle's Communist Party.

Colonel Gheorghe was surprised to see me too, he would confess to me later. I was the only journalist that held an unlimited pass to any prison in the country. We laughed over a coffee in his office when he described our first meeting in hindsight. He had expected someone with more muscle and not a seraphic young woman.

Three months into my assignment, the Colonel invited me for a *walk*. "You give them a good reason to wake up for. Let me show you what we have here," he said.

We passed through a tunnel and a locked gate on the right. It was my first time in this space.

"We use this gate to take them to court," he said.

I smelled car oil and fuel, a stale odor. I coughed. The smell gave me a mild headache.

Then we were in the prison yard, an open space well secured by an electric fence.

"That's the men's section," he said as he pointed to the left.

We took a right. As we got closer to a four-story building, I could see details emerging: clothes were hanging on some windows, plastic bottles were on some windowsills, and some windows had shadows moving about inside while still others held faces looking back at us.

I was still outside in the open air but didn't at all feel like I was in control. The distance to the front door shortened and my anxiety grew with every step.

Before this *walk*, I had spent most of the time in the library, doing interviews or working on their *newspaper* at my suggestion. My group of prospective reporters consisted of about twenty men of all ages; together they had committed a variety of crimes. I saw no sign of Bota in the library again. Maybe he wanted to see how long I would keep going to the prison, I thought. Was he waiting to hear from his *boys* that I wasn't *planted* by any secret services?

I was convinced he was watching me and suspected who his *friend* was, a charming young Russian reporter from Ukraine who had been imprisoned for stealing a car. Igor smoked Assos cigarettes, the same brand associated with Bota's contraband, and I waited for him to make the first move. So, just as I had over the past three months, I kept my mouth shut and didn't mention the Colonel's name. Instead, I kept busy by reading the stories they wanted to feature in their closed newspaper.

Surrounded by about twenty of them I didn't feel *special*. Officer Andrei, a young man assigned to escort me, warned me to be careful, and although he was by my side most of the time, there were moments when I was made to feel very uncomfortable. One time a convict, a former assistant to the first president after the Revolution who had killed his wife out of jealousy, passed me a note with the address and the phone number. The message read, "Please, call my children." He also wanted me to bring him a phone card for the same purpose.

Another inmate, a Greek businessman who had been sentenced for tax evasion in Romania, asked me to help him find his daughter. The girl was the result of his relationship with a Romanian model. I wrote a story for the newspaper about him and found out the mother and the child had left Romania.

After I spoke with Colonel Gheorghe and showed him the note with the request for the prepaid phone card, he told me it wasn't a big deal to bring in a phone card for that inmate. That prisoner had no one to visit him, and since we knew he had kids in school who were living on their own, one time would not break the prison's rule. He appreciated my honesty, and I assured him of my respect.

Children of the Decree

On the day of the visit, I wondered if Colonel Gheorghe was out to test me. One needs tough skin to get inside a prison. First, he brought me to the men's section, and then to the women's building. I saw *everything*. We walked in every hallway and section, library, and eating area. I was prepared to meet serial killers, petty thieves, white-collar criminals, and the wrong-time-wrong-place criminals.

Yet, at the same time, I was there to find answers to my dilemma. *Why do people break barriers?*

We walked to the courtyard and saw the security towers. I wanted to understand where the man and the inner beast intersect, and whether rehabilitation could break or make a person.

At the end of the day, I became paranoid and conscious of my habits, afraid I could lose my freedom and get locked up over nothing. Later, I stopped Adina from crossing the street in an unmarked crosswalk. We were in a hurry to pick her son up from school, and she couldn't convince me to cross the street. "We go *that* way." I pointed to the crosswalk.

She shook her head. "You spend too much time in prison," she told me. She couldn't convince me otherwise, though, so we ended up doing the right thing.

Soon, *prison* became the most used word both in my daily routine and in my nightmares. Awake or asleep I could see silhouettes of men I had met at the maximum-security prison, but I imagined them walking on the streets or living with me at home, coming to me and for unknown reasons calling my name.

I couldn't hide my fears and emotions in the articles or columns I was writing. "Very good," Voicu said every time I handed him a new story. "When will you give me Bota?"

My answer was the same for many months: "when the time is right."

I realize now I was a decent reporter but a half-wit as a woman. One of my jobs, Adina said, was to figure Horia out. "To let him go," she told me.

Chapter Fifteen: The Magic

It wasn't that simple to figure out Horia, but some parts of him were clear to me.

His egotism was mainly a form to protect himself from getting hurt. In his honest words, which still hang over me, I sensed his fear of loneliness and that his younger days would come to an end. Horia, like so many, was afraid of getting older. So, it seemed he wanted to live out the vanity of his glory days, as an attempt to forever pretend to be young. Even an inexperienced woman like me could see his vices: alcohol and women much younger than himself.

Often, he would ask me to write a story about my childhood while he watched television and drank. "Write, don't talk," he would say, pressuring me. Just like that, on his orders, I would produce some prose he'd treasure and share with his colleagues. I remember his reaction when he read a short story about a fawn I had found with Mata Tanta—my earliest memory. I raised the fawn until the morning I found the stall empty. Mama Tanta told me the fawn left, only to find out years later that my uncle killed it for meat.

That essay convinced me that while Horia was a literate person, and enjoyed learning about the Romanian countryside from books, he never had and never would experience that life I had lived up until that point.

I rendered him vulnerable. (We both knew the art of writing reflects upon who you are as an artist, including your vision about life. That the best writers display an intense experience and vision about life and humanity.)

When I was with him, I sensed how much he wished to have had my childhood, or to have been a part of it; to have had the chance to roam free and shoeless, and to have perceived the world's beauty as I had seen it, as a child at Mama Tanta's. I could have told him it was the spirit and not the place. He could have been happier if he'd renounced his foregone perceptions: if you weren't born in Bucharest, you were a peasant, regardless.

~

Children of the Decree

I was writing an essay for Horia's literary pleasure when the news of Romania's new government broke. My second uncle on Tata's side, Radu Vasile, had been appointed Romania's prime minister by President Emil Constantinescu in the first and only government in opposition after December 1989. My uncle, a discreet person, was a senator and a college professor at the University of Economics in Bucharest. An advocate for economic reform and democracy in the liberal party, he was against all old politicians with roots from Ceaușescu's era. Our new president was also a college professor at the University of Bucharest. I met him once in his role as the dean during my studies, never imagining he'd become president one day.

We had no idea how long it would take to clear the government and fundamental institutions from the communist plague. (In one CIA note dated March 1982, Ion Iliescu was mentioned as the possible Romanian president if Ceaușescu were assassinated. Indeed, Iliescu became the first elected president. He was Ceaușescu's right hand man.)

As we watched the breaking news of my uncle's appointment, Horia was on the phone for a long time. Then the surprise took over the country's media. On the television screen, pictures of my relatives were shown along with the new prime minister's.

"Do you know him?" he asked me.

I raised my hand. "My second uncle. But that's all you'll get from me."

His attitude changed. "I'll go to see a woman tonight, so leave," he said.

I promised myself then that I would never go back to see him again. "Idiot," I responded, leaving the apartment key on the nightstand, surprised that I had said such a bad word.

I guess my candor changed into cynicism when I left his fancy place and him, without looking back.

I understood then what Adina had tried to convince me: I had nothing left to share with him.

~

Soon after the breakup, Adina informed me that her husband was going to travel to the United States to stay with his mother, who had remarried a Romanian American man. Adrian needed money for a one-way ticket, and I spared some savings to help them out. America was his dream, I understood, and no one could convince him otherwise. So, the plan was for Adrian to work for his father-in-law's private business in Burlington, Vermont, and to help Adina and their ten-year-old son with money. Intrigued by their plan, I found the tiny state of Vermont on the map. *Too remote*, I thought, but that wasn't my concern. Not yet.

With Adrian gone to America, I started spending nights at Adina's. Our friend, Sadee, joined us after her late shift at the dentist's office on the first floor at Adina's flat.

We were happy. Three women caring for a child and a puppy, saving our energy for dancing and laughing, and planning a whole new series of reportages that even Horia would have been jealous of.

Many of our jokes saw print. Voicu loved those stories about single women and their lives, the struggles to provide for a child, to maintain a professional life, and to choose to go to bed alone. I saw those stories as a reflection of the social class of women in Romania, educated but afraid to commit to a new relationship, or divorced and interested in staying that way. We reached out to others from Sadee's long list of acquaintances, from masseuses to business owners, women who had divorced soccer players, or women who were never married or had endured short-lived marriages like mine. Soon, Sadee became wrapped up in our new passion, becoming our mediator for interviews. She even created a list for us, with possible topics and reasons why women over thirty might want to be alone, most being rooted in her medical practice.

We needed very little to be creative—a tiny spark or idea for a story would come to us, sometimes in jokes first.

One day, while we were hanging out at Adina's after work, Sadee told us about a *magic* woman. "I'm the only one never married," she argued.

She'd already contacted the Roma and made an appointment to find out why her relationships didn't last. Her father, an Algerian businessman, wanted her to marry a Muslim while her Romanian mom, a teacher, wanted her to marry a Christian. She was caught in the middle between religions and parents.

Sadee told us that she had already gone there once. We sat in the living room, Adina smoking her cigarettes, and me outlining a chapter for my novel with a notebook in my hand.

"What did you do?" asked Adina, trying to get Sadee to spit it all out.

Sadee told us that at the witch's house, the woman said some curses in rhymes she couldn't understand, then asked her to burn three matches and toss them into a glass of water. All three matches sank.

I raised my eyebrows and saw Adina doing the same. I put my notebook aside. I knew I wouldn't write that evening and gave her a chemist's explanation.

"The matches sank because of the surface tension. Once the phosphorus burns in the air, it changes its chemical composition, and thus, the mass. Although the burned match has a lower density than water, the surface tension around the uneven match couldn't hold the water molecules around it. That's why it sank."

"Nah! It's magic!"

"Let me show you," I said and asked Adina for matches. Adina found none.

"See? You can't even find matches because there is a superpower who stopped you!" Sadee argued, giving me an evil eye.

Then, in ecstasy, Sadee told us that the matches' ritual meant that someone cast a spell on her.

I tried not to laugh, but Sadee stared at me.

"How could she know if she isn't magic?" Sadee argued.

It didn't matter to her how much we tried to convince her there is no such thing, but only God's will. Instead, she wanted us to go with her next time, just to be *sure*.

"No way!" I said.

But Sadee countered, "Yes, you are my friend. And, besides, you can find out if you'd ever get remarried. I'll pay for it."

Sadee couldn't convince Adina to go, so I agreed to take her. By then, exhausted from arguing with Sadee, I said, "Whatever! But don't tell anyone who I am."

The next evening after work, Sadee and I were on our way to the magic woman. In the taxicab, I couldn't look at Sadee without giggling. When we knocked on the woman's door, Sadee grabbed a package for her. I saw in the plastic bag a bottle of American whiskey and a carton of cigarettes, Kents, long. That was the *shpaga*—or bribe—needed to be seen immediately for our love problems. The woman left us alone for a second to get more matches and two more glasses of water and Sadee gave me a look.

"You better be quiet. If you destroy the magic, I'll never, ever talk to you again." She'd finished the words before the magic woman came back. It was my turn.

The woman had me sit in the middle of the room on an old blanket with camel pictures and started the ritual. Sadee was right. I couldn't understand a word. The Roma burned some matches, said some spells, took my blouse, turned it inside out, and burned another match. She repeated the process three times.

"You'll find your man over water," she said.

Later that night, at Adina's, we went over every word the Roma had said. Sadee had a talent for getting whatever she wanted. One of her favorite things was to have us repeat everything she enjoyed hearing. She kept it up for hours until Adina told her, "Stop! We've told you a million times now. We're not repeating it, and we're done with this subject. Go to bed!"

The next day, Sadee called the woman again to tell her she was ready to finish the magic. This time, the woman told her the price was double and Sadee immediately accepted. What she didn't tell us was that the woman also asked her to buy a new pair of leather boots from Eva's, a high fashion store, and to bring her the most expensive coat she had at home. This was the only way the magic would work, the witch told Sadee.

Children of the Decree

Sadee almost flew to the witch's house, dragging Adina and me along in a taxi. The unusual ritual was held at midnight. We waited for the woman to come, and we spotted her making the cross sign on her chest. It unnerved Adina. She whispered to Sadee, "God has nothing to do with this woman and your stupidity!"

Then, the woman got into the passenger seat of the car. She was dressed in a fur coat and smelled like she'd tried all the fragrances in the store at once. She had a plastic bag with her. Adina opened the taxi's window on our side to get some fresh air. Then the Roma asked the driver to bring us to the closest intersection of four roadways. We had to be there before midnight. The driver asked if it mattered where the intersection was. It didn't, she said.

When the driver showed us the main intersection at the Intercontinental Hotel, Adina and I were almost in tears from laughing. Sadee wanted to find another corner less populated. Still, the clock was ticking, and the magic had to start in a few minutes.

The taxi driver found a parking place a little further down the street, and Adina and I got out of the car to see what was going on. When the university's clock ticked to midnight sharp, we saw Sadee and the woman going into the traffic. We moved a little closer.

"Unbelievable. I can't believe how naïve she is," said Adina.

"Believe it," I said.

Sadee, in the middle of the intersection, had something in her hand. She squatted a few times while the woman gave her instructions. The cars blew their horns, and we became afraid she'd get hit by one. But Sadee just stood there, doing squats and throwing something above her head. When the lights changed to red, Adina and I walked toward the intersection.

Sadee chanted, "So the magic of Venus, come and warm my heart! To hell with all the black magic spell on me!" She repeated this three times each, at each of the four streets. When she got closer to us, we saw a hen in her arms.

"What the heck is that?" asked Adina. Sadee was throwing the hen behind her back, and the hen was clucking. I felt sorry for the hen. Once the ritual was over, we returned to the taxi and dropped the woman off at her place. Sadee asked her about the coat outside the car and leaving the window open.

"I need to keep it one more week so that the magic will work," the woman said. "Call me then."

We didn't talk in the cab, but when we went upstairs to Adina's apartment, we asked her about the woman's fur coat. She told us the truth: that the fur coat on the Roma lady was Sadee's.

"If you don't call in the morning and get your coat back, I call the cops," I snapped, my blood boiling.

None of us slept that night, each for different reasons. Later, I heard a noise in the hallway. It was Sadee's hen, still in the plastic bag left on the floor. The woman had given her the hen to make soup and eat it all by herself. Adina was ready to explode. She took the hen and placed it on the balcony. What happened that night was beyond my understanding. For Sadee, it was the *magic*. For the rest of us it was comical.

I didn't know who killed the hen so Sadee could make the magic soup. Adina believed Sadee paid the custodian of the flat, but I thought she may have done it herself. I later heard from Adina that Sadee got sick from eating that soup three days in a row. Of course, Sadee doesn't remember these details.

The problem was she was expected to keep the bones and bring them back to the magic Roma. Then she had to burn them, and blow the ashes in four directions at midnight, at the same intersection.

I wished that I could have witnessed this magic, but my cousin Nae was visiting and spent the last two nights of his vacation at my place in Bucharest.

The night that Nae had to fly back to Seattle I invited Sadee to stop by after work. Instead of finding me alone, she found Nae watching television and drinking a beer in the living room as he waited for the taxi to bring him to the airport.

Children of the Decree

I watched their reaction when they laid eyes on each other and thought then that I had damn good intuition—the guts I carried with me as a journalist.

It was love at first sight.

As for Sadee's fur coat, she didn't want to get it back for fear of *bad* luck, and because she believed the magic worked when she met my cousin Nae.

Later, I read that some famous artists in Romania went through the same con game as Sadee. As a result, one artist lost an apartment and an expensive car. The truth, however, is that, despite political changes, the Romanian society wasn't ready to give up on its traditions. People still love mysteries and magic when things don't go the way they want. Sometimes, it's more convenient to believe in a spell than to deny or face a cruel reality.

~

Nae called me from the airport to tell me how beautiful Sadee was. I put the phone on speakerphone so she wouldn't ask me what he said about her a million times over. I asked Nae to please send me his e-mail address, and that I would send him Sadee's, so they would be able to keep in touch. He gave it to me right then and Sadee wrote it down as he spoke. That night, Sadee slept over at my apartment, and I felt good when I saw the sparkle of love in both my cousin's and my best friend's eyes.

Arranging their meeting, though, even briefly, took another toll on me, one I didn't expect. I had become Sadee's emissary. The next day she asked me to go to a café on my street and write to Nae because I didn't have Internet at home. My job, she explained, was to write an e-mail to both and introduce them to each other. Looking over my shoulder, she dictated to me what to write about her.

"You know him. Plus, writing is your job. Mine is root canals and pulling teeth," she said.

I wrote to my cousin as if he were an imaginary lover. Whatever I wrote, the effect on Nae worked. He fell in love with Sadee's writing and, thus, with her. At the same time, Nae wanted me to draft some juicier letters for Sadee, because he worked with "screws and bolts," as a mechanical engineer, in her words, "and writing is not my thing. You make a good living out of it."

To save time, Sadee provided me with her e-mail password. Then, when I felt inspired, I'd go to the café and brainstorm a love letter to my cousin from her e-mail address, and then wrote one from my e-mail to him as a draft for Sadee.

I soon felt tired and thought about how to get myself out of this awkward role. I wanted to let them take over, but neither accepted the idea, and I had no choice but to continue to play Cupid.

"What would she think of me when I'll write her short sentences in technical words?" Nae argued. "I am your favorite cousin."

"What would he think of me when I can't even spell correctly in Romanian?" Sadee cried. "I am your best friend."

They were both right. So, I kept writing back and forth until they decided (through my encouragement to both) that it was better they spoke to each other directly over the phone. They loved the idea and I felt relieved.

~

Love takes all the shapes possible I thought as I watched Sadee's transformation. Of course, she wanted to know every detail I knew about Nae, and I filled her in as best I could. But my job, as Sadee's best friend and Nae's favorite cousin, meant that I had to give each of them a clear and fair picture of the other. During the summer of my divorce, while I was staying with my parents, Nae had suffered a car accident.

He had been the driver. In that accident he lost his younger son, who was then about three years old, as well as the neighbor's daughter, a young girl, who was about to start college. They had gone for a ride to a pool, and on their way back to Olanesti a storm came and Nae lost control on a curve during bad weather. Nae's oldest son survived the accident with minor scratches, and Nae lost his front teeth and broke several ribs. The accident happened just a few weeks before Nae, his wife, and their two sons had planned to move to America on a lottery visa. Divorce followed, and only Nae and his oldest son moved from Romania to Seattle, Washington, USA.

In my estimation, Nae was a *shard* of his former self, mourning his son's loss while watching the other grow. He carried the weight of the young girl's death on his shoulders, and he was ever unsure as to which death was more brutal to overcome. I knew there was no answer to that.

"I wish it was me instead of her," he confessed to me once over the phone. He told me about his nightmares, and while he could eat again, having gained new teeth, the crash's impact left him with permanent trigeminal nerve damage. This meant he endured severe migraines, a loss of balance, and the onset of blurred vision.

"Do you think Sadee's capable of accepting me the way I am?" he asked me.

"Ask her," I responded.

And he did.

~

Letting go of some things is essential in life. Otherwise, they'll destroy you from the inside. I bought a two-bedroom apartment in a Victorian house in downtown Bucharest, just half a mile away from Horia's, at the *Romana Square*. The street was quiet although busy, but my apartment was in the back and had a unique privacy. My new apartment was also within walking distance to the prominent stores, a farmer's market, a theater, a subway station, and was just one street away from my office at the *National*.

With the house came a little flower garden in the front, a cherry tree, and an old fig tree that reached my neighbor's window on the second floor. The house needed work, and I hired some contractors to start the remodeling. They changed the floor in the small room where the former owners had the kitchen. I painted everything. My neighbors dropped in to check on the status of my renovation.

"This looks nice, Dana! It smells fresh!"

I truly loved my place. It was perfect for me, and I felt at home. While fixing my house I began writing a novel inspired by my experience with Horia.

I poured my frustration into the pages of that book.

In my novel, the main character—a naïve but intelligent woman raised in the suburbs—gets a job in Bucharest where she meets a controversial intellectual before the Revolution. They marry but she soon realizes that love is not what the man has offered her. Her personality changes, as the country changes after the Revolution. After years of accepting his betrayal and cheating, she leaves him and becomes a successful and independent woman. At the end of his life, he realizes how deeply he loves her.

I called Horia to tell him about the book and he wanted to read it. I invited him to my place and asked him to write down my address, as he had asked me to do long ago.

"What's there?" he asked.

"My house. Kilometer zero point five," I told him.

A half an hour later Horia knocked on my door. I invited him to the living room, where the folder with the printed book sat on the glass table, the book cover on the side. He showed up, looking sharp as always, but now he suddenly looked as old as Tata.

He asked for a beer, and I went to buy some from the corner store.

On the way to buy the beer, I fretted, thinking I was still in love with him. *Why am I so emotional? I won't give in*, I promised myself. *It won't work.*

I woke up in time to avoid my self-destruction.

I knew there was more good in this world than I was able to see in that moment. I had to open and purify my soul to be able to see the world around me differently.

When I got back, I put some bottles in the refrigerator and brought him one. He glanced up but kept reading. I sat across the table from him, my legs tucked under me. I kept bringing him a cold beer as he emptied each bottle. After midnight, when he placed the last page on the table, he asked me to change one thing: the way *his* character dies. I promised him I would.

My biggest surprise was that, after making that comment, he walked straight out of my apartment, and I never saw him again.

I wanted to forget everything about him. But first, I needed to forgive myself and find peace of mind. On the next day I checked in as a guest at a Moldavian church in Iasi named Saint Paraschiva.

I was ready to forgive.

With Sadee (middle) and our friend, Daniela (Black Sea, summer 2000.)

Chapter Sixteen: Making Peace

My physical penance at Saint Paraschiva started with fasting, night masses, and giving up meat. As an occasional drinker or sipper, I had no problem not drinking at all. That was the easiest thing to do.

The hardest part was to quit smoking. I didn't smoke while in Iasi, but soon after getting back to Bucharest, I picked up right where I had left off. All of my friends were chain smokers, and everywhere I went, either in offices or at my girlfriends' places, I was forever in a cloud of smoke.

I tried quitting many times, and after a long pilgrimage mostly on foot to several holy places in Bucharest on sweltering days, with nothing in my stomach but water, I was able to give up that nasty habit. Of course, the pilgrimage on those days gave me a headache, but I continued the holy journey until the pain in my body stopped.

For the soul, I found therapy with spiritual music and asked the priest from the church across the street from my house to come and bless my surroundings. From every church or monastery, I visited, I brought back an icon for my bedroom wall. In addition, I burned incense and holy myrtle from Athos Mountain. The myrtle, however, had to be burned on charcoal and, luckily, all the churches had the proper supplies. One day, while purifying the house in the morning, a neighbor almost called the fire department on me. She saw so much smoke coming out the opened window, she believed the house was on fire. I calmed her down.

Even in that holy atmosphere my soul wouldn't stop bleeding. That was when a friend who had just returned from India after a five-year journey suggested performing incantations. He sold me some quartz pyramids and necklaces and mystic pearls for use on special occasions. I also bought several compact discs of spiritual music and the latest version of *OM*, which at that time cost me about two paychecks. He burned the CDs at home and distributed them to women like me.

The healing would come with patience and faith, he kept telling me. For the record, he was known in that circle in Romania as Gabiji or Gabi the

Indian. We kept in touch during this time, and I bought anything he thought I needed from him. (In the end, it worked).

He also introduced me to his group of healers, members of Universal Energy. I joined the group for a fee, and soon we went to a monastery to open our chakras. I remember kneeling in the church and opening them one by one and experiencing the feeling as if a screw had penetrated my body. Only then did I believe an extra power was both coming from the Universe and going into It at the same time.

One evening at a monastery in Moldavia, we practiced sending out love and peace. We divided into two groups, one inside, while the other was in the town. Of course, we had skeptics between us and, as a Chemistry major, I was the first to need some proof. The outside group had to receive energy from us, the ones inside, and to note when they felt it. The experience was magical.

The effect of this way of life on me was also visible, I soon realized. Many people asked how my face and eyes would gain a noticeable glow. Thanks to Gabi's teaching I became able to send back love and peace to those who had or were currently doing me wrong. I found that to heal my soul was that simple. I no longer saw the mistakes from my past as obstacles in my future, but rather as lessons learned to gain that level of spirituality.

The job now was to keep a balance between my career and my way of living.

That would prove a new challenge.

Firstly, Voicu assigned me to write about vibrators. "What are those?" I asked, thinking they might be an instrument used to measure seismic waves. I imagined how one might stimulate the earth's core and obtain a measurement immediately.

His lips dropped and I sensed his immediate discomfort. "Ask Adina. Or your friends. How old are you?" he said as he looked at me. He didn't wait for my answer, and I couldn't understand what I had done wrong. For the first time I heard Voicu laugh hysterically. I asked Adina and she explained laconic details to me but suggested going to a sex toy store somewhere downtown. At the end of that assignment, I burned all of my myrtle.

Secondly, my diet was of concern. Adina and I treasured this story that many knew back home.

One time she suggested getting some caviar from a lady who was selling it at our office, just so we could change the taste of our daily sandwiches. In my case, those daily sandwiches included bread, butter, cheese, tomatoes, and onions. She convinced me to buy two cans, because caviar wasn't meat, and although I had enjoyed some at embassies' protocols, Adina unlatched in me a deep craving when she made this suggestion.

We usually lived on sandwiches when we wrote, but Adina made a quick soup while I took a shower that evening. I guzzled two bowls of vegetable soup but still felt hungry.

"Why not treat us to some caviar?" she said.

Wearing an oversized T-shirt only, I tucked my legs under the shirt and sat on the stool. First, I cut one slice of bread (one and a half inches) and spread a half-centimeter of butter on it. Next, I scooped two full spoons of caviar and spread it on top of the butter, and then slurped it down in one bite. Then choking, I told her it didn't taste right. "Why do people die for caviar?" I asked her.

She turned to me and saw the slice I ate from on the table.

"You need a few eggs not the whole can."

"You eat it. I don't like it. Give me an onion."

She passed me an onion, and I smashed it on the table as Mama Tanta did all of her life. Then I pulled off the nasty black eggs and decorated the bread with butter and onions. It tasted just perfect to me.

We still argue over that episode. She insists that I had spread the entire can of caviar on one slice of bread. I always correct her—it was no more than half.

~

I remember everything about the day of my book signing, August 15, 1998. It was a Saturday and a holy day, celebrated by both Orthodox and Catholics under the Feast of the Assumption of Mary. In Romanian, we say Maria, just like my name. So, the date was personal and meaningful. And as it was meant to happen on that day, a prestigious library in downtown Bucharest had agreed to host the book launch and signing. The library was situated between Horia's place and mine, just across the street from his office. I had no input on any of that but it made me nervous.

I was nervous anyway. Livia had just been blessed with her baby girl and, of course, she couldn't come, but Mama came the day before. We had anticipated a large turnout through the prelaunch campaign, but as I walked into the library with Mama, my heart jumped from my chest, and the words couldn't come fast enough for interviews. People from all over the country were lined up in front of the library, hours before the ceremony. Television crews, reporters, photographers, people I had invited, and others I didn't know filled the space to the walls. The ambassadors sent their cultural attaches, the mayor of Bucharest delegated his right hand to the event, and most politicians had someone on their staff present. Of course, I looked for Horia, but saw only most of his friends instead.

At a table filled with buckets of flowers, I signed the first book to Mama.

Someone captured that moment in a picture. Looking at it, I see her smiling, although on that day she didn't at all feel well.

As I signed the last books, a lady handed me the phone and said, "This book is for Horia."

"You did it," the voice said. "I heard all about it. I liked it."

That young woman, a journalist from his newspaper, had the cell phone on during the event, with Horia on the line so he was able to hear the speeches that were made. He was too proud to come, he said, but he was also curious, a quality only great journalists mastered when they took a risk—another lesson I'd learned from him. "Weak people don't take risks." I remembered his words clearly.

"Write something nice for Horia, please. Make him happy."

I did, thanking him for inspiring me, gave her the book, and closed that chapter of my life. At least, I wished that action alone had.

The reception following the signing was held at the publisher's villa on Snagov Lake, which is in the most expensive area of Bucharest. He invited businesspeople and his friends to attend the party. A famous hotel, Majestic, where Hillary Clinton stayed during her visit to Bucharest in 1996 when Bill Clinton was president, provided all the food and drinks for my celebration.

I felt overwhelmed by those people, and I left the mansion after I could be assured Mama was in the excellent company of my friend Elizabeta, the wife of the former Argentinian ambassador. She was Romanian, and I loved the love story when the Ambassador saw her for the first time, during the years she was a travel agent. I remember her delicate features, her dark brown eyes and light hair, probably dyed somehow to mask her age. Regardless, I had gained her trust some months before when I wrote an article about her aging husband who would ultimately die in a Romanian hospital. My article included details about her travel to Argentina for his burial.

I then saw Bogdan, the Spanish interpreter. He came with his video camera and recorded every minute of the event, but he was tired from holding the camera on his shoulder by then. In his best suit, of course, Bogdan kept Mama and Elizabeta company and in good humor. George was in my care, because I was afraid he'd leave with the first lady he'd see and spoil the party. I took George out to keep me company, and later Bogdan took some videos of me on a boat ride around the lake. It felt amazing to have two of my best friends with me, both men, for a change and just be myself, without any emotional implications or romantic overtones. If these people had been women, like Adina and Sadee, the effect may have been the same. There were no strings attached on this boat ride and that made it relaxing. (I don't remember why the girls weren't there. They may have been on vacation.)

Later I lay down on the grass, alone. I needed a moment to reflect on the day. While I was modestly proud of my success, I could still hear Horia's voice in my head. I may not have deserved all of the exuberance of the party,

I thought, and found tears running down my face. In the end I knew I was relieved, as though I'd conquered a mountain, but my body had yet to regain the strength to celebrate the climb. I felt a peace inside me grow, somehow liberated from a dream that looked a lot like a nightmare.

When we got home, still in the company of my special guests, Mama recounted how impressed she was, but said she was still not feeling well. She rested a little and then said that she wanted to walk to the library to see the posters. It was a short walk, about a quarter of a mile, through downtown Bucharest. I think she wanted to explore Bucharest at night.

As we walked, I understood what that moment meant to her. She told me that the last time she'd had a similar experience was in college. I kept my pace after hers, afraid I'd destroy the magic of that moment. Soon, we found several people in front of the library's display, looking at the posters of my book and me on the windows. We stopped on the side of the window and waited for them to leave.

"Very nice," a man said. Then he recognized me from the pictures and asked me to sign a book. He had bought it from a street vendor, he said.

When we walked back, my new shoes felt tight, and I took them off. "Look, Mom! All this world is mine!" I said as I laughed, holding my shoes in one hand. Suddenly, my mind felt as free as the time I had walked on the grass at Obogeni. The time of innocence that I loved the most was long gone, but that night brought some of it back for me. I savored the moment a little longer as I walked barefoot through downtown Bucharest, from the most famous bookstore in the country.

A few weeks after the book signing, I wrote an emotional eulogy. It was the last story of the Argentinean ambassador who was dying in a Romanian hospital. Elizabeta, his wife, had asked me to prepare an article about his life. I spent many days with her, helping her get things ready for the funeral, and preparing to transport the ambassador to Argentina.

"It was his wish," she confessed to me.

In those days I got to know her better, and we became close friends. We planned to write her story after her return from Argentina. She wanted to spend some time there and to visit the country.

My book was a success, but I was an easy mark for the publisher. He ran two prints that summer, but I didn't see a dime. Since then, I have trusted no one in the publishing business in Romania. Many years later Adina told me he finished decorating his villa at Snagov and then sold his business—the cowards' way out, partly using money I earned.

~

Mama suffered a light stroke, the doctor said, on the Monday after the book signing. She needed medical exams and treatments. She agreed to stay in a hospital on the condition that I'd stay with her during the day; Voicu granted me my first vacation of my career.

"Take care of your mom," he said.

I spent many hours visiting with her and did what a child should do. I brought her sweets and food, newspapers to read, went for short walks, and even took some naps in bed next to her. I remember her face, and how her deer eyes melted when she saw the nightgown and the bathrobe I bought for her.

"How much did you pay for it?" I laughed and didn't tell her. "Is it expensive?"

Sometimes she asked me to bring her a drink from a vending machine and insisted on leaving my cell phone with her. She used the phone to call Tata, who was still upset with me because it appeared I had given up completely on teaching.

When the doctor said Mama was safe to go home, I brought her back to Dragasani.

Tata waited for us at the gate and all of us cried. In the two years since I had seen him last, I found him slanted, his face wrinkled, but his eyes were the same. We sat on the bench, at our spot, while Mama went to check on the house. I asked him about Passiflora since I hadn't been able to see it in its place.

"It died two years ago," he said.

I felt sad, learning that Tata's favorite flower died when I was gone, just after he and I had that heated argument about my new job as a journalist.

"You look like you know what you want, so I give your job credit for it. If you're happy, I'm happy," he said, seeming to conclude his thoughts. It was then that I really felt at peace.

For the next two weeks I kept busy during the day around the house. I fed the chickens and the pigs, ensuring Mama stayed out of the sun. I even took on cooking since Tata loved seeing me in the kitchen. Every time, he would get in my way and would keep asking me what I was making; we kept each other company as in the old times. We laughed so much, too, remembering all of the jokes and pranks through the years, and how we left Maita Maria, his mother, on the top of the roof, upset because she didn't give me any walnuts.

After we laughed our way through our memories, we got back to living without artifices, and when Livia came home with her baby daughter, I understood how much I'd truly missed in those two years away from home. We all tried to give Livia some time to recover from sleepless nights spent as a new mom.

I loved holding my baby niece in my arms, and putting her to sleep in the afternoons, when I watched her breathing and mumbling her innocence in her dreams. While she slept, I realized how much she meant to all of us, as we all fought to be with that tiny miracle. I acknowledged then what I should have never doubted: love comes naturally; love can't be forced.

In the late evenings and early nights, when my parents and Livia retired, I sat on the bench into the night and listened to the crickets. It felt as though my soul was composed of that song, one I knew and longed for and carried it inside with me to Bucharest and back. *How could I have ignored who I really was? Why did I have to try becoming fancier than I was?* I rediscovered this song and let it roar, louder and louder, in the middle of that August night, there on Mama's 57th birthday.

I wish time had stopped at that moment. It was so peaceful after we finally rediscovered the harmony we had all been seeking. Even Tata agreed.

They had subscribed to my newspaper and constantly were looking forward to reading my next articles.

With Mama (right) on my book launch.

Children of the Decree

Maria D. Holderman

Chapter Seventeen: Iron Cribs

This is the horror I that I helped reveal when I began reporting on the orphans of Romania.

Much like the rest of Romania, I first learned of these atrocities committed during Ceaușescu's rule by watching television. It was the winter of 1998.

Hungry and peeling potatoes in the living room, I turned on the television, the sound on low for background noise, the phone by my side. I had been waiting to hear back from my mother regarding Tata. A few days before Mama told me he was ill and was not getting well. The doctor in Dragasani had suggested an MRI at the university hospital, as none of the treatments seemed to be effective, but Tata was stubborn, and a trip to Bucharest to see a doctor was unlikely. Unless my mother could convince him to make the trip for me, to see me.

As I peeled potatoes and waited for the phone to ring, a gruesome image flashed across the screen that caught my attention. My stomach lurched and I dropped the knife I was using peel potatoes. The knife clattered to the floor at my feet, forgotten.

There on the television, crowded, bold, and naked, sat children on the floor or tied up in beds and chains, bumping their heads against walls. Some were clearly soaked in body fluids, or on uncovered mattresses in iron cribs.

I gasped, unable to look away, my trembling hand covering my mouth. It seemed as if I was suddenly watching a horror movie, as if young actors were playing roles in a disturbing story and a narrator spoke in English overdubs. I saw something then I couldn't understand. *Who were these children?* Then I heard women speaking Romanian, and my mind struggled to catch what they were saying. I grabbed a cigarette and lit it unconsciously, inhaling great wafts of smoke as I tried to understand what I was seeing happening.

When I crushed my third cigarette, I realized it was a documentary aired in America and being replayed by CNN International.

Children of the Decree

The documentary told a story of Romanian children tormented and trapped in horrific institutions. But my question was, *why did Romania still have orphans? And how many?* Then I remembered the English interpreter, and the American family willing to adopt a child but simply couldn't find him.

That was a sleepless night for me, the first of many to come. I stared at the flames of the fireplace sparkling in the darkness, my mind whirling at what I'd witnessed. Even crawling off the couch into bed seemed impossible. I was in shock.

In the morning, I stumbled to the phone, delirious from lack of sleep. Mama said Tata was feeling better that morning and that he'd decided not to come to Bucharest. I sighed in relief, glad he was well and relished that I had the day to myself.

It was still dawn, and the clouds predicted a steady snowfall outside my frosted windowpane. I stormed into the office, barely noticing there was no one around.

Desperate to know more about the children of the documentary, I turned on the computer and Googled *Romanian children*. The search showed pictures of us, my generation in pioneer uniforms, gathered all around Ceaușescu as he grinned.

My throat tightened and I wanted to scream. I could only stare at the pictures for several minutes, seeing children smiling and looking happy just as I was at that age, back when I believed Ceaușescu was our father. It seemed like a time so long ago.

With shaking hands, I typed: "Romanian children. Documentary. America." Several links opened to the same black and white picture I had seen on television the night before. I was compelled to watch the entire documentary again.

I clicked *play*.

More children appeared before me, their images haunting. They were out of any human sight, far from anything that seemed remotely humane. Ceaușescu had been dead for ten years at this point, and while the Decree

770 had been long abolished, its effect remained as though nothing had changed.

I tried to guess at the children's ages, and while I'd realized some were likely to have been born during communism, most were likely to have been conceived after the Iron Curtain's fall. We, the Children of the Decree, were thirty-one or thirty-two years old at the time.

With a handful of hair in my hand, my scalp hurting from pulling it, I concluded that I could have been one of their mothers. One generation destroying the other, on the screen before me. I saw a full circle that started with my parents, then me, and now these children.

My generation was responsible for them, the post-communism, Romanian, disabled children, discarded as too unhealthy to serve in the new democratic society and thus locked up in institutionalized centers built by Ceauşescu's regime and maintained after its fall.

On television, the only orphans I saw that looked happy and cheerful were around Michael Jackson during his two concerts in Bucharest, in 1992 and 1996. The news reported then that he had donated $10,000 for the construction of a playground.

How was it possible, and who was responsible for these children on the screen? And why was no one talking about it?

Within moments I was on the phone with the social services office, searching for more information. They passed me from one office to another, but no one wanted to talk. It was a dead-end.

I could have stopped there but I was driven to know more.

As I crossed out names and institutions, I considered what steps the best reporter I knew would take in this situation—Horia, the man I had fallen for — and it was then that I remembered the family I had met at the court archives just a few weeks previously.

I had been reading Colonel Bota's deposition and across from me sat a tall man and a petite woman about my size, looking much like a husband and wife, who told me they were both Hague Human Rights Committee's lawyers. They handed me a business card. She was the President of the Association for Human Rights in Romania, a Helsinki (APADOR-CH) division. I was intrigued by them, thinking of how petite women can and do change the world.

They were my chance to understand much more about Romania's orphans.

The husband answered his cell phone, surprised to hear from me so soon. Yes, he knew about the documentary and, hours later, I was glad to find myself in their office.

I learned that they represented several American families in the adoption process who had found that while some adoption cases in Romania were successful, most weren't. Many couples found they couldn't finalize an adoption because of an old law, a loophole allowing parents to change their minds about signing adoption papers. Common practice in Romanian adoptions often involved this legality, bribes, or both. Or, instead of adopting a child that couple had fought and paid for, they'd discover a switched baby, and that their kid was long gone.

Some Americans spent a month in Romania, they said, spending thousands and thousands of dollars in bribes, or waiting for the court to rule on their case, only to be made to wait for another month or more for a final decision, with still no guarantee of success. The process matched exactly the description I'd heard from the English interpreter.

Hundreds and hundreds of children found homes overseas, most of them in America, after the original airing of the documentary. Kind people had given a chance to some kids, and I was grateful to them, but there was much more to what was going on.

The system was rigged, and the authorities were hungry for money and, after international coverage, they were looking to capitalize on the ongoing tragedy. Still recovering from the economic disaster that followed the fall of Ceaușescu, everyone was desperate for stable American dollars. Now they knew how to get them.

"You need one more of this, translated and notarized," and so on, the vultures squawked.

Maria D. Holderman

It was around that time that I tried to access the orphanage that Michael Jackson had visited, but after the explosive American documentary, no reporter could even get a pass. Desperate, I asked Irina to help me, since her name was more popular than mine. Plus, everyone knew who her father was. She couldn't get access either.

The biggest surprise came when Voicu told me again, "Who cares?"

"I care!" I exclaimed.

"Find something interesting, bring me more stories from prison, and the first interview with Bota. Or write about kinds of condoms," he said.

I would have to find another way to get the whole story.

I would have to persist.

There was no other choice.

~

I had a plan in mind: if I gave Voicu the interview with Bota, maybe he'd let me go find out the truth about missing children and Romanian adoptions.

I hoped I'd discover something of great importance in my digging and figure out what exactly was going on. My break arrived one afternoon when a reputable colleague gave my newest colleague, Viorel Ilisoi, and me a phone number, saying, "this is the director of *Dracula* magazine, Alec Macri, a former caricaturist. He admires your writing and wants you to collaborate with him. You'll like him."

The next day, we showed up at Macri's office behind *Unirii Square*, in a house transformed into an agency on a quiet street. A couple of redactors were bent over a pile of letters and greeted us. We then met with Alec Macri and his editor-in-chief, a woman in her early thirties who was dressed in a pantsuit.

Macri looked highly professional, in his early fifties, and carried with him a bit of an old-school attitude, which only added to his charm. His exaggerated politeness and diction, coupled with a naturally exuberant personality came across during his short tour of the establishment. There everyone seemed preoccupied on a task but was friendly enough to welcome us. I was convinced the stars had aligned in my favor.

Children of the Decree

We continued our discussion over wine and delicious food at a high-scale restaurant that I had only seen from the boulevard. By dessert, I understood what Macri and his group wanted from us. "We read every letter and respond to each. Our readers want more stories, and now it's time to publish paranormal stories everyone adores and wants more," he said.

Immediately I understood why they wanted me. "You touch that human part with such emotion and reflection that goes to your heart." The same was true about my new friend, Viorel, who was a master in relating to other people through words.

Macri, an elegant and literate man turned into a businessman later in his life, tried to convince me to sign on: he offered me a new cell phone, excellent pay, and a car to go wherever I wanted to find stories. They'd pay for all of the expenses, and even more, if I'd accept to publish with my name and picture. While I agreed to write "stories," Viorel decided to inaugurate a rubric called "Nothing About Paranormal." Viorel kept his promise and wrote satire instead. And I kept my word.

Macri celebrated our verbal agreement with a bottle of expensive champagne, and I felt drunk after the first sip. "Come tomorrow to sign your contract and get your cell phone," he said as they dropped me off at home. As I look back, it was the best deal that I could have ever made.

I continued going to prison for three days a week and wrote spare interviews to justify my physical absence at the office while I was away on assignment to produce the stories for Macri. He had suggested that the best stories would be in small places in Moldavia, as almost every village had something unique in it, stories we often today call legends. My task list for *Dracula* meant finding the tales, bringing them to life, giving them space and dimension, and finding one or two locals who could tell me the story, and taking a few pictures.

Moldavia was the region of Romania with the most significant number of orphanages and children's homes. Even my new friend Viorel grew up in one of the homes, in the north part of Moldavia, until he graduated high school. His sick father was out of work for many years, and five of the twelve children were sent to a home for children. On some weekends and vacations, he'd go back and visit with his sisters and brothers. The children's house became his second home, and, in time, he'd learn how to avoid starving and the beating from both the personnel and the other children.

As my first trustworthy witness, he recounted for me dramatic episodes that he desperately wanted to forget. His voice drawled, and his eyes became lost as he remembered times he had longed to forget.

To my surprise, there were some small victories that he candidly remembered of that system as well. These included the librarian who had instilled in him a love for books, and a couple of friends with whom he had played violin at school events. But as much as I wanted to know more details, I couldn't corner my friend in his moments of vulnerability brought on by his experience. I couldn't even tell him why I had developed a sudden interest in such a sensitive topic.

Only after I visited several orphanages did I understand why no one wanted to talk about those children.

Nearly three decades after I was born, the Romanian institution had about 800,000 orphans. I found some naked and filthy children in iron cribs, remnants of Ceaușescu's time. These children made no eye contact and showed no expressions, and I found some so drugged up that I thought they were dead.

I asked about mortality, but no one could give me an answer. One evening I stayed overnight and went to the local bar. I learned from some locals who had family members in the system that some children there died from simple health issues, such as cataracts or anemia. "Who can take care of two hundred children at once?" one local told me. Without many words, I came to understand more about why so many children had died due to of lack of care.

In other places I visited I saw children tied to their beds, left to wallow in their urine and feces or restrained by their own clothes. "Why?" I couldn't stop asking the ladies in charge. "We have things to do, and those don't stop fussing," they would tell me.

As a result, these children suffered from developmental delays, along with malnourishment. Sometimes they contracted diseases from the use of dirty medical equipment.

After I saw those places, I couldn't tell if I had a heart or not.

One woman who worked in the orphanage told me that the only thing that had changed from Ceaușescu's regime was the donations they received from other countries. "We have powdered milk and diapers, more medicine and syringes, but the same number of babies and personnel," she said. She invited me to see the kitchen, and I saw a boiling pot on top of the stove. I asked what was for dinner. "Nutritious food from our donors," she answered. I waited for a moment of distraction and looked around. I found several tin cans discarded in the overfilled garbage.

"This is cat food," I almost cried.

"Yes, but it contains the most nutrients," she said, trying to push me aside.

The answer I needed came from a caregiver. "It's a cycle," she said. "These are children of the orphans or of women with less education or stable material situations."

My parents' generation perpetuated the cycle to mine, and we did the same to the younger children, who are passing the abuse on to this day.

It became that simple to understand, but in my core, it remained as difficult to understand as ever.

~

Before my commitment to *Dracula* magazine Voicu didn't care whether I was present at the office every day or not. He wanted *stories* and I had to search for them. After my position changed from reporter to special reporter (my name was on the editorial box now, and the new position title also meant more compensation), he expected me to find more exclusive headlines. Like the editors at our competitors, Voicu loved and treasured the oblique and exclusive kickers on the front page. Sometimes I could understand how he moved around the headlines and subheads, to intentionally power the front page with eye-catching news.

Not everyone was aware of my collaboration with another outlet. Voicu's right hand since the times of EVZ, a tall, skinny man with a voice like nails on a chalkboard, had a group of favorite reporters he tried hard to promote. Rumors said that this man shared his office with a much younger girl that he was in love with. That part was true. He had pulled some strings to send her to the Cannes Film Festival, but she overstayed her visa and later married another guy. After that Voicu's right hand lost his mind.

I remember this man's hysterical reaction once when we crossed paths in the hallway. I had no idea he read *Dracula* magazine, which had in the editorial box the names of the best journalists from each newspaper in the country. Viorel and mine were listed under Macri and the editor-in-chief.

"You write for them and not for us?" he screamed in front of Voicu's office, fluttering the latest issue of *Dracula*.

I knew I had to please Voicu and so I wrote even more stories than he demanded of me just in case I was busy traveling to write stories of ghostly places and people; and my real intention was to learn more about the orphanages and the scheme of international adoption in my country.

At that point, I needed two more missing pieces of information that no one yet could tell me: how children were selected for international adoption, and how they and others sometimes disappeared from the centers in Bucharest.

One night while I stayed at Sadee's, I remembered Mama telling me that our godparents' son was a doctor at an orphanage near Bucharest. I asked Mama to find out from his parents where he lived. I needed an address, to be able to meet him at his home.

"I'm not doing it, Dana. I don't want to get him involved in a scandal," she told me.

"If you don't find the address for me, I'll find him at the orphanage. Better help me, please," I asked.

I knew Mama would give me the address. I packed for a few days and rushed to *National* with an interview I saved for emergencies, with a serial killer known as The Death Taxi Driver. Like Ted Bundy, he was an intelligent man, an engineer who killed three women for sex and revenge, women he had picked up with his car from the train station in Bucharest. When I met him in a conference room, it was with two armed officers standing behind him on both sides, just a week after he'd arrived at Rahova. He was a *lifer,* since Romania abolished the death penalty after the Revolution in December 1989. I was in court on the day of that sentencing.

Of course, the press considered him a high-profile case, and many journalists tried to interview him. I planned to wait for his sentence and to do the first interview with him, in his words and on my terms. The shackled man on the opposite side of a long table analyzed me from head to toe. His aquamarine eyes penetrated mine, as if he wanted to know if he could manipulate me and get me to publish the neatly handwritten notes he wrote for me.

As I listened to him, I sensed no remorse in him for killing the women. "Why did you kill the last one, Mariana?" I asked, looking over my notes with the names from his file. "She stole one of my gold rings to escape," he told me. While he tried to convince me that she deserved to die over the stealing of a ring, I could not help but imagine her last breath as he strangled her.

"Were there other women?" I asked, looking straight at him. He masked a sarcastic laugh, and the officers moved one step closer to him, probably afraid he'd try and do something. I knew he would not answer, but I wanted to get his reaction, to describe in my exclusive interview. With his tongue he wet his upper lip and then his eyes fixed on my mouth. *He would have killed me, too,* I thought, and I ended the interview wishing him a *good stay*.

Those eyes sometimes haunt me in my dreams.

~

A few hours later I knocked on my godfather's door. I found him changed since I had last seen him at his wedding. At that time, I thought he was too slim. Now, his hair looked almost gray, and he gained some weight which made him look sharp and alert.

"I just got home. I knew you're coming, so I grabbed something for dinner. My wife will be here soon," he said. She was a doctor at a nearby hospital.

The varied hues of brown in his eyes emanated peace and I felt comfortable.

I complimented him on his look and the house, a new two-story villa.

"So, how can I help you?" he asked. He grabbed two glasses and a bottle of wine.

I explained what I needed, information on how children were added to Romania's international adoption list.

"No names, right?"

"No names. I promise you."

That evening, I came to understand how the system worked. Some social workers would visit orphanages and find the best-looking children. The highest demand was always for blond kids with blue eyes, or anything close. He believed the recruiting social workers were, in fact, part of an organized group supervised by someone at a triage center in Bucharest. "Something for you to figure out," he said. The recruiters visited two or three times each year. Then other social workers would come take the children late at night—most of the time, with no paper trail left behind.

"Listen, I am just the doctor. I don't know how this thing works; I didn't see any transfer orders. I guess. You go figure out because I want to know what is going on. I never saw those kids come back, and to be honest, I have no idea where they went. But this I know: one day, a mother came to see her child, and the kid was gone. She had no clue."

I wasn't surprised to hear that. All I had was a supposition, and I needed the proof. I couldn't use my godfather's name in my reporting.

My job now was to find that triage center and the person or people in charge.

Again, I reached a dead-end.

Children of the Decree

Chapter Eighteen: The Truth

I had a premonition, or it may have been something that was just meant to happen on an early February day. I woke up singing. I also remember my strong desire for crepes and coffee as I waited for Sadee to join me. She was getting ready for a new day at the dentist's office. Side by side, we looked into the large mirror and laughed. She dressed in an elegant V-neck black dress with green high heels and a necklace, her hair long and curled. I wore gray wool pants, a black sweater under my jacket, and black boots. With makeup and burgundy lipstick, she looked perfect. I only combed my hair.

"What's on your schedule today?" Sadee asked as she sipped from her teacup, looking a bit concerned about my plain attire.

"Prison day," I smiled.

There was one thing I learned from my trips to prison—dress modest and look dull. With my reporter bag on my shoulder and Sadee with a designer purse, we shared a cab.

I dropped Sadee off at her practice, promising we'd talk later, and then kept on to my destination.

The city glittered in a white coat as I watched the view from the back seat. I saw a few children walking to school, playing catch with snowballs. Two girls bundled up in pink hats and snow gear, taking turns riding a sled.

What a beautiful day, I thought.

I gasped the last fresh air of freedom as I dragged myself toward the prison's front entrance, ready to step into a different world.

As always, Captain Andrei escorted me to the library. The inmates probably found out I'd arrived earlier than any other day because they appeared in the next few minutes.

I opened a pack of cigarettes, served them, and left it on the table for later.

"How about we interview you today, Ms. Dana? Everyone talks about you here. Why don't you tell us your story?" one said to me.

The idea brought a smile to my face. Of course, I didn't expect to "give" an interview, and at that moment I envisioned Sadee's face after I would tell her of this encounter. I also heard Voicu's sarcasm in my head: "You are famous now."

Even Captain Andrei agreed with the idea. "Go for it and teach them something good," he said. I thought I could use the occasion to practice the art of interviewing, the sequence of questioning, and the final write-up. "Why not?" I exclaimed.

I gave them time to work in groups and come up with the questions, and soon I told them about Obogeni, the sister I never fought with, and the watch Tata bought me after I saved enough from selling flowers. I told them about how I became a journalist and what I had to give up—the teaching job. Some just listened to my story; others wrote down my words and got lost in them. I kept talking, my spirit high in the smoking cloud above our heads. When I finished, I divided them into two groups to write the interview, and then each group would share their version, and that would be followed by discussions and critique. Halfway through the write-up I heard a voice behind my back.

"Someone wants to talk to you," the Ukrainian journalist whispered.

I turned my back, looked around the library, and saw a group of inmates playing chess. Then I observed a waving hand, as if to say, "look here."

There he was. Colonel Bota smiled from a distance, a golden tooth shining in the light. I waved back, raising my palm, and mimed "five minutes." He acknowledged that he understood my gesture.

Captain Andrei patted me down. "He's ready!" I heard someone say. Somehow, I felt nervous but calmed down instantly, took a deep breath, and told the writing group to keep working. "I'll be back," I said.

Conscious of my every step, as if I was measuring the length of the aisle at my wedding, I walked toward him. He watched me coming and moved to another table by himself. I felt uneasy, curious about what made him change his mind and come out from his bear den after more than a year. *Holy crap! I'm five feet apart from one of the best anti-terror agents, a spy, and I don't know what to do with my hands.*

I was five feet away, and he rose.

"Good morning, Ms. Achim. Colonel Bota." He extended his right hand.

"Dana Achim," I said.

He took my hand and kissed it, the highest respect for a woman in Romanian custom.

"Have a seat!" he said.

He pointed to the seat across the table and then slid the chair under me as if we were having dinner at a restaurant together.

Dressed in military training camouflage but without the ranks, he kept his hands on the table. I saw his gold wedding ring, a pack of long menthol cigarettes, and an ashtray with half of a cigarette still burning on his side of the table. He inhaled once and blew the smoke to the other side.

"You are popular here. How are you today?" He leaned back to watch my reaction.

"All is fine, thank you," I said.

"What's new in Dragasani?" His eyes measured me.

"Same as in Buzau. Same old, same old."

We kept talking like that for some time, his questions showing me he knew who I was and my responses showing that I knew a lot about him. I could say and ask a lot without a blink. His smile convinced me that he seemed pleased with me, and then he handed me his pack to offer me a cigarette. I saw there was only one left and refused. In Romanian custom, a woman never takes a man's last cigarette. If one does, it means that they accept his invitation to get closer than is permitted.

"Do you have questions for me?" he asked.

"No. Not at this time. But if you want to tell me something, I'm listening," I said.

"Good to know," he said. "I know my situation *here* is of interest, but I also know journalists speculate. I like honesty."

"You'll have it if you want to talk with me," I responded.

"We'll see how it goes."

We discussed what we each liked about Proust, Camus, and Kazantzakis, and how the movies made after notable literary masterpieces—

Zorba the Greek, for example— missed some of the core beliefs of the characters.

I found he could talk about anything. I knew he was testing me on every level of intelligence and knowledge and whatever else he may have been looking for. It was a test, of course, that I had to pass.

When facing him every nerve and muscle in me tensed when he wanted to hear me talking, and the pace he installed in our conversation made me relax a bit. I wanted to hear him talking nonsense, saying something to make me rebuff him, but I found him well-rounded and eager and charming and totally unwilling to be heard sounding anything but intelligent. Of course, because of who he saw himself as, he had to act this way, I realized.

One hour later, and before lunch, I grabbed my coat and bag to leave. I guessed that I passed one of his tests because I never took my notebook from my bag. "Nice meeting you, Ms. Achim," he said. "Come back soon."

Holy crap! I couldn't wait to tell Voicu about my short visit with Bota.

"Write!" Voicu demanded.

"He's testing me. Not yet."

I saw Voicu's eyelid pulse, but also his temple.

"I'll write a good story, but I won't mention him this time. Give me two more weeks. I think I got him," I said.

Voicu finally understood and agreed to my approach.

A few days later, in the office, Adina handed me the phone.

"Good afternoon, Ms. Achim. Colonel Bota. I loved today's article. When do you come back?"

I had to sit and concentrate.

"Tomorrow? Same time?"

"Sure. I'll have something ready for you. By the way, I loved your book, too. I just finished it."

I felt a knock in my head. The day I had been waiting for was on the horizon but something in me felt dead. Why wasn't I more excited for the interview that Voicu had wanted for more than a year?

I wasn't sure how Bota's interview would end, or if he would change his mind, until I arrived the next day. I was sure of one thing: I passed the tests, thanks to Horia's lesson: "don't show weakness. You hold the pen."

It worked.

~

Piles of snow on the road slowed the drive to Rahova the next day. *The road to Hell,* I thought, remembering Chris Rea's song that I still love. I debated if I should call a photographer or not, but my guts convinced me not to. I had the feeling Bota wouldn't like his picture taken in military attire, without ranks, so I decided not to call anyone to join me. Not even Voicu, until I was done writing the article.

I found Bota in the library, handwriting papers on the desk, glasses on. We exchanged a few polite words while I placed my notes with questions and the files about his case next to his papers.

"Should we start?" I asked.

"Why not?" he answered.

I asked the first questions—whose initial idea it had been, and why he had accepted to be part of trafficking cigarettes. "I am a man of honor and respect the authority" He said sternly. This meant someone in a higher position gave him a command and he obeyed the order.

We talked about the night when the scheme was discovered. "Three Colonels knew about it. Only two were removed from their position." I figured which one was left—*anti-terrorism, still in charge. Aha!* It appeared that the anti-terrorism Colonel turned the other two in. The Army Colonel, who supervised the military base at the airport, went down too. "The Secret Services is left," I concluded for myself.

His answers weren't straightforward; I had to read between the lines and to ask clarifying questions, but we agreed to leave some responses just the way he had wanted phrased. I knew what these verbatim phrases meant to him: they were secret codes to his people and the world that was out there waiting to hear from him.

Bota's was the most intriguing interview I had ever accomplished. On my way to the office, I thought the Colonel was proud and smart, and there was no surprise there. But his steadfast claims that he was a man of his word, and that his ranks and the uniform meant there was honor in the creed: no matter what, you obey the order.

That's precisely what he did, and he assumed full responsibility for his actions. I couldn't figure out what deal he had made in exchange for his silence, but at that moment I didn't care. My mind's focus wasn't in this interview, but to find the *triage center* for the orphans. I knew I would.

~

Not long after the interview with Bota, Voicu asked me to help one of his relatives, a widower who was raising two children. The man had tried on his own to solve his problem but had little success. He came to *National* and talked to Voicu. He seemed very polite, and his first words were about God and religion, and he admitted he still cried for his late wife. I wasn't sure how to console him, especially there in Voicu's office.

Then, Voicu told me to listen to him, and to write a concise article about his cousin's problem. This was the first situation where I had to write something so plainly, and I didn't then understand why my boss didn't get someone from the *social* department to cover this story. Then, in Voicu's office, the man complained that the water pressure in his apartment on the last floor was weak and that he had had no water for weeks.

The brief regarding this story appeared on page five, in a small print to fit in the next day's designated space. That was the first time my name appeared on that page and not in headlines touting my exclusive interviews or stories.

Two days later, after I met Voicu's cousin and wrote the brief, I got a phone call on my cell from the mayor of the first district.

It was still early in the morning and daylight inundated the living room. The mayor said he wanted to talk to me at his office if possible, and that he could send his private driver if I preferred, to get there as soon as possible. Or, he said, I could take a taxi, and he'd reimburse me for the expenses. My house was also in the first district, just like Voicu's relative, which I assumed was the reason for the call. Based on my location, I was under the jurisdiction of George Padure, the mayor's real name.

I announced myself at his office and the mayor invited me into his private office. He said he wanted to meet me personally. Until that day I had only seen him in television commercials, appearances in which he was either promoting his furniture stores or running for mayor.

The mayor's elegance staggered me but, of course, he could afford anything he wanted as the CEO of a profitable business.

He said he had the furniture in his office decorated with colorful orchids because he wanted to feel at home. Afraid I'd bump my knees on the delicate coffee table, I sat on a leather armchair.

"I'm a big fan," he started, looking at me from his desk. "I applaud you for all you do, and I want to assure you if you ever need anything, I'm here to help. I sent some people to solve the problem with the water but, next time, please, call me before you write something negative about district one."

And then my brain clicked. "The orphanage Michael Jackson visited twice is under your jurisdiction, right?"

"Right."

"I've been trying to get in, but the director denied all my requests."

He paused and grabbed a cigar and handed me one. I refused politely.

"What's the story, Ms. Achim? Why do you need access?"

"Well, I've been working on something for some time, but I need to keep it confidential until I'm done."

I did mention to him the money Michael Jackson had donated for a playground, and I wanted to know where the money had gone because the playground was in fact not a playground but a couple of cheap slides. That was all I could tell him, and it was the partial truth. I didn't tell him my real intentions because I was unsure if I could trust him.

"Well, I can't promise you much, but I think I can help you. Give me two days, okay?" he said.

Children of the Decree

We made a deal, and I was on cloud nine because I knew he'd find a way to direct me toward the missing pieces of my investigation. After all, he had reached out to me.

That night Sadee and I spent the night at Adina's. "We have to celebrate my divorce," Adina told us. We danced to Latino music and *Mambo No. 5* until we got dizzy, and I still remember the thrill of that Ishtar Alabina's *Loli Lolita Lola* night: Sadee teaching us Arabian moves, all three of us in pajamas, turning and sweating, and feeling free of men and compromises.

Even the dog joined us in our beautiful craziness.

~

The phone call came later, and it was one I had been waiting for. Every time my cell rang, I wished it was the mayor. Then, one day, I received a phone call without an ID. It was Colonel Bota, "Don't cross the street between two cars," and I panicked. Other times no one said a word.

When the mayor finally did call to invite me to a meeting at his office, I shortened the phone conversation to its very minimum.

That was when I observed cars parked for a long time on my street, with the driver inside, reading a newspaper. Sometimes I saw the same white car parked on the same spot; then I would take a cab and go to Adina's or Sadee's. Sometimes different drivers took turns sitting, reading in the white vehicle.

I took a trolley to the mayor's office at the last minute, pretending to look for a cab. Once I was sure no one was following me, I ran to his office. The mayor introduced me to two women, both nurses at the orphanage, each in their early fifties. One of them was still on the job while the other had been fired a few weeks before.

They said the money for the playground went to other departments, to build offices for the director and his protegees, among whom were several family members—a priest hired to give blessings to babies and a bodyguard to protect them. I learned then that the director had signed a contract with a circus to bring the babies and children under age two to the shows. He also had a villa that was under construction.

Only then did I ask all of the questions I needed answered to complete my investigation. For example: "How does a child come to the center?"

"Through a separate placement center, situated on a different street in sector two." The children my godfather had mentioned arrived there first.

"They arrive late at night and leave early the next day. One morning, I observed the name of a child crossed out and the child gone overnight. So, I asked, where's this one? I was told to mind my own business, but when the second child disappeared during my night shift, I went to the director and insisted he tell me what happened. So, I got fired. But my colleague can tell you what's going on now."

I sensed the mayor's tension. It was too late to stop me, I thought, and I told him, "It happens in your district. Did you know what was going on?"

He said no, and I believed him. "It's new to me. I will support you and back you on this story." He didn't sound happy.

The second woman described a wing for children under one year old. Those children received the best food and clothing, vitamins, and enriched formula. "The healthiest, best-looking children. Kids for export only. Only foreigners could visit them. They are the ones that disappear."

In the end, the mayor gave me an official statement and promised to commence a formal investigation. I protected the identities of the women but mentioned the presence of the mayor during the interviews. "We are in this together," he assured me. His words gave me peace of mind and, importantly, a kind of protection.

Now, my job was to write the story and convince Voicu it was necessary to publish.

~

I couldn't sleep for a long time and didn't leave my house for days until I finished writing, surviving on bread and butter, and coffee. I don't need much, to be honest. But I knew the story's weight and the anticipated consequences were keeping me motivated and awake, and no one could convince me to give up the assignment—especially not after discovering the ongoing truth. I wanted to be sure the aftermath of this article would not jeopardize my career and, as much as I trusted Voicu, I had to protect myself. With the final version of the article in my handbag, I knocked on the door of the office of the lawyers from the Hague Committee. They were, after all, the best of the best.

We sat around the table. They read each page as I waited for any response. They began by suggesting changes in verbs and took out every adjective, adding the mayor's comments right at the end as a credibility bonus. "If they need someone to blame besides you, they can find him first. He's powerful and rich," one of them said.

Even then I kept the article a few more days. Bogdan read it too and then we met with the English interpreter, who read it, and then exclaimed, "Wow, what a mess." He confirmed the parts he knew of, describing again the way the child he had promised to the American couple had vanished.

During this time the mayor grew nervous, calling me every morning to ask why the article wasn't in the newspaper. "I'm still working on it," I answered every time.

Two weeks later, the underground schemes of adoptions in my country came to light. The article was published on June 1, 1999 – International Children's Day. This was not at all a coincidence but clever planning on my part.

After he read the text, Voicu asked me to give him a *good* story.

I slept unturned on the sofa and woke up early when Voicu called. His voice sounded harsh, and I sensed fear.

"The orphanage's director called the office. He was mad."

"Is there something I didn't know?" I asked.

"I guess not."

We were sued.

Gheorghe Voicu, the editor-in-chief of "National" daily, in his office.
(Photo: Florian Gheorghe.)

Maria D. Holderman
Chapter Nineteen: Finding Freedom

By the end of 1999, I thought I accomplished what many journalists strive to achieve, but only a few actually get to accomplish in their lifetime: to find that unique story that needs to be remembered. *You have to open your eyes and listen to others*, I read once in a journalism book. *The best stories are nearby.*

Perhaps I have had some luck coming face-to-face with people who have walked around previously unobserved, and I was there to discover who they were and the importance of their actions. For example, who would have believed that the soldier who had arrested the Ceaușescu couple in the forest after they fled the Palace at the onset of the Revolution was a disguised taxi driver I met one evening? Or that in a secluded location near the airport, over fifty Kurds pleaded for their safety, to remain in Romania and not to be extradited to Turkey and face death? I was there to take a photograph one night, of the word "HELP" written in their blood on a bed sheet propped on the window. I know I tried to do all I could to help avoid their extradition, but all I was able to do was buy time until my uncle, the prime minister, told me, "I'll push the delay for as long as I can. You're right—they don't deserve to die. But I can't promise you anything."

A few days later, I walked into the dilapidated building with my new friend, the Hague lawyer, who had prepared an official representation letter. "You start writing their names, and we have a case," she told me. I never saw her so determined, so furious, and so emphatic.

I had written several episodes about the unfortunate Kurds and their quest for freedom of speech and religion. And while their personal stories could move a mountain, the pictures of their faces with saw mouths with nails and curtain wires determined the Romanian authorities' call for a press conference. They promised help and protection.

"You saved fifty lives," Voicu said after he read the text about the protection's promise.

"*We* saved them," I responded. "But we need a law. There are more."

Voicu's upper eyebrow raised. "That's a lot to ask."

Not long after, the detainees received political asylum, and the government looked into a new law to protect immigrants from Africa and Middle East. And while I thought I couldn't find anything of the same significance—saving people's lives—I came across a neatly handwritten letter from prison.

It read:

Dear Mister President Constantinescu,

My name is Simona Gologan. I am 20 years old, and I grew up in an orphanage. I have a small daughter, one year and eight months old. I was sentenced to three and a half years in prison because I was convicted of stealing two meters of copper cable from a construction site on my street. I didn't steal it; I found it and recycled it to buy one liter of milk for my daughter and half a loaf of bread for me. The police arrested me at my home during the night. I wasn't present at any of the hearings of the court. I beg you, please, pardon me so I can see my daughter! I did nothing wrong.

Respectfully,
Simona Gologan

My plan to leave early changed at that moment.

I reread the letter—the words *milk*, *bread*, and *daughter* sticking in my head. I knew those words well since I was a child, and had been fighting for them, getting bruised and bullied for demanding those basics. I knew this was *something* I wanted to investigate. What I didn't realize at the time was how it would change my life and others.

The next day was the National Day of Romania, December 1, 1999, and Voicu's birthday, just a week before mine.

"Do you know her?" he asked.

"No, I found this letter among the other letters for my column. I think we should publish it separately."

His left eyelid pulsed, precisely what I'd expected.

"If this is true, it would be a great case for the newspaper," I assured him. "I think I should call the director of the prison and see what he thinks about this girl. I could talk to Officer Andrei, who gave me the letter. He must know her."

"Do you think you can find anyone at the prison now? After 7:00 PM?" Voicu asked me, excitement in his voice.

"Someone must be there. It's a prison, not a library. They watch them 24/7," I snapped.

"Okay, call now." He handed me his phone.

One officer on duty answered and gave me Officer Andrei's cell phone. He had left for the day. Voicu put the phone on speakerphone so we could both hear.

"Yes, I took the letter from her and placed it in a pile with the rest," the officer said. "Yes, what she says is true. She's a good girl and loves her daughter. All she does here is make clothes for her baby. No, she didn't steal the damn copper cable, she found it. I know because I saw her file, and the construction company owner didn't file a complaint, the cop did. So, yes, you can see the file when you come here next time."

I paused. Voicu made a sign with his hand for me to hang up.

"Have a seat," he said, as soon as I put the phone down. But I couldn't sit. We never sat down in his office. He didn't insist.

"Look, Dana, this might be the story of your life," he said. "You could become the best journalist ever. But, if she's a liar, you'll go down. No one will ever trust you."

"But what if it is true?" I looked to see if his body language would reflect his emotions and if his eyelid flickered, the sign he was excited. It pulsed.

"Okay," Voicu said, "but I don't want to hear I didn't tell you the risks. So, we'll make it the front page. "Letter to the President on the National Day of Romania.""

And this story became mine—*my* fight over milk. I prayed that I'd succeed.

~

At first, Simona's letter to President Constantinescu looked like a joke in the media world. "How could you ask the president to pardon a thief?" another journalist said, with an emphasis on the word *president* when I waited at the elevator the next day.

I squeezed into my office and asked Voicu for a photographer and a car to the prison. He gave me his driver and told Fane, our best photographer, to go with me.

At the prison, Fane took some quick shots of Simona holding our newspaper, the headlines regarding her letter to the president. "Who would believe a convicted jailbird? You're wasting your time. And mine," Fane whispered to me as he left.

Fane had taken the newspaper's car, so I had to call a taxi to get back to my office. Then, holding Simona's file on my lap, I skimmed the pages, looking at the *findings*. It was then that I got the idea of what to do next.

Voicu waited for me at the elevator, and I saw on his face that he was excited and impatient. In his office, the pictures Fane had taken were laid on his desk. "She's pretty. We are lucky. People will like her. How's the story coming?" I knew Voicu liked blonde girls just like that one, and I thought for a moment that luck was on my side.

I handed him the court sentencing order. "It matches her story."

"Write it up. Have it done in one hour, or I'll fire you!" But, of course, I knew he was joking.

On my way out, I turned and said, "Happy Birthday, Romania! Happy birthday, boss!"

I gave him the story three hours later, but not before Adina could grab it from my hands to read it first. She couldn't wait. A few minutes later, Voicu showed up in the office, facing me.

"It's good! What about tomorrow? Can you see her daughter and the father of the child? What do you need?" Voicu asked, his eyelid jumping.

"I already planned on it. Send me a car and a photographer at 9:00 AM at my house." I spun on one foot and left for home, wanting to spend the night alone.

I couldn't sleep that night. The case took me back in time. I saw myself as a little girl, fluttering on the hills at Obogeni and wearing the *wings* shirt Mama Tanta didn't like—the only freedom I knew then. I recollected the morning of the fight, holding on to an empty jar as I was defeated and bloodied. Now, I had someone's freedom in my hands, and although I wasn't sure if she stole that copper or not, I knew I was her only chance to get out. That thought terrified me. *What if I fail and give her hope for nothing?*

At six o'clock in the morning, I ran to the closest store to buy the newspaper. The first-page headlines pronounced in giant letters: "Simona Wants to Be with Her Daughter This Christmas." There were three pictures of Simona, and the story took up the whole page. I read the article as I walked home with the same curiosity as if someone else had written it.

A few hours later we found Simona's place. It was now an abandoned flat, ready to collapse, with a painted red triangle on the wall. The triangle meant "Building prepared for demolition." I couldn't imagine anyone living in those conditions: no power, no water, and no windows. A woman entered the building at the entrance, carrying an unwrapped loaf of bread, and I asked her where we could find Georgiana, Simona's daughter, and Cornel, the girl's father.

"From the newspaper? God bless your heart!" she said. She directed me to the third floor, second apartment on the left.

When we entered the apartment, I realized there was no flooring but dirt and a moldy smell. Plastic covered the window frames. An old metal bucket sat in the middle of the room, used to bathe the child, I guessed, but also to collect the water from the ceiling when it rained. A fire had burned recently, and the ashes were still red, but the room was frigid. The vapors of my breath formed a silky cloud.

Cornel was on the bed, rocking the baby girl on his legs. Wrapped in several layers of clothes, she'd sucked on a dried slice of bread. Cornel later told us the only difference between living there and not on the street was the leaking roof over their heads and a bed where they could sleep. I believed him.

Fane took some pictures right away, but he didn't leave this time. He waited for me to finish the interview. Georgiana, the little girl, was still sucking on the bread. I couldn't stand her crying, so I took my winter scarf and put it around her neck. She seemed to like the touch of cotton and maybe the fresh scent of my Versace perfume. She called the scarf "Bebe." I held her and rocked her, kissing her dirty cheeks until she fell asleep holding my scarf. After that I didn't take it back.

"Does Georgiana know she has a mother?" I asked before leaving. I pulled some bills from my wallet and left them on the table. "For food," I said.

"The only words she knows are Tata and bebe (baby)," I was told.

Searching the place again, I couldn't see any toys.

A few blocks away, on my way to the office, I saw a new building under construction, the place where Simona had found the copper. I memorized the name of the construction company and planned to take on that part of the story: did she steal the copper or not?

~

The following morning's headline was "Please, Pardon My Mother," and featuring images of Georgiana crying on the bed and Cornel holding her between the window's frames. Beneath the story, a note read: "Call our office to leave a message of support if you want this baby to be with her mother."

I never doubted that Voicu was a genius. For the first time in the Romanian press, he invited our readers to become part of the story, encouraging them to use their voice. That was a smart move.

I was sipping my coffee when my cell phone rang.

"Mr. Voicu wants you to come here now," his secretary said. She sounded concerned.

My watch showed 8:03 AM. It was very early. We always showed up after 10:00 AM. *What's wrong?*

My first thought was something from Simona's past that I may have missed, and it had just surfaced; something unexpected that could destroy my work. Then I remembered the *risk* discussion we'd had about the letter for the president when we went ahead with the story. I accepted the risk then, but now, I wanted to take it back.

I saw Voicu pacing in the hallway, which was unusual for him. Usually, he'd be in his office reading all the newspapers but not so early in the day. *He heard the elevator and came to meet me,* I thought.

"Come," he said.

We walked to his office, him in front of me, his hands behind his back. He didn't sit.

"Guess what? Over two hundred phone calls already. People are going crazy. They want her out!"

"That's good," I said, anticipating some bad news.

"We need to keep the story going. Go to the prison and do a second interview. Take my car. Fane's waiting for you. I want a picture of her with our newspaper showing the kid crying. I want more emotion, more background."

"Got it! That's it?"

"I guess you have enough on your plate for now."

The effect of my sleepless night was visible. A tear appeared in the corner of my eye. He didn't miss it and handed me some newspapers.

"For your friends," he explained. He meant for *my* inmates.

I was still in the hallway, not sure if I should leave or not. It looked like Voicu had something else on his mind.

"Don't look so discouraged. One day, someone on a white horse will come to rescue you," he said.

The driver called the elevator and Voicu watched us leave. Mid-distance while I sorted Simona's papers on my lap, the driver said to me, "He calls you Cinderella." I smiled.

~

Officer Andrei agreed to let me interview Simona in her cell this time. Before that day, a guard had brought her to the conference room in the main building to meet with me. He reached for his pager, and I knew he wanted to announce to the women's section the change of plans.

"No. I want to see what she's doing there. No rehearsal. Just the real deal."

"Dana, I don't think you'll like to be locked up in there. They have to lock the door, you know, right?"

"Let's go. I know."

Andrei stopped in an office, exchanged some words while I waited, and soon, a lady followed us who was holding a large key chain. We kept walking down more stairs and hallways, passing cells all on the right, and I even heard my name called several times.

"How did they know who I am?" I asked Andrei.

"They talk at night from their cells and pass each other the newspaper."

I found Simona sitting on her bed, knitting a sweater for Georgiana. Her face glowed when she saw me, her hair in a ponytail, and she placed the plastic needles to the side. Next to her sat the *National's* morning edition. Three other women occupied the cell, all on their beds.

"I sent it to her this morning," Andrei confessed when I stared at the newspaper.

After Andrei left, the guard, a slim lady around forty, opened the cell door, let me in, and told Simona my plan. Then she locked the door behind me and waited in the hallway, facing the cell.

Look at me; I am locked up now, I thought, and felt a lump in my throat.

I couldn't find a place to sit, so I unfolded my notebook and the files I carried with me on the floor, Simona at the edge of her bed. If I'd reached out my hand, I could touch hers.

"I want the whole truth now. I want to help you, but you need to be honest," I started the conversation.

"Ms. Dana, are you sure you have time to listen?" she mumbled.

Her story started in an orphanage, soon after her mother was diagnosed with cancer and waited to die. Her father was absent in their lives, and there, in the iron cribs of the communist system, Simona had to watch over her little sister. She loved school and wanted to become a teacher, but then she wanted out and met Cornel at fifteen. They moved into the abandoned apartment where I had met Cornel the day before. On April 23, 1998, she gave birth to Georgiana. A year later, on the same day—her daughter's first birthday—the cops broke into her place, handcuffed her, and brought her to jail on alleged charges.

A month later, she was an inmate at the Rahova Maximum Security Prison and was sentenced to three and a half years. She had served nineteen months at the time of this interview.

While I listened and took notes, I realized why Simona's story was so important to me. It exhibited everything that was wrong with our society, starting with kids in orphanages, to lack of parenting, to ignorance as to how to procure a proper ID without having an actual address, to how not to become a young cop's trophy arrest in their hopes of boosting their monthly tally.

I thought Simona was not the exception to what was happening in the country. She was the rule. People like her, now jailbirds, have had no one to assist or guide them. Many were the victims of an outdated and unjust judicial system and were sentenced to prison for stealing a loaf of bread or a jar of milk while corrupt people who made millions in illegal schemes received similar sentences or none at all. I wanted to change that.

~

I kept Simona's story going. Convinced I was on the right path, I experienced something new the next day.

People brought had brought Georgiana food, laundry detergent, and clothes—I even saw a salami on the only bed. A few dolls sat between loaves of bread and a stack of powdered milk. Holding what she could grab, sitting between all these goods, food or dolls were the same as my scarf.

By the end of the week over one thousand people had called the newspaper's office, and over one hundred letters were arriving daily. Voicu hired a third person to answer the phone, and he gave up his direct phone line to take messages. The secretary had to work on Saturday to answer the calls.

The effect of the last story and the two pages with messages from people published over the weekend created a national movement. This national movement then became an international movement. While the mainstream media let my newspaper take on this battle alone, I knew the cause that I was fighting for was larger than just me or my newspaper. We were giving the people a voice and they wanted to talk. They weren't just the Romanians living in the country, but from all over the world. Their message spelled: "Mister President, help this unfortunate mother to be with her daughter. Those who deserve to be arrested are still free."

The last time something similar had happened was during the Revolution, a decade ago.

Still, no other newspaper or television news station took on the story. It worried me, but Voicu said the risks were high from the beginning, and as with every media competition, every outlet wants to be the first to report any story. There's no second place in the press. We found ourselves leading the very first "press campaign" in Romanian history.

On Monday afternoon, while I was writing the story after I returned from Simona's cell, Voicu showed up with a fax, his face glowing and his eyelid twitching.

"The president asked to review her case. It just came in. We are moving forward," he said, looking over my shoulder at my computer screen.

I stopped what I was doing to read the press release, anticipating how Voicu had envisioned the next edition, with headlines about the president's request and, separately, pictures of Georgiana and Simona, with two pages of messages, and the announcement. "We'll keep this story going!" I said out loud.

On an invisible chess table, President Constantinescu had just made the first official move. It didn't surprise me.

The following day, still early, Voicu called me from his office. He said the Minister of Justice, Valeriu Stoica, called a press conference for 10:00 AM. The Minister's office left several messages for me to attend.

"How about I'll come to bring you there to save you time? We can talk in the car."

"Great," I said.

One hour later, in Voicu's car, he handed me a different cell phone.

"Keep it on so I can hear what's going on. Then use your phone to text me."

I laughed and he wanted to know why. I briefed him on how Horia used the same technique at my book signing. The two had known each other well, but Voicu thought I deserved better than Horia; as he reminded me, I should be waiting for the man on the white horse.

"Ready?" he asked. The car stopped in front of the ministry.

It was my first time there, never having been accredited to visit any ministers. If I was one of those certified reporters, I would lose my ability to work in the background. I feared exposing myself and being forced to play the political games I so hated.

I found the floor of the conference room in another building attached to the main one, based on Voicu's detailed description, provided so I wouldn't look lost. Now, with my head up and carrying my reporter bag, I walked the long hallway, trying to stay calm, passing dozens of other reporters on my way. With my hand clutched on the cell phone in my jacket pocket, I saw people move in and out of offices as if something big were about to happen. Then I heard my name.

"Dana, come here!"

It was the Romanian General Director of Prisons, just leaving the minister's office.

He opened the door to an empty office and was straightforward.

"I'm not sure how this conference will end. The minister is waiting to meet you. We just spoke. But there is a law in place, and until this law is revised, we can't do much. Don't lose faith. It might not be what you expect to happen, but we are now discussing proposing a government review of this law. Let's go."

I was sure Voicu heard every word and I waited for him to text me. "Tell your story. Make your point clear."

After the minister briefed the press about the case and called on me, I stood at my table.

"With all the respect for your kind words regarding my work on this case, we need to recognize the problem. Thousands and thousands of Simona Gologans are crowding the prisons instead of being home raising their children and working. They are all poor people who did something stupid. Theft is theft by definition and law, but if society had a plan for them, most of them wouldn't be there. I have received similar stories every day since we started the campaign, and we will keep it going until something changes."

"However, the difference is this: Simona Gologan did not steal the copper. I went to her place and saw the construction site where she got it from, materials on the street. I could grab a brick or something. The owner of the construction site didn't file a complaint. We need to bring justice and hope you will reflect on it, make the right decision. The president is waiting. Let's not be blindfolded. It's in the name of that word you rule over. Allow me to spell it for you: Law."

Immediately, the General Director of Prisons stood and agreed with my argument, blaming the law. However, he also pointed out that, based on his own review, there had been no official complaint filed.

Soon, Voicu texted me to leave. With all eyes on me I grabbed my things and left. I realized I was shaking when I called the elevator. Voicu waited for me at the front entrance.

"It's a matter of time now. But we did everything possible," he said. "Good job!"

Chapter Twenty: A Birthday Present

I was still sleeping when I got the call at 6:00 AM, two days after the press conference. On the line was the General Director of Prisons.

"Guess what I found this morning on my fax machine?" he asked, his voice sounding delighted. "We won!" he cried, not waiting for my answer.

"What? No way!" I screamed.

"Happy Birthday, Dana! The date is on your birthday, yesterday, but they faxed it late. Still, how do you feel about this present?"

"I don't know what to say now."

"Here's the plan. First, I'll send the paperwork to Rahova. Colonel Gheorghe is on his way there. We all agreed you should be the one to tell her. And write the end of the story. Would you do me this favor?"

I cried and screamed, I don't remember in each order, and even now, I still weep to think of this moment, more than twenty years later. It was too early to call Voicu, but I called Fane.

"She's getting out. Let's take her home. Don't tell anyone. I don't want any other press there. I'll take a shower and call a taxi. See you in one hour at the prison."

After the shower I grabbed my cell phone and saw three missed calls from Voicu. I answered when he called again.

"Fane gave me the news. I want pictures when she leaves the prison and some of her and the baby at home. Bring her here when you're done."

He didn't say "bye."

~

I hastened to get ready and forgot my cell phone. Fane waited for me, talking to Voicu. At least one of us was able to be in touch with our boss.

I walked again through the tunnel, this time with Fane and the prison director, but I smelled nothing this time. I was running a fever, and my nose was clogged.

We passed cells and believed all of those women realized something big was happening.

"Good job, Dana. Thank you!" I heard coming from the cells. We kept going.

Simona was in the same position as I left her, working on the pullover for Georgiana. Then, finally, the director opened the door, and we all walked in, my heart jumping and tears coming.

"I came here to take you home," I said. I didn't want to exploit her feelings any longer.

"Are you serious, Ms. Dana? When?"

"Now. Colonel Gheorghe can confirm it."

She looked at him and saw his smile while he handed her the official paper. Her hands trembled, her feet dancing. It was then that I heard her give out a scream that one could hear all the way to the entrance of the prison.

"Pack your stuff. We have the paperwork ready for you," the director told her.

"I am free! I am free!"

The news echoed through the cells, and we heard excited voices, "She's free!"

Simona turned as she wanted to hug me but hesitated. I held my hands toward her, and we hugged, everyone there watching. We stood like that for some time, and when we released each other's hands, our faces in tears, the sleeves of my black jacket were wet.

While Simona packed her few things, which was enough to fit inside of two plastic grocery bags, I couldn't take my eyes off of her happy face. Then she surprised me, leaving to one of her cellmates her best T-shirt. By law, she was entitled to some money upon her release—just enough to buy two loaves of bread.

It was her first step out of the gate that I wanted Fane to capture. The boundary between freedom and confinement, the fortunate and unfortunate, and this young woman crossing over it.

"I can't believe it," she said, elated. "Thank you, Ms. Dana."

She didn't look back.

~

When I got to the office with Simona and Fane, Voicu said he wanted to talk to me alone. The mayor of the first district of Bucharest had papers ready for Simona to sign, to give her a subsidized two-bedroom apartment. I was happy to hear this news.

"Are you okay?" Voicu asked.

"I think I'm sick. I can't hear well," I said.

"Write the story and go home. Take off as much as you need. But before you write, stop at the business office. They have something for you. Then open it when you're alone, okay?"

The "something" from the business office turned out to be an envelope with my name on it. I ran back to finish writing, and Voicu checked on me several times. As I typed the last words and gave Voicu the pages, he walked next door to the tech guys in charge of editing the newspaper. My text was the last thing they needed to send the edition to print.

"Come," Voicu said.

On a computer screen, I saw the headlines.

"How's that?"

My voice had disappeared, and my head pounded. Finally, I mumbled, "Great." Then he sent me home in his car.

"Thank you, Dana. Don't forget the envelope."

It was my first bonus, all in new bills.

I then slept a whole night and a day, not knowing that I had pneumonia.

In all that time, sick and congested, I had one picture in mind: a little girl breathing again in her mother's arms.

The road to freedom takes a fight, I remembered reading somewhere. Now I understood more about what that meant. Freedom meant the most supreme rising of a human being. It could mean the way to take a lead and the sacrifice to get to it and keep it. Or, as some might say, *the calling*.

I was very sick for the first time in my life. My chest was congested, and I had a constant cough and wheezing that kept me up most of the night. I wanted to sleep during the day, but I had chills and tried to get warm in front of the fireplace. But then I felt my body on fire, and the fever continued for hours until I felt cold. My nose continually required blowing, but after days I regained some of my voice. Worried, Mama wanted to come to stay with me until I was over the symptoms, but I refused, afraid she'd get sick too.

I didn't leave the house for two weeks, forcing myself to eat even though I had no appetite. I didn't want coffee either, which I knew was a sign I wasn't doing well.

"Maybe you are cursed," Sadee told me over the phone. "I'm coming over after work. I think I know what you need."

She came prepared with a bag of incenses and myrtle and asked me to lay down on the sofa. I watched her burning some charcoal on a spoon, and then she placed some myrtle over the incandescent cinder. Then she spread the fumes over my body, from head to toe, invoking superpowers and heavens, the very good spirits she said I had to breathe in. She said the evil spirits would leave my body when she counted to three. But every time I forced myself to exhale the evil spirits who made me sick, I choked harshly and expectorated green mucus.

"See? It works," Sadee said, trying to convince me to stay still. She didn't blink once.

When she decided all the evil had left my body, she opened the living room door to allow the spirits to leave the room. She pushed the fumes with a towel through the tiny window in the kitchen and came back with a boiling pot.

"You need to open your lungs, so you keep your head over this holy water," Sadee ordered me. I kept my head over the pot, and she covered my head with a larger towel. After a few minutes the cough accentuated, and my teardrops fell into the pot. Then I was able to sleep without any disturbances.

Every three hours throughout the night Sadee repeated the same ritual and when the alarm woke us in the early morning I got up and took a shower. I felt rejuvenated and alive, feeling like Sleeping Beauty.

"What did I tell you? You were cursed!" Sadee said to me, with a large smile on her face.

She left for work after I promised I would use the holy water to wash my face to keep the nasty spirits away. I knew it was her love and friendship as much as anything that cured me and got me back on my feet.

Then Voicu called me.

"Feeling better? The Minister of Justice wants you there. His secretary insisted that you attend. I can send a car to bring you to the Parliament."

I agreed.

The event, a simple get-together with the accredited journalists before Christmas, became an informal celebration of my work. They were waiting for me with questions and champagne.

~

The minister had promised to make reporters' jobs in accessing court cases easier. That alone was a win. I was dressed in a winter coat, smiling, while Valeriu Stoica and his staff lined up in front of me. Next to him, a young girl was dressed in a plaid shirt and wore a leather cap — his daughter, Andrea, who insisted on meeting me.

Soon after I left the minister, something happened at the prison that I would remember for the rest of my life and would serve as inspiration throughout my career.

The invitation came directly from the General Director of Prisons Mihai Eftimescu, a former judge, who was also my pass to access prisons. "They (the inmates) put up a show and wanted you to come. Would you do me this favor?" he asked.

I couldn't deny this special request. The show was to take place in the cafeteria, on an improvised stage in the middle with bleachers around. On the left side, on chairs used at meal time, sat the dignitaries—my reserved chair between the director of the Rahova prison and Eftimescu. I felt awkward.

Inmates watched, waving to me, and while I contained my desire to get up and talk to some, I understood the mission for that day meant to just sit and watch the show in front of me, surrounded by the people who trusted me as a journalist and a human.

But something felt strange. I didn't have any desire to reach out to the VIP inmates, and while I checked quickly to see if Bota there, I felt relieved when I couldn't find him.

My thoughts tangled around the unexpected situation, and I wasn't sure why I'd lost interest in him. Instead of searching around to find familiar faces in the crowd, I relaxed and allowed myself to feel an inner softness when I saw and listened to the women's carols. This event, produced for me, may have been the first time when men and women in the prison were in the same place, breathing the same air and checking out the opposite crowd seated on their section of designated bleachers. Between the rows, armed officers stood, unmoved by the performances.

Just when I thought how strange things were appearing on that day, I saw them: a group of elementary school students and their teacher, on the opposite corner from my seat.

One tiny boy dressed in a red winter coat stood and waved. "Mama," I saw him say. I watched as the boy sobbed and cried while the mother forced herself to sing along, tears coming down her face. (Officer Andrei mediated for the school to attend the event, he'd tell me later.)

There was no dry eye around me, and for a moment, I believed I witnessed a happy ending story, the reunion between a mother and her son. My brain couldn't accept another ending, and I let myself picture them around a real Christmas tree in their home.

"This is why I wanted you to come, Dana." Eftimescu spoiled my fictional dreams. "What you've done is called *prison reform*. The minister is pushing for it. I am providing evidence. We all thank you for that."

But those words sounded like an echo and did not represent the reality I was witnessing. Maybe I was too humble to realize the enormous impact of the press campaign, and the long road it took to change laws and orders. I became impatient, grabbed my notebook from my bag, and started drawing to keep my hands and mind busy. All I knew was that I wanted to bring the mother and the child together right then and, in my mind, I played out scenarios that gave them the news at the end of the show that they could go home. Of course, I knew then that I would work to bring them home.

The couple who introduced the performers mentioned Adrian Stroe, The Death Taxi Driver. He directed and played in a comedy and recited some personal poems later, with no shackles on that time. He scanned me several times, his eyes so indiscreet that I had to turn my face away, and even Eftimescu observed him give me the *look*.

"Don't worry," he told me. "They are all curious to see you."

It was Igor, the young Russian male dancer from the Moscow Ballet, that I couldn't convince to talk to me, who stole the show. Dressed in an authentic ballet outfit, he performed a solo from *The Nutcracker* and, for a moment, I thought we watched one of the finest performances, delivered on an acclaimed theater's stage. Perhaps my eyes became wider in admiration because the general director whispered, "double homicide." He knew I hadn't written his story.

Then, hand-in-hand, appeared the Chinese couple who had killed a business associate and dismembered his body in acid. Together they performed a native dance. I knew their story from Officer Andrei, who told me that every night, from across the yard, you could hear one or the other calling to each other through their windows. Their nighttime routine became so known in the prison that no one would fall asleep before they heard the calling. I read their criminal case, which was filled with gruesomeness and details of hatred, and I saw the dreadful pictures attached to the file. Now, their eyes and hands and bodies absorbed each other's scents and images until the following Christmas, when they could meet again if they'd behave over the next year. For now, they'd met a few minutes after the program, a reward for participation and good behavior.

I couldn't write a word that evening at Adina's. That night, I reflected on the day, and realized the discrepancies of a wasted life behind bars. Part of me rooted for the artists while the other argued that they put up a show. In the year I had spent going to prison, I realized how thin life's razor blade could be. One day, you're the star, and the next day, you're the criminal.

And only the strong ones stop at the right time.

"I think I saw all I needed in prison," I told Adina the following day. Before we left for the office, I handwrote my last story. In simple words, I portrayed the mother and the child I'd met, and how old her son would be at the end of her sentence. He'd be too old to remember his mother's love and touch, but young enough still to forgive her and to choose the right path for himself.

And then I thought again, *Don't we all want the right path?*

But Voicu wanted more. He suggested we should follow up with Simona's story and write the end of it. "Simona and her family with their first Christmas tree in their new place."

I still have the newspaper as a token of my first *true* battle of freedom, giving Simona a chance to breathe free as if I saw myself fighting over that jar of milk as a child. On the right bottom corner there is a picture I had to remind Voicu he'd promised me: "Dana Achim, the journalist who conducted the successful press campaign."

And then I spent New Year on the streets with Sadee and Adina and maybe one million more people who wanted to be together on the first second of the year 2000.

The last year before a new millennium.

A new adventure.

With the Minister of Justice, Valeriu Preda, at his office, His daughter is on his right.

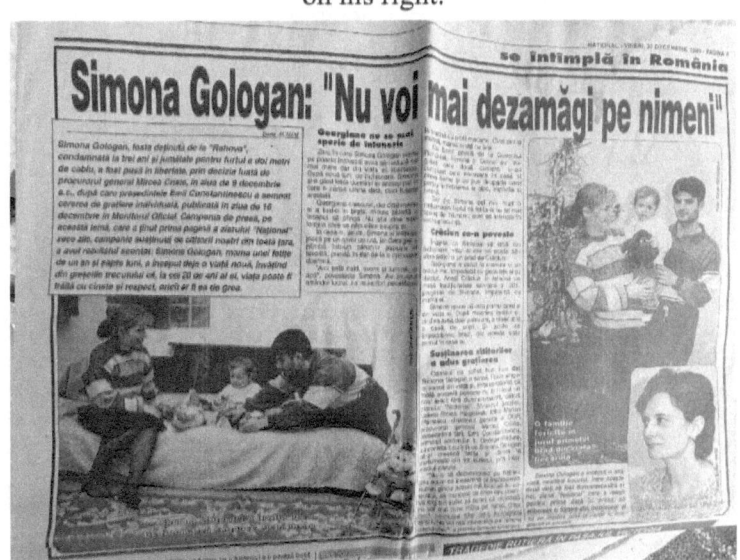

"Simona Gologan: I Won't Disappoint Anyone."

Children of the Decree

Chapter Twenty-One: New World

On the second Thursday of January 2000, we waited at Adina's for my first documentary to air at 6:30 PM sharp, just before the 7 o'clock daily news. The commercials for the show I named *A Chilean in Bucharest* had started a week before, and my heartbeat raised in anticipation. *Would it be good enough? Would the people watch it?*

Adina finished redacting her page in advance. We left the newspaper together and grabbed some food for the watching party.

In the building, Adina checked in at the dentist's office to remind Sadee to come upstairs. "I'm finishing now. I'll be there," I heard Sadee's voice.

As usual, Adina didn't take the elevator, so we climbed up the four floors with the shopping bags and our reporter bags.

Bogdan switched his radio program with a colleague so he would have the afternoon free. He arrived in a taxi with the protagonist, the Chilean whose story I'd be presenting to the viewers.

At 6:20 PM, everyone waited in the living room while I prepared sandwiches in the kitchen.

"Are you nervous?" Bogdan asked me. He brought a bottle of red wine and wanted to open it.

I gave him the opener. "It's my first show. I am."

He grabbed the opener from my hand and then placed his hands on my shoulders. His face almost touched mine, and an electric current stroked my body.

"*Bésame mucho*," he sang in my ears and kissed me on my forehead. "It will be amazing, don't worry."

Bogdan introduced me to Juan Retamal right after Augusto Pinochet was arrested in London in October 1998. He was so excited: "I have a great story for you: a former consul in Allende's government, now a lawyer in Bucharest, tortured by Pinochet's militia and later extradited to Argentina," Bogdan pitched the subject to me. Of course, I was intrigued. I remember crying when I listened to Juan the first time. We managed the interview over several days, and while it was so much information for me to grasp, I remembered the nights I wrote the story with Adina.

Now, two years after our first meeting, in the same living room where we'd started, Bogdan poured wine and helped me carry in the platter loaded with sandwiches.

"Do you remember the first time we met?" Juan asked Bogdan, grabbing the wine glass. We all knew how much Juan loved good food and refined drinks, and that evening we wanted to comfort him.

"*Noroc.* Cheers. The first word you wanted to learn in Romanian," Bogdan laughed. Then he dropped on the floor next to me, between our friends' legs.

"*Noroc*," Juan said. "And you need a larger sofa," he told Adina, who sat next to him and Sadee. Then, upbeat chords announced the start of the show.

My voice took over the screen, introducing Juan and continuing with the story: from an educated politician married to Sylvana, a journalist, to his arrest and torture in Quiriquine Prison. His conspirative name was Camilo Fernadez. Sylvana, the love of his life, hid with their daughter at Juan's parents while he fought in the resistance against Pinochet.

One day, Sylvana came to the apartment in Concepción, hoping to see Juan, and when she switched on the lights, the apartment blew up in an explosion. He found out about the explosion that killed his wife a few days later. His anger grew. His soul died, he let his guard down, he was arrested, and subsequently he was shipped to the notorious prison for political prisoners in Quiriquine, the Chilean version of Guantanamo. No one came out of there alive.

For more than a year, squeezed in a tiny cell with nothing on him or around him, they tortured him. First, they pulled out his nails one each day, prolonging his desperation each day. Then they removed the hair from all his body and electrocuted his genitals. His torso became ashen. When they ran out of ideas, they sank his head in the latrine bucket. "Papa good," his voice quivered, and the image zoomed on his nailess hands. "We (the resistance) prepared ahead for interrogation.

They couldn't get a word out of me. And in all this time, I thought of my younger brothers fighting in my place. That thought was enough to keep me alive and speechless." A tape ran in the background on his home TV—Juan behind Allende when Chile was safe.

Then, one day, they sentenced him to death and asked for his last request. He wanted to see his parents and daughter one more time, but they denied it. "Write them a letter," they told him. So, he wrote a goodbye letter for his daughter, fully aware they'd read every word.

On the day of the execution, they walked him to a wall, the first time seeing the daylight, and he felt blinded by so much light. He remembered the cries of the seagulls and the last picture in his mind of his parents and wife and daughter. "Fire!" he heard, and then he fainted.

When he realized he was alive, he was in a coffin on the back of a truck. Two men carried the casket on a shoreline, and Juan wanted to get out. "Stay still," they told him. "Don't make a sound."

The resistance had organized his escape with a fake death by a firing squad, he understood in Argentina. It was his last destination after four years on the run, hunted by Pinochet's military juntas.

"I guess the resistance didn't want to tell me or anyone about my escape, afraid they would conspire somehow, and the plan could fail," Juan explained on the television.

From Buenos Aires, he went to Dakar, and then Frankfurt, and Zurich. At the airport in Zurich, he met the Romanian Minister of External Affairs, who told him, "You are now under the protection of the Romanian government." Then Juan followed him to a separate plane en route to Bucharest and saw two blindfolded men escorted from a car.

"That's when I knew they exchanged me for two dissidents. I never knew their origins," the Chilean explained on the screen from his apartment.

In Romania, Juan remarried and became a father again, to a daughter. But a car killed her on a crosswalk when she was six, and Juan lost his mind again. A divorce followed, then a law degree, then another marriage, another divorce. He remarried a much younger lady, Lucia, and their five-year-old daughter, Elba, smiled in pictures I used as backgrounds in the television segment.

"I learned Romanian from the women I loved, and I earned my place in this country. At fifty, I wouldn't feel at home if I'd go back to Chile. Romania is my country, and I love it more than many Romanians do," he said.

In the last images, Juan watched his daughter and other kids sliding in the snow from a distance, his Araucanian profile accentuated, and then the image moved onto the kids and his back.

And then the news started, about a minute late. "What a story," the anchor said with a trembling voice, announcing the latest news and, somehow, explaining the delay in the program behind her hidden tears. We became close friends not long after this first show.

I waited for Juan's reaction — any reaction, to be honest, — but his mind was far away. I could move my hand in front of his face and was sure he wouldn't see anything. No one moved a finger until Adina turned the volume down.

"Very good," Juan said after a while as he broke the silence. Then he continued, "I'm hungry," he said, and grabbed a ham sandwich from the platter. Our cell phones rang for an hour. Everyone wanted to say something to one of us.

The show director called me to say, "that was an amazing story. Well done. People call for a repeat. We'll air it again tonight," she said.

"Congratulations," the Chilean ambassador told Juan.

"Your father cried," Mama said.

In the middle of the living room, Juan demanded, "Let's dance. Enough with the phone calls."

He handed Adina a CD and we followed his directions, lining up one behind the other with a hand on the one in front's shoulder. "Like this," Juan corrected until we all danced to his liking.

Even Bogdan followed the instruction. "He's dancing his life," I whispered to Bogdan. "I guess so," Bogdan responded.

And that night, Juan taught us the fighting fire of Lautaro, the Araucanian hero and what his Araucanians people do when celebrating life and death—dancing their love and pain.

It is, in the place where he was from, the reason to resist, to die heroically, and to live again.

~

We dropped off Juan and then Sadee. At the last turn on my street, I asked Bogdan if he wanted to come over. He got out in front of my house and opened the back door for me and paid the driver. "Not tonight," he said, and kissed me on my forehead again, holding my hand for a few seconds. "You need rest," he added. Then he walked away, and I stood there until his silhouette dissolved in the street, hidden by the new moon.

It was past midnight and I turned on the fireplace, leaving the door open so I could warm up quicker. Then, wrapped in a wool blanket, I watched the flames illuminate the room. I couldn't decide how I felt yet about the day, and I tried to let my thoughts settle and find their place in my mind and soul.

Some interesting thoughts kept me awake that night while I was watching the fire. First, I opened my sixth kachra, the one on the forehead, and started the mediation, inhaling and exhaling in three steps as my spiritual friend Gabiji had taught me. A flow of energy entered my body, and instantly I got warm. Then some discreet shapes appeared in the fire, and I moved them with my mind from left to right or higher, and soon I observed a woman's silhouette. "You didn't do anything wrong," I believed she told me. "Forgive yourself and others, and then you'll find happiness." It was the younger version of me calling to my then thirty-two-year-old self.

No, I wasn't afraid to be alone, I said to myself, wondering why I had invited Bogdan inside. All I needed, I thought, was the human touch, the cuddling I missed most—the *connection*.

I felt lost, dehumanized, nobody.

"What's wrong with me?" I kept asking myself. My inner voice responded, "you are fine. The problem was never yours, but his." I immediately thought of Horia and the way he had mistreated me. I saw myself shivering in his hallway when he passed me after he invited me over, saying "I'm going to see someone tonight. Go home." Then I saw the inside of his apartment, where I'd heard, "I was born in Bucharest. You're a peasant. Don't talk."

Just as I peeled the layers of an onion, I dug into the layers of my experience. I wasn't afraid this time. Instead, the inner me deciphered what Horia told me. Except for Adina and George, none of my friends were born in Bucharest. But that aspect didn't stop Bogdan from becoming a respectable man. Or Sadee, who studied Medicine in French as an international student, and was now a doctor with an elite clientele.

"No, it's not where you are born, but what you become in life," I kept arguing with myself.

"So, what was my problem then?" the younger me asked my older version.

The flame changed the shape, and I saw myself reading Stendhal, Guy de Maupassant, Balzac, Proust, and the Russian authors. First, I tried to make sense of the image, wondering why it had appeared during my meditation. And then I understood my upbringing skipped over childhood. In fact, since a very young age, I had to watch over the house, all the animals, and Livia. *I grew up too fast, for sure.*

"So, why did I ask Bogdan to come over?" I pushed.

I want intelligent people around me. That's why I could love him. I could love Juan too. I could love anyone who intrigues me and challenges me. It's that simple.

An astonishing truth arose then: the feeling of *love* meant admiration and attachment, and I felt I never loved anyone before. I only remembered playing backgammon—the only good thing from my short, long-ago marriage. *Forgive yourself; you're a child.*

In the morning, I was happy Bogdan had gone home. I couldn't have forgiven myself if something had happened between us. He was, indeed, the smartest of the two and kept in touch with me, without ever opening that subject again: how I chose him to get intimate.

~

A few days later, Adina showed me an e-mail from her ex-husband. "A new friend here, at IBM, wants to write to Dana. We work on the same shift, and I'm keeping him informed about what's going on in Romania. He followed Dana's press campaign. It's like he's in love with Romania. Do you think she would be willing to respond to his e-mails? Tell her he's a very nice man."

"Not interested," I told Adina.

She typed while I watched her: "Dana said she's not interested. She's *very interested*. Send him her way."

"You're crazy!" I screamed.

"What's to lose?" Adina smiled. "Let's see what happens." Then she lit a cigarette and looked at me as if I annoyed her. "Don't you have a show to get ready for?"

"Right," I answered.

"*Alea iacta est*," (The die has been cast,") she said, watching me leave.

I went to the TV station to schedule the filming for the following week and ignored her calls for a few days, which was the best and only way I could let her know I was mad.

A few days later, I found this e-mail sent by Lyman2b@yahoo.com: "I am Lyman, Adrian's friend. He talks so highly about you and your work. Do you want to correspond with me?"

I responded: "Sure. Why not? I like meeting people from all over the world. I learned so much from their cultures. Tell me your story, please. Cheers to you and Adrian. Dana."

My first impulse was to write a story for Voicu *if* Lyman became interesting enough, so I decided to wait for his reply.

~

A few weeks later, I found the first postcard from Lyman in my mailbox—an image of Vermont's picturesque mountains covered in orange colors. He signed it, "Sincerely, Lyman."

Ha! There's some beauty there!

I placed the postcard on my writing table to look at for inspiration. In return, I sent Lyman a card featuring downtown Bucharest and the University of Bucharest. It was founded on July 4, 1864, when Europe wanted to prosper, and America was fighting its Civil War.

When I mailed the subtle message card, I hoped he'd see the significance of the dates and their meanings, one ocean away and one hundred fifty years before our time.

~

Lyman sent me three more cards and several e-mails over the next month. *Vermont* was the keyword now, and I wanted to know more about this state and its beauty.

"Tell me more," I asked Lyman. He wrote about being a single father, raising girls on his own, the night his ex-wife left them in a pick-up truck, the girls crying and asking for their mother. He wrote of his dreams to find happiness "someday," and why now was the perfect time.

I couldn't find anything about him that would make a story for the newspaper. He was just an ordinary man in a faraway place. The best stories were around me, I knew, and my fans wanted more.

Around spring, Tata came to Bucharest for some medical tests. His voice sounded harsh, and his doctor had sent him to see a specialist. Having him over meant working longer hours, to accommodate Tata with doctor's visits during the day and taking walks in Bucharest in the evenings. I showed him my favorite places and had dinner at a Lebanese restaurant. On one of those days, I found him fixing the bathroom door. He'd fixed nothing at home, and I found it strange seeing him with tools he had in the trunk of his car, Maricica.

He was a few feet away when Lyman called for the first time. I didn't feel comfortable talking to Lyman in front of Tata, and his face turned red from hearing me speak in English. I told Lyman that Tata was over, and I couldn't talk longer, and to Tata, Lyman was "a friend of a friend," but he didn't buy it. "You sounded *too* excited," Tata said. His words resonated somehow but I had yet to figure out how or why.

After Tata left for home, I didn't write to Lyman. I was still getting postcards in the mail and found my correspondence with Lyman was a waste of time. My last e-mail was, "I'll e-mail you when I have time. I am swamped now." What I meant I knew Lyman understood: "Leave me alone."

Still, occasionally, I checked my e-mails and found several from Lyman. I read them in order. "How are you? Is everything all right?"

"Why don't you answer? I didn't hear from you in three weeks."

I felt pressed to answer. "Working on a sensitive story. Three orphan siblings raising each other, sharing chores, and going to school. One brother just died. I can't take my mind off these children. Please, understand it's nothing personal. I just don't have time. Have a nice day."

But Lyman understood my work. He felt compassionate and encouraged me to keep working and I loved his comments. Again, I took a break from writing to him, except this line: "I'm super busy."

He persisted, and every week I'd get a postcard from him as a reminder he existed and that he wouldn't give up.

I could've told him the truth: while I had worked my way up to becoming a successful and some would have said dangerous journalist, I was a mess as a woman, and while I loved the wrong guy, part of me hoped I still could change him and show him it was okay to love me. While the scandalous newspapers and magazines wanted to portray me as an insensitive woman, I avoided gatherings and exposure, keeping my life private among my small circle of friends.

There were rumors that I was an agent, and one day a reporter asked me if I had graduated from the spy school. Of course, I laughed because everyone knew I was a chemistry teacher—it was written in my employment card, but because of my affiliation with Horia and his entourage, the stories about me wouldn't stop with my simple denial or the explanation that I had no idea where that school was even located. In one magazine, there was a picture of me talking to the best show producer in the country, at an award event.

He looked entertained and was looking at my hands. I was probably explaining something to him. Overnight the press ruled us a couple and while I denied it, it didn't matter. Another story was about a cultural attaché who invited me to some events. We went together to a private club and the next day there was a picture of us dancing in a newspaper.

I had the feeling Horia was behind some of these stories when one of his buddies told me, "He's planning to destroy you. Be careful." I believed him.

A few months later, Lyman wrote: "Adina told Adrian you work too much. I think you need a vacation. Why don't you come over for Christmas?"

This invitation puzzled me. I didn't respond for a few weeks. Then, one day, I ran to Adina's office, a big smile on my face. I posed with a leg in front of the other, hands clutched. "This girl is going to…" And my eyes opened wide, waiting for her to complete the sentence.

She guessed the first time. "Vermont."

The only thing I needed was a Visa.

A few weeks later, I waited in line in front of the American Embassy in Bucharest. I applied for a two-week tourist visa and had the interview that same day. The American Embassy building was right behind the Intercontinental Hotel, across the street from the university. It was 5:00 in the morning and I saw hundreds and hundreds of people holding onto files with their documents. The line of people crunched shoulder to shoulder in two directions on the sidewalk, and then stretched out across two streets, and then folded back again toward the embassy. There, squashed again, the flashback of when I got hurt over the jar of milk rose in my mind. *That memory is part of my destiny,* I thought.

This time, I was in line for permission to visit America. "This is my third time," a mother whose son lived in America said. Another lady, whose daughter studied at Harvard, wanted to spend the holidays together. She wasn't sure if she'd get the visa. Only three people from that forest of humans received permits before me.

I walked in convinced I'd get the visa and composed myself in front of an American consul who looked at me over his glasses and asked for my name.

"Are you a journalist?" he asked. On my passport, my name was Vasile.

"Yes, I am. This paper is from my TV station, this one, from my newspaper."

"Who is *Dana Achim*?" he asked.

"I am. It's my pen name."

The American officer examined each file on my passport. There were visas from Germany, Switzerland, Spain, and entry-exit custom stamps from Poland, Turkey, Ukraine, Hungary, and Czech Republic.

"You may reapply in six months."

The consul placed a *denied* stamp on the last page of my passport. I couldn't believe it. Some people outside told me I was young and too vulnerable to be trusted to visit the United States as a single woman. Others said, maybe I stopped those adoptions, and Americans didn't like it.

Whatever the reason was, I was angry as never before.

Walking home with my head down as if I had somehow failed a test, I shouted a few swear words to cool myself from that humiliation. *"I can't visit the country of freedom!"* I cried.

I saw the travel agency on the other side of the street where I wanted to get my ticket to America. I walked in and said I wanted to book a flight and hotel to Paris for my birthday. The lady at the travel agency recognized me. I showed her the denied visa on my passport, tears in my eyes, and only then I realized my hands were trembling.

"I am so sorry. Let me see if I can offer you a deal to make you feel better."

After a few minutes, she said, "I found you a half-price ticket. You'll stay at the Montpensier Hotel. You'll love it there. It's downtown Paris."

Children of the Decree

With my plane ticket for France in my hand, I promised I'd never apply for an American visa again and e-mailed Lyman. "Can't come. No visa for single women like me. Going to Paris."

I wasn't sure what hurt me more: not getting the visa or that it was the American Embassy denying it. *Liberty doesn't come easy, not even fighting to visit America on a tourist visa.* It wasn't *me* Americans needed to trust. It was *my country*.

"I'll come to Romania," Lyman responded in his next email.

Juan Retamal and his family, the exclusive story I wrote with Adina Mutar. For the first time, Gheorghe Voicu allowed two full pages, as mentioned in the headline.

Chapter Twenty-Two: Lyman

Bucharest, March 2001

    The taxicab dropped me off in front of the International Airport in Bucharest a little before noon. It stopped raining just before the plane landed, but the sun was rising over the clouds and formed a hugging rainbow over the airport. I stopped to watch the rainbow and saw others doing the same. I wasn't going to miss it.

    As Sadee and George had suggested, I wore an executive suit, but it was the wrong choice looking at the other people waiting there.

    When the first passengers passed the exit door, I got closer to the waiting area. With my glasses on, I examined the faces of the men coming out, my heart banging in my chest.

    "Lyman," I shouted when I saw him in the crowd.

    He hurried over and hugged me, then he kissed me on my cheek and stepped back to look at me. He said Adrian told him how we greet people.

    "Wow! You're beautiful!" I wasn't sure what my first impression of him was.

    We headed to the exit for a cab. I observed that Lyman was overdressed, wearing winter clothes. He apologized for his appearance, explaining that it'd been cold and snowing in Vermont when he left. He surveyed the parking area and saw the trees blossoming in pure white colors and the grass sprouting on the greens.

    Once in the taxi, I was transfixed by his hands, which looked like leaves with veins starting from the middle. His nails were cut short, but their nail beds were wide and long—the perfect nails for someone who would want to show off the beauty of well-done nail polish. His hair, golden brown, was a little longer than I liked, and his eyes were bright blue. His eyebrows spread above his eyes, making him look concerned. Ten years older than I was, he was in good shape, athletic and energetic. He laughed with a full face, rubbing his hands as if it was cold and he wanted to get warm.

    It was past noon, and the traffic was heavy. Lyman stared out the window and admitted he would have a hard time driving in Bucharest.

"Look at these cars. They pass on the left and don't even wait for the green light," he said.

When we reached Aviation Avenue, I showed Lyman where I worked, pointing to the TV station on the right, and then I showed him the Press House with the *National* logo on the right corner. The taxi driver, who recognized me, asked in Romanian who Lyman was.

"A friend from America." The driver told me how much he and his wife enjoyed my documentaries on television. I thanked him for his kind words.

We stopped near the first district police station in front of the Academy of Political Studies, preferring to walk a few blocks rather than disclosing my address to the taxicab driver. I paid the driver a tip and helped Lyman by carrying his lighter suitcase.

The lilac scent of fresh-washed drapes covering the tall windows in the hallway pleased me when I opened the door. Everything looked clean and fresh, the windows cracked, the laundry ironed and folded on the bed.

"This is a really nice place," Lyman said, looking around my apartment. From the tall ceiling hung antique lamps, and the expansive windows had original handles that I had repainted myself, and the framed door made the space large and comfortable. At first, I thought Lyman was old-fashioned or too modest to be an American working for one of the best computer companies in the world.

However, his attitude and gestures made me feel like he didn't realize how simple he was in comparison to Horia's arrogance. Lyman walked around the house and took the time to analyze the Oriental art displayed on the wall and the Gallé vase I had purchased at an auction. I thought he wanted to make me feel good about my place.

I opened the door to the living room and invited him to take a seat on the sofa while I sat on the love seat, the glass table between us.

"I brought you something," he said, and opened one of his suitcases. He handed me a black velvet box. I opened it and saw six small perfume bottles, Guerlain collection. One of them was *Samsara*, the Buddhist word for *continuing life*, one without beginning and end. It is a mirage one wants to chase because the shape changes again and again, and is perpetual and innocent, and continues forever into a new form one thinks is attainable but is not. I thanked him but didn't want to talk about the meaning of *Samsara* or anything about my spirituality just yet.

"Adrian helped me pick these for you. He said you have fine tastes," he said. I smiled. "His wife is expecting, did you know?" I remained silent. But then he said, "87 to 103." The numbers sounded like a score, and I couldn't make sense of the meaning.

"That's how many e-mails you and I wrote," he stated and handed me a three-hole punch binder. "I saved them all," he said.

Why in the world would someone print those e-mails? I wondered.

"That's the testament that we have a relationship," Lyman explained. "In case we need proof."

Flipping through the pages, I recognized some of the words that kept me up at night, romantic plans he wanted to happen, and the seeds of courtship I couldn't explain or understand yet. But now, he was here, sitting in my living room, and I couldn't hide anymore.

It was as if I uncovered my face to show my real self to someone who had only dreamt of me, who now wanted me to become part of his future because I fueled the dream with fancy words I translated before sending out an e-mail.

I could hear the water running in the bathroom, and I quickly called Sadee to let her know he had come, and we were home. All she wanted to know was, "Did you have sex yet?"

I felt annoyed and answered, "Yes. In the taxi."

Lyman appeared in the living room wearing a pair of blue jeans and a T-shirt, his hair wet and lined on the back, and I felt cramps in my stomach. No, he didn't have the look of a sexy guy one might see on book covers, but rather a sensual appeal and calming, unforgettable energy that made him likeable, even loveable. As I look back on that moment, I think people find a gesture or a small detail that sparks their falling in love. For me, it was the second when he appeared in the room without socks, half-wet, half-dry, sleep-deprived but fighting to stay awake, probably thinking, "What the heck am I doing here?"

Coffee, yes. I needed it to compose myself and calm the beasts in my stomach, the little devils wanting to be loved and hugged, that were at times more like phantasmagorical creatures who tried to remind me, "You're a woman. You could be loved for once."

I recognized the cause of those cramps because I had them when I asked Bogdan to come over, but he was smart enough not to follow me inside, and probably afraid of what we would do, how we might have looked at each other and where that might have led.

This time I was sure I wouldn't regret anything, and more than that: I could see myself waking up next to Lyman the following day and loving it. I couldn't look at him without thinking of him as my lover. The tension grew as I watched him sorting some clothes, perhaps to keep his hands busy. "This fantasy is getting real," he said.

He wanted some coffee, too.

In the small kitchen at the end of the hallway, I boiled water on the stove and added a little sugar and four spoons of coffee. Then I added more coffee, making sure it would be strong and tasty. Finally, I added two drops of cold water to settle the grounds and poured the coffee into two tiny teacups.

Back in the living room by the coffee table, he took a sip and grimaced as if he was chewing something bitter. Finally, he asked for some milk. Then he asked for a larger cup.

After I had brought him everything he asked for, I watched him pour the coffee from the small cup into the big one. Then he added milk until the cup was full, took a sip, and asked for more sugar.

"This is Turkish coffee," I said.

"Why do you boil it? We use coffee makers," he said. He seemed confused.

"This is how we make coffee here," I laughed.

"We drink lots of coffee, in big cups, and always with cream." He must have realized we were different, starting with the way we prepared our coffee, an essential task.

What the hell had I been thinking? The stronger the better did not work for this man.

"This is my first trip to another country. Americans think they are the center of the universe, and they can control everything in this world. They were all immigrants at some point but have forgotten their history," he said. His words hit straight to my heart.

I could've kissed him then.

But Lyman waited for the right time, I guessed. *So, he didn't kiss me after six hours together,* I imagined later telling Sadee. Then I remembered writing to him that I wouldn't do anything without God's approval, and with the priest's blessing from across the street to approve our union before anything, because my true religion held in it not only wanting to love again but to bring God with us to guide us in the journey.

This idea came to me on a road trip with George. He was my therapist when I needed a break from my work, and we usually took long drives around the country on weekends. An excellent driver, George hated those who didn't respect the traffic rules; on those occasions, I heard him swear. Naturally I didn't like that, and he apologized every time.

These outings were meant for us to enjoy the scenery together, and we always took a different route. My friend needed my company, he said several times, *just to talk*. During the week, he had many adventures but *needed* someone to talk to and discuss life and love and everything in between. Sometimes, we shared books and used the trips to discuss our understandings, and one day, we talked about Plato's *The Republic*.

"By the way, do you know what platonic love is?" George asked. "It's not what people think, love without sex." I didn't understand how that was possible.

"There are three types of attraction," he explained. "In the first one—physical attraction—couples confuse love with sexual attraction. They see each other, they like each other, and then they jump in bed. Later, they discover they have nothing in common. The second one is more complex. They like each other, have great sex, and have many things in common." It sounded reasonable. "The third one is the hardest to achieve—they thank God for that."

The morning after Lyman's arrival, I did just that. I thanked God for sending him my way. He was perfect.

~

Lyman quickly learned about Romanian money and soon he could shop alone without getting robbed by people who realized he was a foreigner. He enjoyed speaking English with people he met in stores and loved that many Romanians spoke his language. Sometimes, he'd wake up early in the morning and walk to the nearby McDonald's to get his coffee.

It took several days to adjust to Lyman's presence in my tiny house. He wanted to visit the country but explored Bucharest first and carried an English-Romanian dictionary for tourists in his pocket. He even purchased a book, "Things to See in Romania." I promised I'd take him places and show him the country, and I scheduled a short vacation. I had enough work finished ahead of time so I wouldn't have to worry about my upcoming segments on the show.

On the following morning, I prepared Lyman's coffee with lots of milk and made mine the Turkish way—strong, a little sugar, and no milk. He liked it.

"Are you ready to see the town?" I asked.

He finished his coffee quickly and brought a light jacket with him.

Lyman was all ears, trying to understand each word I said. Sometimes he'd stop me and asked specific questions. We passed the Ambassador Hotel on the left and kept going down the Magheru Boulevard. The library where I had my book signing was on that side of the street.

In front of the Intercontinental Hotel, Lyman took a deep breath and looked around like he wanted to recognize the pictures he had seen on the Internet. But instead, he stopped in front of the wooden cross marked by candles and flowers. An old Romanian flag fluttered. Someone had ripped off the place for the hammer and sickle, the symbol of communism. But ripping off the sign wasn't enough to change the country's mentality. It needed more. It required reforms and actions as a start.

"*This* is the place I saw on the internet. People died here." He didn't ask; he was sure and frowned, his eyes pacing around. I gave him time to absorb the view, and he took some pictures.

I sat down on a water fountain wall and watched him. Then Lyman sat down next to me. He wanted to *feel* Romania, he said. A few children holding hands complained about a test. The strident voices on the streets coming from the subway faded with the mild wind. Some flower petals flew down the sidewalk, carried by the wind.

"You don't see people dressing like that in Vermont. Do they dress like that every day?"

"Most of the time, yes."

"It looks like they are going to a fashion show," he said, looking puzzled.

"Just for a walk. To the park or just here, on the Boulevard. We call it a "promenade," a way to show we enjoy being outside."

He wanted to know what happened after I published the article about illegal adoptions in Romania.

"Many Americans came to Romania to adopt children," he said. "I know a family. They adopted a child, but the kid had so many problems, so they had to return him." I didn't tell him the orphanage director sued us.

We stopped at Pizza Hut to get something to eat for later and, on our way home, I bought tickets for the evening show at the National Theater.

Lyman didn't mind that the show was in Romanian. He said he could read the actors' expressions and could sense the play. I guessed that sometimes words aren't necessary to show emotion.

The following day we were in the car with George on our way to Dracula's Castle.

George spoke English and entertained Lyman on the way to Bran. Once we got in the mountains, Lyman couldn't stop praising the views.

"We have mountains in Vermont, but not as high as these."

We made quick stops, got coffees and snacks, and listened to George's lessons about the old history of those places in the battles against the Turks.

"Vlad the Impeller got his nickname because he opposed the Turks trying to settle on our land. If it wasn't for him, we could be part of the Ottoman Empire, and our long traditions and religion would be gone."

Lyman was all ears and said, "I couldn't choose a better guide."

"Vlad had brilliant ideas and was a great commander of his army. We have lots of legends, but they generated from his imagination, trying to fool the Turks."

We walked to the castle and paid for an English interpreter for Lyman. Every time we moved to another room, Lyman kept saying, "Wow!" His favorite place was the secret stairway that connected the living rooms to the cells where Vlad incarcerated prisoners.

"This is spine-chilling," Lyman laughed, making a face to show us he was petrified.

"Something strange is in the air," George told me in Romanian when we got behind Lyman. "He's in love with you," George said. I blushed.

From each angle, Lyman shot two rolls of film, from the top of the castle that showed the mountains to every detail of the artifacts displayed in the sealed showcases.

"History!" he explained, rubbing his hands as he had won the lottery.

At a gift store outside the castle, Lyman bought a scarf for his mom.

Going back to Bucharest, Lyman wanted to stay in the back seat.

"That's how I take my nap on the way to work and back home," he said. A few minutes later, he was deep asleep.

George and I listened to Elton John for a while, taking turns to smoke—I'd started smoking again—and we both sang "I'm still standing."

I asked George how he knew Lyman was in love with me.

"It's body language, a man's body language." Then he added, "You know what's crazy about you? You can read people very well, but you suck as a woman."

Later that evening, Lyman and I had dinner at my favorite Lebanese restaurant. We sat next to a window, at a table with two seats. I could feel his tension. He wanted to say something, but it looked like he had forgotten the words. Neither of us touched the food.

"I am back on my feet now. I grew up poor, raised my girls, and now, I am ready to start a new life. We say, 'Show a man love, and he'll move a mountain for you.' It's true."

Then, he talked about his work at IBM in his second year, which involved testing the chips produced during the day.

"I live in a place that doesn't have good-paying jobs. There's not much to do there, so I must commute more than one hour each way, but I carpool with two other men to save on gas and driving. It's a good job."

I agreed and told him I would do the same if I were in his place, but I couldn't pinpoint where his background story was going.

"I am not rich, but I have a good heart. I don't have a diamond with me, but I'll give you all my love. I want to build a life with you. So, Dana, would you marry me?"

The entire world collapsed. I wanted to say no. Everything I had and loved was here, in Romania. Even my dreams were here, and he appeared in them as nothing but a fantasy. I liked him, but I wasn't ready to marry him. I wanted the courtship to continue, for him to come to Romania several times before I could commit in that way.

"I like you very much, but I don't think I can right now, Lyman. Romania is everything I have—my family, job, house, and friends."

"You don't need to answer now," he said. "Take your time." His eyes turned red.

"Let's see how it goes," I answered. "Let's be in love."

We tried to eat, but every time we stared at each other, we stopped. I wanted to leave, and I guessed Lyman felt the same way. My feet turned restless, my head spinning.

We walked home without saying a word. I didn't turn to see his face and kept one hand on the purse, and the other, in my blazer. At home, I ran into the bedroom and locked the door. I heard the television through the thick brick wall.

There was something inexplicable about him, and the feeling was there, a sprouting seed after a dormant winter. Initially, his innocence or simplicity intrigued me, but I wanted to learn more about his world once I discovered he was anything but a simple man. It attracted me. I recognized his unflashy love for nature in his stories and saw myself watching the Big Dipper at Obogeni on the darkest nights. His stories were somehow similar to mine, to a point.

When he talked about his farm, it was as if I was speaking—the long nights, the seasons changing, the harmony between man and universe. It intrigued me to hear how he worked his land with simple tools and felt he competed with nature against all the odds. He loved his life and confessed he wanted to find his life partner, a woman who he could trust and grow old with, a soulmate to share the good and the bad.

We were falling in love, *I* was falling in love, but I wasn't ready to marry him. Not yet.

~

On the following morning, a sunny day, I sat outside having my coffee and a cigarette. I wasn't sure if Lyman was home or not, and I tiptoed to avoid a discussion or to see his face so early. Never in my life had I ever contemplated leaving my country and family behind.

Thinking more profoundly, it was out of the question that I'd marry a man and leave everything behind. Even if I had known him for a year, and the attraction grew since we had met, there weren't enough reasons to change my mind. Yes, I could be in love with him and maybe try again to get a visa, but I simply couldn't bear leaving my parents and family.

I belong here, and Romania owns me, I concluded, and I promised not to even think about this idea again. *So, I'll just wait until he leaves.*

My plan took a different turn that day at the lawyers' office when discussing the next day's court hearing about the orphanage director who was suing me, the mayor, and the newspaper as he'd promised Voicu he would. We knew he would do that. The lawyer couple decided on representing me pro bono, while the newspaper hired its own separate lawyer. I had to testify, and we went over possible questions and responses that would help make my point clear.

They didn't see any surprises with the case, but I was concerned all the same. I reminded myself that until that day, only my friend Viorel Ilisoi had received thirty days in a county jail for an article he had written, but he was released after a week. I wasn't afraid I'd be found guilty but was afraid of the bad press I'd get.

When I came home, I grabbed a chair from the kitchen and went outside, smoking a cigarette and thinking about the next day. About half of my colleagues had similar cases in court, and they all had said that it was no fun to go to court. I relaxed and spotted the first snowdrop flowers and tulips in the garden. Sitting on my knees, I bent over to smell the snowdrops. I knew that fresh smell well.

"What are you doing, Dana?" Lyman asked. I didn't hear him coming.

"Smelling flowers," I said, not knowing the right word for "snowdrops."

We sat outside, the temperature dropping, and I covered us both with a blanket. I didn't want to give him a reason to bring up the marriage proposal again, so I did all the talking. The only thing that came to me was Tata's passion for flowers. I told Lyman of the wildflowers I loved at Obogeni, or the ones I took on the trips with Tata, to bring the roots home and acclimate them.

"I have lots of wildflowers in Coventry, on my farm. Black-eyed Susans, daisies, and many, many more."

I closed my eyes and imagined Obogeni in summer, the hills dressed in green, and me—dancing with my *wings* shirt on. Now, I was sitting next to a man I liked, our shoulders touching under the blanket, his breath heavy.

"I have something to do tomorrow morning, so enjoy your morning alone," I said and grabbed the blanket. "Good night," and I walked the hallway to my bedroom.

"Good night, Dana."

Children of the Decree

I locked the bedroom door and cuddled in my bed, listening to the TV in Lyman's room muffled by the brick wall.

The following day, passing Lyman's room, I observed that the TV was still on, and that he had slept in the chair. I tiptoed again, making my coffee and getting ready to leave for the hearing.

In front of that courtroom, several reporters waited in the lobby. My lawyers were already there, and we went to the side of the hallway.

"Don't be nervous. Just relax. Tell your story. We have the facts. Okay?" I said, "Yes."

"Let's go."

~

When the judge called our case, I answered the questions and felt an inner power to speak loudly. Then, in cross-examination, the director's lawyer, an exquisite man, asked me several questions, and I answered them, looking directly at him. I saw the director there, standing next to his lawyer, dressed in Versace and posing proudly. Did someone pay me to write the article? Of course not. How did I decide to publish it on that day, June 1st, 1999? I answered truthfully—the International Children's Day.

"I was aware he would sue me, as he mentioned to my boss. I think we all know the effect of his actions, and while there is an investigation from the government to look into it, his immediate resignation speaks for itself. He didn't resign because I wrote the article; he resigned after he had learned there would be an investigation."

I saw the director giving interviews outside and we left. Few people followed us, and we walked into the lawyers' lounge.

"Wait here, Dana, until they are gone," one of my lawyers said. "We'll bring you home."

When I got in their car, I heard a voice, "She's leaving." We then took some back roads, my legs shaking.

In front of the house, I got out and rushed inside and locked the front door. Lyman was reading in the living room. The hallway smelled fresh, and I saw several buckets of snowdrops in the kitchen.

I crashed on the bed. Then, breathing slowly, I closed my eyes and began questioning how much my life had changed over the past year. I didn't feel safe, was afraid someone would kill me, as Bota had warned me over the phone several times. "There are two kinds of security: those who want the truth and those who oppose it," as he told me in our prison interview. The old and the new security are forever stepping on each other's feet, he had explained to me. There was no mercy for those like me, fighting for people's freedom and the underprivileged.

I knew that because of my journalistic investigations, I had become the target of the underground adoptions mob. What I didn't know yet was that my investigation was on the European Union envoy to Romania's desk. Since my story had become so public, the European Union had pressed the Romanian government to stop international adoptions and pass a new law that included strict accountability for children.

I don't want to live like this, I thought and surprised myself talking out loud as I crashed on my bed, tears on my face. I wiped my tears, got up, and knocked on Lyman's door.

"May I come in?" I asked Lyman.

"Sure! What happened? "

His hands reached to offer me a chair.

"Did you see the flowers? I bought them all from a lady," Lyman asked.

"Thank you! Why do you want to marry me?" I asked out of the blue.

"Because I love you. I have loved you since I learned about you. You are special, kind, and generous. I know I can make you happy."

I waited for my head to stop spinning and then I said, "I'll marry you."

He screamed, "She said yes!" and jumped from his seat and danced with me in his arms. "I am the luckiest man alive."

At that moment I feared nothing and the brick wall between us was gone. I allowed myself to be loved and happy for once and left behind the protective armor to my heart. It was a new beginning that I'd grow to accept and cherish; the opportunity to be myself. That step would prove to be the hardest one I had yet to take.

~

In all the books I read and all of the stories I wrote or heard, there was nothing to advise me on what to do next. My faith said that if it were God's will, then all doors would open to it. No obstacles. With that faith, Lyman and I entered the American Embassy and returned five minutes later with a signed paper from the consulate. He was free to marry anyone he wanted.

"What's next?" he wanted to know.

We went to the town hall in the district where I lived, and met a new mayor this time, but he promised to have everything completed in one day if we were indeed ready. We weren't. We needed to tell my family, and I couldn't do it without Livia's help, but Livia simply hung up the phone, saying, "You're doing it. You better tell Mama and Tata!" When I called Mama, I made sure she had a seat first. Then I said, "I'm getting married. In a couple of days. To an American."

There was a pause, and I asked if she was still on the phone.

"Do. What. You. Want." Then she hung up just like Livia had done, and I couldn't explain why they both had to respond in that way. To me, marrying Lyman was the right thing to do.

While I dealt with Voicu and the director at the television station and tendered my resignations, Livia jumped on the train and went to Dragasani. Later that evening, she called me to say that my parents respected my decision to marry Lyman but complained that it was too quick for them to be prepared for the marriage certificate that we would sign in two days. I promised we'd go home soon after the ceremony to spend time with them.

~

On the day of the ceremony, Tata, Livia, and my brother-in-law came in one car.

I wore an elegant black pair of pants with a white silk shirt and a salt-and-pepper blazer, and Sadee did my hair.

Lyman had on a gray suit and a white shirt and greeted Tata outside, in the garden. But Tata wanted to go for a walk with me, so we stopped across the street at the church.

We bought some candles and I saw Tata on his knees with his hands united under his chin. I melted. There was no one in the church but us. Time stopped. I joined him, prayed for him and Mama to keep strong, and asked God to heal him. His voice wasn't getting better. Was he praying for me?

"Time to go, Tata," I said.

Lyman saw us coming and hugged Tata. "I know it's hard to see her go to America, but I promise you I'll take care of her!" he said, and George translated his words. Tata shook his head, meaning, "I got it."

We drove with George to the town hall, and there, my friend volunteered as Lyman's interpreter.

Before the official ceremony started, Lyman told me he'd pray not to cry. I wasn't sure about that—his eyes sparkled, and then he wept. He was not the only one.

Tata and Livia wept discreetly, and I was about to burst into tears just looking at their faces. I knew they saw me happy as I never had been before, but my leaving to America killed the joy of the moment for almost all of us. It felt like one eye was for happiness, and the other for regret.

Only Lyman seemed on his way to heaven.

~

Two days after the wedding, I surprised Lyman with a room for three days at the Royal Castle Pelisor at Sinaia. We spent days walking around and Lyman, the early bird, shot two more rolls of film with his camera.

When we got back to Bucharest, I had my interview at the American Embassy for my visa. However, the American consul wanted to speak with Lyman first. So, when it was my turn, I showed them my report from the police—I wasn't a criminal—and answered all the questions. I knew all of his daughters' names, their ages, where he worked, and the name of his town.

Eventually, they said I would get my visa in two hours. That was a quick deal since many Romanians had to wait weeks or even months before getting the temporary visa for America. When you leave everything in God's hands, I guess, that's the way things turn out.

Children of the Decree

Outside, Lyman jumped in the air a few times and we hugged and kissed. After a few more formalities, including a medical record, everything was sealed in an envelope at the embassy and ready to present to Immigration. Lyman bought me a one-way ticket to New York.

We went to visit my parents. Tata had waited for us at the train station, dressed in his best suit and tie. Mama waited for us on the bench in one of her elegant dresses. She smiled when she heard us talking on the road and came toward the gate. She said, "Matzer Vivi," to Lyman, and I hugged her tightly. I told her in Romanian how funny she was. We all laughed.

We entered their sparkling house. I inhaled the discreet smell of lavender Mama kept in the dressers and saw the impeccably ironed bedspreads on the bed and flowers in a vase in my childhood room. Mama served us several meals and appetizers, cakes, and drinks until Lyman said he couldn't eat anymore.

It was a warm atmosphere and they kept it calm. On one side of the table, my loving parents saw me in love and happy as never before. Next to me sat Lyman, the man from the United States, who would take me with him.

I was in the middle.

~

The night before the flight from Bucharest to America, I had to decide what to bring with me. The rule was that I could only carry two suitcases. I opened the dressers and picked two designer suits. From the two lines of Italian high-heeled shoes, I decided on four pairs. I wanted to take my cozy bathrobe, but it occupied too much space. I decided on some books, newspapers with my favorite investigations or articles, a copy of my book, pictures, and other pretty little things I made, wrote, or loved. I sat on the suitcases to close them and looked around my house like a stranger. My past was packed in two bags, ready for my new adventure in America.

The morning of my departure, I had the last coffee in my house with Sadee and George.

"I lost my kid," said George, sipping his coffee.

"I lost my best friend," Sadee continued with tears in her eyes.

Only Lyman kept track of the time. I locked the door and put the key in my purse, and left the second key in a flowerpot, ready for a colleague to move in.

Sadee and George accompanied us to the airport. Luckily, George kept talking and asking Lyman questions about cars, and I watched the view from the window.

One by one, we passed the places I knew, and I stared at my newspaper's building on the left, and soon, the television station on the right. Lyman gazed, knowing I was looking at the last picture of Bucharest I could carry. At the airport, I felt I had betrayed my family, friends, and country. Finally, Sadee asked me if I was scared.

"I trust Lyman," I told her. I couldn't say it aloud, but I also thought, *But I know I trust God more.*

Once on the plane, I wept. Flying over the Carpathians, I saw the mountains covered in green and the blossoming trees like snowflakes. "Everything will be alright," Lyman whispered. That was the last image of my country I took with me on my way to America on April 8th, 2001.

March 21, 2001. Bucharest.

Chapter Twenty-Three: Billy Boy

When the snow melted at the end of April, I went to the farm with Lyman for the first time. At first, I thought of him as a cowboy as in *Dallas*, but Lyman couldn't break a horse or ride a bronco. The cows were his pets, and I felt like he didn't have it in him to ever butcher them for meat. It reminded me of Tata's nonsense, when he bought a goat and made a pond for it that couldn't hold water.

The farm consisted of a runoff trailer with a well down a slope. A large area to the left was once a cemetery.

I stayed in the car with the music on and waited for him to feed the cows left loose in a fenced perimeter on the other side of the property. Something had happened, I guessed, since I'd been waiting for some time and had lost my patience. I stepped out and saw three cars on the right side of the gray trailer. I started my way to the trailer and followed the path Lyman left behind, and then I saw four more cars. And there were more hidden between the bushes and tall trees. In the end, I counted thirty-four old vehicles and a school bus. I couldn't believe my eyes. So, when Lyman saw me in the middle of the property, he hurried.

"Thirty-four cars. Why so many?"

"For fun," he said. "One day, I will fix these cars and get rich. Then I'll be a landlord and buy Perkins' farm."

Perkins was a neighbor who lived farther up Lyman's private road. He was Lyman's nightmare because he had the reputation of locking up escaped cows and selling them at auction.

Thinking of how much trouble the cows were, I was surprised to hear that Lyman never milked them.

"It's too much work. You have to milk them twice a day, and I can't do that," he said.

Even though he was serious, looking from one end of the property to the other, to the sky, and then to me, I couldn't help but laugh at his ambitions.

Children of the Decree

"We need to support the farmers, buy Vermont milk, cheese, and hay to help the local economy," he said.

"Why do you keep them?" I asked.

"They mow the lawn for free, plus they look nice, don't they? And they make shit, good for the lawn."

I couldn't understand why someone would spend so much money on hay during the winter and fortified grains all year round if they weren't going to use the cows for milk. Everyone in Obogeni raised cows for milk. I laughed, listening to Lyman's arguments, and then I understood: he is a true American.

~

One morning, on one of Lyman's days off in early May, he came in beaming with joy while was I painting the kitchen in the trailer.

"We have a baby boy!" he exclaimed.

Curious, I ran with Lyman behind the trailer and up the hill and then climbed over the barbed wire fence, my black shoes soaked by mud. And there he was, a little black creature lying next to its mother. I moved around the calf and touched him on the head. Two wide eyes tried to look at me.

"He's *too* beautiful. His name is Billy Boy," and I sang a song I had learned in elementary school:

"Oh, where have you been, Billy Boy, Billy Boy?
Oh, where have you been, charming Billy?"

Lyman joined in singing with wide eyes, and we danced around the little boy as if we were in heaven.

Billy Boy turned out to be a reason for me to go to the farm every day. I checked on him and watched him grow and get stronger. I also liked going to the farm because I came to understand how important that place was to Lyman. Except for his red Toyota, the farm was the only thing he had owned in his entire life: eleven acres of land in the middle of nowhere, an old trailer, thirty-four junk cars, six cows, and Billy Boy. There he looked and felt rich and powerful.

"Here, I am close to God. Do you feel that?" said Lyman one day.

We looked out at the view atop the hill. The lakes in the distance looked like drops of rain in the early morning. A mild, warm breeze coming from Canada and the smell of fresh grass reminded me how I used to get on my knees while watching my uncle's cows in Obogeni just to smell the grass. After so many years I felt at peace. I thought Lyman had brought me here to learn again how to be me. No more Bucharest fashion, no more hunting for stories for my show, no more investigations for the newspaper. Undeniably, I finally understood Coventry was his paradise as Obogeni had been mine.

I accepted that I was in the place where I needed to be. It was God's will, and it had happened.

~

With the coming of the late spring season, my life with Lyman became full of action. I read my Romanian books and worked on my novel while he was at work. My newfound confidence in crossing the border by myself was my main accomplishment. Not far from the American frontier there was a natural park with benches. I loved to write to my parents under the trees there, far away from the road and, sometimes, when the grass looked dried, I would sit under a pine tree. The fresh scent of twigs reminded me of the terpene alcohol I synthesized long ago in college while studying chemistry.

But it was the resin oil that triggered my memories from Obogeni. I wrote a letter to Mama Tanta, telling her about all I'd found in America. I knew she would read the letter again and again, before bedtime, storing it under the mattress.

The other place I loved was the Haskell Free Library. Like our apartment building, it sat half in the US and half in Canada. There were two computers that I could use to e-mail my sister Livia. Soon, I made a new friend, Janet Hartley, a Canadian who lived in the countryside outside Stanstead, Quebec, the place I visited with Jack and Joyce. Janet was in her late fifties but appeared to be much younger, with short, silver hair, a cheekboned, fair face, and emerald eyes. She was tall, well-shaped, and wore slacks. I loved her British accent.

"How are you, Dana?" she would ask me. Except for Lyman, she was the only one who could pronounce my Romanian name. We bonded and looked forward to sharing our stories.

The library had a Queen Ann style and looked like a palace. In the reading room, my favorite place, there was a black painted line like the sign out front—one side Canadian, one side American. A large table sat in the middle, straddling either side of the floor's black line. Janet told me that in the '70s when John Lennon had problems entering the United States, he met there with the other three Beatles—Lennon on the Canadian side, Paul McCartney, Ringo Starr, and George Harrison on the American side. No pictures of them hung on the walls, but the story intrigued me, and while Janet went to her desk, I researched it on the computer.

I found out that in March 1973, John Lennon received an order of deportation from the US to England, based on his conviction for possession of marijuana in 1968. It was possible for this secret meeting to happen, at the perfect geographical place between two borders, in a discreet library that may even hold other conspiracy secrets. Two years later, Lennon's expulsion order was overturned.

The journalist in me wasn't at all dead. Curious, I wanted to find the librarians from that time, to hear the whole story for myself, and to write it up for my old newspaper. That's what I did in Romania. The rumor mill worked for me, but there one had to know where to start and, when to walk away from the story before becoming the story oneself. If done right, then it becomes your story forever. But first, I needed to earn people's trust and to learn more English.

Something else disturbed me when Janet wanted a cigarette, and I went with her outside.

"I can't consider Canada my home," she said.

Her home was Britain, even though she hadn't been back in over fifty years. A hidden sadness appeared from the corner of my eye, and I buried it, keeping my eyes glued to the leaves of the trees. Memories rose one by one until Janet shook my shoulders.

"You're gone, my friend," and she stepped inside.

My cigarette burned out. I lit another one and gasped the first smoke and wondered if I would ever consider America my home.

~

The trees blossomed in May but only later did the wildflowers appear. I glowed when I discovered the violets that smelled the same as those that grew in Obogeni. I'd watched the flowers grow in Jack's garden and the trees bursting with leaves. In my mind, I'd found a piece of Dragasani, Tata's flower gardens and the fruit trees. I couldn't name all the flowers in English yet but was determined to learn those first: daffodils and hyacinths. I already knew the tulips and lilac.

Around that time, Lyman brought me to Burlington to order our wedding bands and to visit Adrian and his new family.

"Hey, guys! I asked Dana to take care of you, not to marry you," Adrian said when we stepped in, and we all laughed.

I understood then why Lyman fell in love with Romania. Adrian's new wife, Anda, displayed what Lyman considered the hot Romanian look—a light tan face and dark eyes and hair. It was that extreme of colors that made her face glow. We kissed on the cheeks—our Romanian tradition—and Lyman jumped in, kissing everyone, laughing to have the chance to kiss Anda in front of Adrian. Adrian didn't mind.

Adrian gave me a tour of his two-story house, and I saw Adina's son playing video games in one room. Happy to see him, I wanted to hug him and noticed he was taller than me. He was growing a mustache, and I found it funny. I asked him about school, and he said it was easy.

"Next summer, we'll go back to Romania," Lyman told them.

We ate Romanian sausage and learned there was a store in Williston that sold European food. I felt *home* for two hours and didn't want to leave my Romanian friends. Lyman let me enjoy the visit.

Later in the car Lyman said I had the same look as I did in Romania. But it was something else that brightened me—it was Lyman's look. We weren't yet in the same spirit we had in my country before we flew to New

York, but we were getting closer to covering the gap of my first two months in America.

That evening I cooked *mici*—skinless sausage, while Lyman read the newspaper in the kitchen. I kept Romania's smell in the house for as long as I could, playing my Romanian music and singing in two tones. I saved the dessert, *Eugenia*—rum and chocolate between shortbread. It was my favorite snack when I was a kid. I ate one piece, saving most for later. The taste of it brought me back in time, and I felt at home in my town for a moment.

By late May our vegetable garden was ready. I learned that in Vermont, farmers waited until after Memorial Day to plant their crops. I couldn't believe that Lyman took less than a few hours to have everything ready for the vegetables. All of the work looked effortless for him. He attached a plow to his John Deere tractor, went over the land twice, and then spread the manure while he sang and sipped his alcohol-free beer. I didn't even finish painting one wall in the trailer.

The next day, we headed to a community shelter to pick up seedlings.

"Making Vermont strong and healthy," Lyman chuckled when we walked out with two hundred tomato plants, cucumbers, eggplants, and green peppers. At the farm, Lyman said we should divide the work. He would take care of the corn, beans, cucumbers, and herbs, and I would care for the tomato plants. He saved the end of the parcel for potatoes. He would cut the big potatoes into halves, making sure each slice had a bud, and bury those at an equal distance.

"They will never grow, Lyman. They will dry out," I told him.

My mother used to plant potatoes in one piece, and indeed we harvested potatoes in the fall.

"Watch me, baby. There's nothing I can't do," he chuckled, rubbing his hands.

How could you cut the potatoes like you were frying them and expected them to grow into plants? I couldn't understand that part of Lyman's farming.

We spent the evening planting six rows of tomatoes, six rows of potatoes, and six rows of corn, each fifty meters long. I encountered a strange feeling working with Lyman. I saw myself at Dragasani, helping my mother in the garden, and loved the closeness of that thought.

The tomato plants received special treatment. Lyman made holes in the plastic foil, and I lodged all two hundred tomatoes seedlings in those. Lyman even embedded the bean seeds around the fence—Mama planted those in rows. *If nothing grows, no big deal. It must be another strange thing Americans do.*

On the right side of the driveway, Lyman buried pumpkin seeds. He made the holes with a stake and counted five seeds until he used the seeds from two packets.

He watered the rows with water from the well. Fifty meters by eighteen rows, a lot of walking. Then he walked the same route over again, placing black plastic over the seeds.

We returned to our apartment feeling good about a job well done but tired.

A few weeks later, green stems poked out from the ground: first radishes, and then the herbs. But my real job started as the potatoes budded and developed.

"We have to watch for the Colorado potato beetles. They will kill the plants," Lyman advised me. But, of course, I knew of the Colorado bugs, having seen them at Mama's.

He was right. I picked bugs every day, but the next day there were more. I became obsessed with the beetles and laughed many times when I thought about how much my life had changed. Just a few months ago, I was in my office at the television station editing segments for broadcast. Here I was now, in a bathing suit, killing Colorado bugs in a soda bottle with gas. Later, when I realized the paradox between my two lives, I laughed more, and more loudly as I realized there was no one to hear me in that wilderness.

~

Lyman surprised me again. He brought logs from the other side of the property with his John Deere tractor, and then he asked me to come with him. I jumped up behind him on the tractor, he pushed on the gas, and we went up to the top of the mountain where I saw some big stones along layout strings.

"This is where our new house will be!"

I saw that almost half of the foundation had already dried between berry bushes, pine trees, maples, and weeds. I tiptoed with Lyman around the foundation, holding hands. That was the moment I realized he was never afraid of the future.

He showed me the blueprints he kept in his pocket—three rooms downstairs and a kitchen and living room upstairs, so we could see the view from the top of the mountain between the tall birch trees and pines. I watched as he dragged logs from the other side of the hill with a chain until there was a considerable pile, ready to dry. He then attached a wagon behind the truck and appeared with loads of stones and other things he needed for the foundation. The only thing he would have to buy was cement.

"This place has everything, I'm telling you. By next spring, the house will be ready." He looked wistfully over the land.

After working for a few hours, Lyman went behind the trailer, disappeared into the berry bushes, and returned with two cold alcohol-free beers from the well.

"My well gives me the beer. What do you say about that?" He giggled and opened one bottle with his teeth.

He kissed me on the way to the tractor. I jumped on behind him, and we went to get more logs. I put the other cold beer bottle on his neck. He made a noise like he was hurt and drove faster. He chased me on the other side of the property like we played tag in the mountains. I screamed and climbed into a tree. There was that Obogeni feeling of freedom I knew and had found again after almost three decades.

We didn't bring any logs back, only played. That may have been the moment when I fell in love with Lyman for good.

~

With the warm weather came longer days and more work at the farm. It was almost summer when I finished painting and cleaning the trailer, but my job working outside had just started. I wished I had some ragged clothes and boots to protect me from snakes and other creatures that I was afraid of. I found some old clothes the girls had left behind. I looked like a Pokémon dressed in giant garments, but there was no one to see me. Sometimes, I tanned almost naked on top of a car.

Lyman owned a sawmill. It was a bulky Woodmizer style, perfect for the work we needed for the log cabin. We used a generator to power the machine. He explained the process. First, we cut the two by fours and let them dry. Then we'd get the flooring ready. After that, he said he could work inside during the winter and prepare the first-floor structure for the first snow. I loved the smell of fresh-cut wood, and the stack of logs was growing every day.

Lyman wanted to finish the foundation first and get the lumber ready. I didn't know much about concrete and cement for the foundation, but I carried water from the well. On sunny days, we poured concrete first and let it dry. Then we moved on to other projects, like bringing logs from the forest and stones for the fireplace. Digging for rocks in the mountain was my favorite activity. It felt like I'd searched for gold and found a treasure.

I called it scavenger hunting and found the clues by looking at the shape of the terrain covered in moss and ferns. If there were spaces between the spots, and the soil sounded hard when I kicked it with my shoes, I'd get a shovel and start digging from one side. Either granite or mica would separate into layers, and I cheered each piece I pulled out.

"Look! This one!" I'd scream to Lyman.

"I told you this land has everything!" he'd respond, taking a break from cutting trees.

We needed rocks for the foundation, granite for the garden walls, white stones for the fireplace, and trees for lumber and floors. And that land did indeed have everything we needed.

My job was designing the fireplace. First, we drew a plan, and once we decided the right place for my master project, I selected the widest rocks for the bottom. We used the top of the woodstove from the trailer and surrounded it with thermal bricks. I measured the surface, determined how many layers would go on top, and sorted the stones by colors and smooth edges. It felt like a puzzle using rocks, a new experience that made me giggle at times. But I was determined to complete my project and planned to take a picture at the end to send to Tata for appraisal.

"Our love is written in stones, Lyman. Here's my favorite one," I said, rubbing my palm over a large topaz-amethyst rock I placed as solid support on the right edge.

"One day, you'll tell your grandchildren the story of this fireplace, the story of each stone you handpicked on this property," he said. Still, I guessed we both left our thoughts to travel in space and time, as if we were invincible, as if no one, but no one, could destroy the legacy we began cementing together.

During this work my mind wandered back and forth between countries and places, recalling people I missed, and things I wished I had done or said. Part of me lived in the past, bringing up memories I treasured. The future looked promising and, every day, the bond between Lyman and me grew stronger. I imagined myself reading in front of the fireplace, discreet lights around the living room, and I was thinking of having a child for the first time. I shared my idea with Lyman.

He said we should keep the upstairs for our child's bedroom.

"Can you imagine? Our child would see all this wildlife and animals and grow up strong," he said.

But before the child, we needed our space.

"We'll do it together, you and me. People hire contractors, but we'll finish our log cabin by ourselves. Then we can tell our child we did it. Can you imagine that?" Lyman said.

His enthusiasm was contagious, and we kept working on our dream house.

Sometimes, I saw Lyman watching me. I probably looked concerned sorting rocks, measuring two times before deciding on the next layer. As a perfectionist, I had to complete the pattern I'd design, and sometimes it wasn't easy. Either the size, color, or the surface of the rock wouldn't let me make progress.

Sometimes I puzzled. *This is the easiest thing I've done,* I thought, considering some of the tough college exams I took and what I'd experienced as a journalist. Now, if the rock didn't fit, I could find another one behind our mountain. In the past, one possible mistake meant ruining my career, or worse. Now I didn't want to imagine what would have happened to me if I was still in Romania.

On Lyman's days off, we stayed longer at the farm, and we'd grab something to eat and burn a fire with the leftover wood. The truth was that I loved the sunsets over the hills and mountains, loved watching the last rays disappear under the sky and on to the other side of the Earth. Every evening in America marked a sunrise in Romania, and I wondered if any of my family members looked at it at the same time as me. Sometimes I cried.

With Billy Boy at the farm.

Maria D. Holderman
Chapter Twenty-Four: When It Rains First

My first fall in Vermont was astonishing, and I could start to see more clearly than ever where my life was taking me. I had published two stories in the *Barton Chronicle*, gave a couple of interviews about my work as a journalist, started college to improve my English, and got a job teaching at the local high school. As I watched the maple trees turning colors, I thought I had never seen such an original palette of red, orange, and yellow in my life. No wonder people from all over the country came here during the foliage season to take pictures. They parked on the side of the roads with cameras in hand when Lyman brought me to Stowe.

On one of those days, Lyman brought me a driver education booklet. He said I needed a driver's license to go to my classes and to become *independent*, as I liked to say. That was a hard thing to do. First, I found the language in that book ambiguous. I had never driven in my life and had no clue what the technical words meant—clutch, brakes, ignition, acceleration. I could identify flowers and mushrooms, wild berries, trees, and birds, but never in my life had I been interested in cars. However, Lyman helped me understand some of the theory and quizzed me before the test.

He was disappointed when I didn't pass the first time. I told him about the friendly clerk who recognized my accent and went over the questions that I missed with me. I still remember one. "When is the hardest time to drive?" The answer was, "when it first rains." But the question and the answer puzzled me for some time.

I memorized the answer, and, on the second try, I recognized the question about the rain and passed the test. But Lyman's Toyota had a standard transmission, and the clutch and the brake looked the same to me. I couldn't remember which one was which, or how to press on them, and when to release my foot. I tried three more times and gave up, crying, "I can't do it!"

"I'll fix up the black Mercedes for you. It's automatic, so you don't have to drive a standard."

He started work on the Mercedes as soon as we got to the farm.

"I'll get something from the older cars and make you the best car," he said.

I could see why he had all those cars. You never know when one piece of junk could replace another.

~

On the weekends, I went with Lyman to the farm. I couldn't help much around the farm during the days and I missed it. When I called out Billy Boy, a bull now, he would jump on his feet and come closer to the fence. I fed him right from my hand. While I was in school during the day, Lyman picked the vegetables. He brought big baskets to his friends at work and to Jack and Joyce. We made eighteen jars of ketchup with fresh tomatoes, the first time doing this job without Mama and my sister Livia.

It surprised me how much value Lyman's garden had to people. Jack and Joyce loved to receive free, fresh vegetables in massive quantities. I felt embarrassed to ask them to take more since we couldn't cook it all, but they never said no, and Jack preserved everything we gave him. I was happy, and Jack and Joyce were delighted, and that was all that mattered.

~

It had not even been a week into my new job when the astronomy teacher opened the door unexpectedly and told the other teacher to turn on the television. It was September 11, 2001, and I was supposed to help one of my students in that class. Instead, CNN showed several images of the Twin Towers collapsing. We learned a plane had hit one of the buildings, and then another plane hit the second building. During that time, a third plane crashed into the Pentagon. Soon, all was dust and debris.

On that day there were no classes.

"Did you hear what happened?" I asked Lyman when he picked me up after school.

"Yes, I heard on the radio going to the farm. I didn't feel well. I just checked on the cows and came back to sleep, but I couldn't. I wanted to come to school and get you home earlier, but I knew you would be upset missing work for no reason." Indeed, his face was pale.

"Are you sick, Lyman?"

He paused, taking my hand in his, and quietly said, "I can't believe what just happened."

I wished we had cable television in Derby Line. In the following days, I listened to the news at the library while I waited for Roy, the student I tutored, but there were many words I didn't know, and I didn't understand the whole story. As a journalist, I needed details. It was easy, however, to get the sense that it was pretty bad.

America was in tears, and so was the world.

~

Lyman didn't believe in cell phones or the Internet at home. "I am around computers at work and need none at home," he had said to me many times before. By the end of the month, Lyman agreed to allow his daughter, Pearl, to move to her mother's. A strange silence conquered the apartment, and only the sound of the river reminded me where I was during the times when I fought back memories of home.

I'd sensed my parents got accustomed to the idea I was away, and while I called them every week, the distance didn't matter much. By then, Tata got his diagnosis—ALS. I was glad it wasn't cancer, although this disease was deadly. It had no cure.

Looking back at that time, Tata was the most unselfish person you could meet. Nothing made him happier, even dealing with his disease, than knowing I was going to college and getting a school job as a paraprofessional. It paid $7.54 per hour, but I had my own health insurance.

"We all have teaching genes in our DNA," he said when I gave my parents the news.

I promised my parents I'd come home for Christmas. I already had a debit card where I deposited my first paycheck, and the money was growing. Lyman looked for a good deal on the tickets and bought them when the price was in our range.

I also contacted my lawyers in Bucharest about the case with the orphanage director who'd sued me, and the illegal adoption scheme I stopped in Romania.

"You won! Did you know they put a ban on all the adoptions right after you left?" the lawyer said when he first heard my voice. In the back of my mind, I was concerned about this case and didn't want the judges to believe leaving Romania was an indication of weakness in this case. Romania was corrupt, and so were some judges. Winning this case was like winning the lottery. Relieved to put the matter behind me, I concentrated on my career and Lyman. It was then we decided to have a child.

Around the middle of November, I knew I was pregnant and couldn't wait to tell Mama.

"You'll be a mother now. You'll be a great mother," she said, crying.

My body's response to the pregnancy was clear: nausea, tiredness, and aversion to smell. Lyman took me to the gynecologist to register me as a new patient and decide on a doctor. We filled out all the forms, and the receptionist scheduled my first visit on the last day of November, right after school.

It was a foggy day as I waited for Lyman to pick me up from school a day before my first appointment. He was late. I crossed the street and walked down the hill, and then I saw his red car making the turn at the intersection and waited there for him to stop and pick me up. He gave me a quick kiss.

"A cop just stopped me. I didn't have my safety belt on, but he didn't give me a ticket." He looked like a farmer in blue jeans and a T-shirt under his brown coat. His hands were rough and dirty, and his face was pale from little sleep. A bandage on his hand looked soaked with sweat and dirt.

"I did a lot. The sidings for the floor are done and brought the lumber to let it dry over the winter," he said. "The house will be done next year, Dana." Then, holding my hand, he asked about my day.

"I was tired, almost fell asleep in science class, but I managed to work on a paper due tomorrow for my English class."

Something else crossed my mind and I wanted to tell him.

"I had a strange dream last night," I said. "I dreamt there were snakes in our bedroom. I counted seven."

Lyman thought for a minute. "Dreams, baby."

He told me he'd spent part of the morning looking for the cows and had found them a mile away in someone's woods.

"Billy Boy acted crazy. He stayed in front of the car and didn't move. I tried to move him twice, but he kept sticking his head on me like he wanted to knock me down. Maybe he ate poison mushrooms."

At home, he made cheeseburgers and asked if I could take the bus to work the following day for my English class. My class started at 8:00 AM, and Lyman wouldn't be home until around 8:30 AM since one of the carpooling guys was working overtime. I agreed to take the bus, but that he'd pick me up for the doctor's appointment. Then we talked about baby names.

"If I have a boy, I'll call him Lyman Roger Dezotell II," I said.

"I don't even want to think how happy I'll be with a boy. Maybe you are the one who could bless me with a son. But I think the name is confusing. We'll think about it," he said.

"If God loves you because I know He loves me, you'll have a boy."

"What about a Romanian name?" he asked. "Something like Andrew, for example. How do you say it in Romanian?"

"Andrei. But people will have a hard time calling him this name."

"Maybe like your father, John." Lyman chuckled.

"Maybe," I responded.

"Well, we'll wait and see, okay? We have plenty of time to think about the name."

The smell of autumn entered the kitchen, fresh and sweet like the leaves of the trees. Ready to leave for work, and we hugged and kissed at the door, and Lyman made his way down the stairs. Halfway down, Lyman called me.

"Give me one more hug." I walked down the stairs, and we hugged and kissed one more time. As I climbed back up to the apartment, he turned around again.

"Don't get wet when you walk to the library. It started raining," he said. He ran down the stairs, looking at his watch, and zipped his coat.

~

I was sleeping when I heard knocking at the door. It was about 10:30 PM, and I tried to look through the little glass knob, but I saw no one. But the knock repeated.

"Who's there?"

"It's me, Jack," I heard. I didn't recognize his voice.

"You can't be Jack," I said. "Who's there?" I asked again.

"Jack, tell her to come downstairs." I heard Joyce's voice like an echo from somewhere.

Then I opened the door. Jack's face looked like he was holding either a laugh or a cry.

"The father called. Lyman had an accident."

I couldn't understand if Lyman or his father had the accident. I took a while to realize what he was saying.

"How's Lyman?"

"The father said he's dead."

"The father? Lyman's father?"

"No. Lyman."

"You joke. Stop this stupid joke. He can't be dead! We have a doctor's appointment tomorrow. He left for work. Look, here are his glasses."

I argued with him, showing him Lyman's glasses, which he'd left on a dresser in the lobby.

"Danielle, the police are on the way to talk to you. They will explain everything to you. Please, come here now," Joyce said from the bottom of the stairs.

If someone had struck me on the head with a hammer, I would have been more coherent than I was at that moment.

"We called Janet to come here to stay with you," Joyce said.

I couldn't see my slippers. Just when I put my winter boots on, I heard the noise of the front entrance. A police officer, a woman, talked to Joyce, who pointed to me. As I came down the stairs, my unzipped boots made my walk sloppy, but I didn't pay attention until I had to crawl on my knees all the way down.

"Danielle, stay there!" Joyce screamed. She climbed the stairs and supported me from under the shoulders, helping me take one step. The woman waited at the bottom of the stairs. I knew there were seventeen stairs in all. I used to count them when there was no light on in the lobby.

"I am an officer from the state police. Mrs. Dezotell, do you understand me? I know you are an immigrant," she said. She looked into my eyes.

"Yes, I understand."

"We couldn't find your address—this address—since Lyman's driver's license is in Coventry. And you have no phone. No one at IBM knew where you two live. One of Lyman's friends said he heard him say you go to the church here, in Derby Line with your neighbors downstairs. So, we got in contact with the father."

"Tata?" I asked. "Or Lyman's father?"

They exchanged some strange looks.

"Father Royer, the priest," answered Jack. The officer turned to Joyce, whispered a few words, and then she faced me again.

"Lyman, Dino, and Kevin had an accident going to work at IBM, somewhere in Johnson. A young man crashed into their car, and all three are dead. Do you understand that?"

She spoke slowly. When I finally understood what she was trying to say, I collapsed. Janet was next to me when I regained consciousness, sitting on her knees in the hallway and rubbing my face.

"Poor girl. Oh, Lord," she said.

I remember nothing, but the officer told my friends the state police had called Lyman's parents to let them know about the accident. Janet brought me back to my apartment, helping to hold me up.

"Stairs, Dana, two more," a voice said.

The newspaper Lyman had read that day, and his spare reading glasses, were still sitting on the kitchen table. I told Janet it couldn't be real. She couldn't stop saying, "Oh, Lord. I am afraid it is real, Dana."

I knew nothing about death. I remembered when, as a child, I saw my great-grandfather in the coffin, the first and the last time I saw a dead person up close. Then I recalled how people in Dragasani brought their loved ones to the cemetery behind the train tracks. They used a truck decorated in black fabric, and a picture of the person hung next to the head of the dead. The coffin was always open, but I was too small to see what was inside.

Sometimes, I could see the white fabric and shoes. Other times, I could see a cross over the hands. I never saw the face. With that thought in mind, I took the framed wedding picture from our bedroom, placed it on the hallway table, found a scented candle, and lit it. Janet watched me and said it was a good idea.

I looked for scissors but couldn't find any. Janet found them, but she didn't give them to me until she understood I wanted her to cut my face from the picture. "What is dead cannot come to life again," said Janet to herself. And she added again, "Oh, Lord."

We stayed in the bedroom, and the silence became unbearable. I was afraid Janet would leave me alone. I dreamed with open eyes.

Two hours later, I heard another knock at the door. "We need to take you with us for the funeral," Lyman's adopted daughter, Beth, said. His parents decided to have him buried around their area, and I was told to bring some clothes with me for a few days. She helped me pack the clothes and asked me to choose a set for Lyman. I opened the walk-in closet and saw Lyman's suit from our wedding, the blue chrysanthemum pinned next to his pocket, right where his heart would be if he had the suit on.

In the middle of the night of November 29, 2001, my life collapsed.

~

It had stopped raining, and the night was cold. A sharp wind blasted the leaves across the parking lot. The full moon illuminated the cars and the wind howled. *What am I doing here? Am I hallucinating?*

I peeked at Jack's window, thinking it was irrational for me to be in the parking lot at that time. I saw Jack and Joyce coming. They hugged me, and my body cringed. "So, it's true," I heard them say.

I grabbed Janet's hand when one of them opened the trunk for my luggage. "I'm not going anywhere. I have my English class in the morning. Lyman is bringing me to the doctor after school."

"Oh, Dana," sighed Janet.

I asked Jack to let my new friend from school, Pam Wade, know why I wouldn't be there to ride with her to school on Monday. She was giving me a ride on weekdays when Lyman got home late.

It was Jack who got me in the backseat.

"Danielle, you have a baby. You need to take care of yourself," either Jack or Joyce said.

Where am I going?

I'll wait for the funeral and decide what to do after.

My head was hurting, my brain was on fire, and my whole body shivered. For five days, the denial of my husband's death took all of the shapes described in books. And while the family planned the funeral and made phone calls, I sat on the sofa, half-dead myself, refusing to eat and speak. At one point, I thought I miscarried, and for a moment, I wanted it to happen. Maybe the pain would be easier on me. But I didn't lose the child, and then I asked God for forgiveness and forced myself to eat a sandwich because I wanted to survive.

The moment I received Lyman's belongings I understood he wouldn't be coming home to me. I was sitting on the floor next to the entrance door at Beth's. Her future mother-in-law, a kind woman with a lot of energy and a straight mind in those circumstances, tried to make the situation fast and easy for me. She had an empty trash bag, the ones people in Vermont use for leaves, for the things I didn't want to keep. In fact, I was the wife and had to go through the bag from the morgue.

She took out Lyman's black leather jacket first, cut it into pieces along the sleeves.

"You don't need that, Dana," she said and took the jacket from my hands and put it in the bag. The black corduroy slacks he had worn to the airport in Bucharest were next, each leg cut in half alongside. Then she tried to move even faster, putting them into the trash bag. My heart sank when I saw the white shirt and his sneakers with bloodstains on them. I kept only his belt and watch. I saw her outside, carrying the trash bag to a dumpster.

I'll never see Lyman again. I lost consciousness.

A few hours later, Beth handed me the phone. It was my cousin Nae. Surprised to hear him, I spoke in Romanian, everyone watching me as if I was an alien.

"How did you know? I haven't even told Livia yet."

"From Sadee. And Sadee from Adina. And Adina from Adrian. From IBM. I checked the newspapers and saw Lyman's name."

He told me that I could move to Seattle and have the baby there—my choice.

"We will survive, Passy. I know how hard it is."

His voice emerged from my childhood, the turning wheel of life into death.

"Let me tell Livia, please. Don't call Mama Tanta or your parents. Don't tell anyone. Let me do it."

He promised it to me. I bit my lips, sobbed, and hung up.

~

On the morning of the funeral, I woke up smiling from my dream, feeling a real kiss on my face. It didn't feel like a sting but a gentle touch. I wanted to keep that moment longer, but it disappeared, and I couldn't get the flare back even with my eyes closed. First, it ached. Then it stung me as I remembered my mission, which was to say goodbye to Lyman and to go back to Derby Line without him. My body throbbed and tears rolled again.

Beth said we'd go to the funeral home for a wake. I wore the same black pants and a blouse with a black coat as at our ceremony at the town hall in Bucharest, and a hat I'd bought at the mall with Beth.

"Open casket for the family," she added. Then she opened the door for me. I walked out, carrying my luggage, and saw a half of the sky covered in dark gray clouds. My heart mimicked the darkness—I had nothing to look forward to.

The funeral director waited for me and said, "Mrs. Dezotell, I know you are pregnant. Lyman doesn't look well, although we did a lot of cosmetics. I don't think you should see the body. Please, have someone else put it in if you have anything to leave, such as a letter or anything. "

The formaldehyde smell almost knocked me off my feet. So many people were in the room, all of them dressed in dark colors. My mouth dried, and I spotted a water fountain in the hallway opposite my chair.

After a few sips, I peeked over at the coffin. Lyman looked like he was asleep in profile, and I saw his mother taking pictures of him.

Then the funeral director asked me if I wanted to leave the wedding band with Lyman or wanted it back. I said, "With Lyman, please."

He doesn't even have shoes on, I realized.

We were in the first car behind the sizeable black one bringing Lyman to his grave. His last trip. His last time before getting buried in the darkness of the earth.

As we got closer to the Hope Cemetery in Barre, I felt colder and held my breath, praying I wouldn't collapse again. The sky darkened and my ears drummed. My teeth shuddered and I couldn't control my body. Even my seat vibrated with me.

The car turned onto the cemetery's alley and then it made a left.

I saw an immense crowd of people. Beth said, "Gee, all Dad's ex-girlfriends are here." When I got out of the car, I saw Pam Wade and Gwen Bailey, my colleagues from school. Then Jack, Joyce, Janet, and Lyman's friends from IBM, including Jim, the guy who brought us from the airport when I arrived in America. They all told me the same words—if I needed anything, to let them know.

The funeral director and Beth helped hold me steady in the seat by the grave. I don't remember what the preacher or funeral director said. Someone put a long black coat over my shoulders, but my body felt cold regardless. I was told to put a rose on the casket, and Beth helped me walk to the blue coffin. I touched the casket and said, "Goodbye, Lyman."

Several snowflakes melted on me. I stood next to the casket and watched the snowfall for just a few seconds. I looked to the sky and saw a bright spot above. I knew the snow was Lyman's way to say goodbye. When

Children of the Decree

I went back to my seat, the snow stopped. I prayed, my eyes closed, asking God to guide Lyman and me, and more tears rolled on my cold face.

Soon, Beth walked me to her car to grab my suitcase from the trunk and moved it into Pam's. In her van on the way back to Derby Line, all of my friends kept quiet. I still remember that silence.

Janet said I could spend the night at her place in Canada, and I believed they planned it. I don't remember anything else but Janet's cold bedroom. She didn't want any heat upstairs and she had a broken window. I didn't want to sleep alone and felt warm water bottles under the bedcovers. I remembered how Livia and I used the same method when we were young.

When I woke up, it was mid-morning. I found Janet downstairs in the kitchen reading a book. She made me breakfast and said we would go to Derby Line. She had to work the afternoon shift, and I had to go back to my apartment. In Derby Line, at the library, I e-mailed Livia about what had happened. I still remember the lines: "Lyman died last Thursday and was buried this Wednesday."

I asked her to understand that I needed time to think and told her to take care of our parents. They needed Livia to help them grieve. As I wrote the last sentence, my body shivered as I pictured my parents' reaction when they received the news.

I said goodbye to Janet and grabbed my suitcase, my mind on my parents, and walked to the Canadian border with tears jammed in my throat. Then crossing the bridge, I blanked. *Where am I going?*

I opened the apartment door and, after six days away, I felt like a thief. I left the suitcase in the hallway, the door wide open, and walked around the apartment. It looked like a different place, from past times. *I don't belong here!* I was a stranger.

A few seconds later, I knocked on Jack's door. They expected me. While they watched the *Wheel of Fortune* show I went into the sunroom, and Jack brought me a blanket.

I asked my old friends if I could sleep on their sofa, in the living room. "Of course," Joyce said. Then Jack asked me about my plans.

"Still going to Romania for Christmas?"

I pulled the plane tickets from my purse and laid them down on the table in the sunroom. Then, sipping a coffee, I stared at the tickets and thought.

The answer to that question came later.

"No. I'll cancel the trip until I'm sure what I want to do."

So, I stayed, knowing the pain would take over my head again and again but, at that moment, I was willing to take the pain and pray like Maita Maria, on my knees, that my child would help me heal.

That would be my only way to move forward.

Three days later, I'd turn thirty-four. My soul seemed old and tried in battles I owned. Some contests I wanted to remember and some I tried to forget. But as I finished the coffee in Jack's sunroom, I remembered my life with Lyman. The first e-mail. The first kiss. The ultimate and unfinished dream.

How am I supposed to fight the memories and care for my pregnancy alone?

For a moment, I knew I could handle it all, but soon, I wasn't sure. I had to start from a point, but which one?

From the night when I decided to stay in America, the last thing I remember was sleeping in Lyman's T-shirt I grabbed from upstairs and how Adina, Sadee, Juan, and Bogdan appeared in my mind. We were dancing after watching Juan's show.

Then I heard a voice. "You can dance Lyman's death. But keep dancing your life."

My life.

Children of the Decree

Epilogue

The international adoption of Romanian orphans stopped two months after I left for America. It would take another four years for a new law to be passed that protects children. The director of the orphanage appealed the court's ruling all the way to the Supreme Court of Romania but lost.

The last smuggled children from the orphanage in Bucharest were found in Italy, part of a child trafficking ring.

Over the years, several pedophiles (including from America) have been arrested in Bucharest.

No one knows the number of children trafficked, but we know some found homes overseas. You can read about some success stories on their Facebook group, The UnForgotten Children of Romania.

In October 2002, the Romanian government pardoned 2,629 incarcerated people for crimes similar to those of Simona Gologan's. At the same time, new legislation was put in place to curb prison sentences for petty theft and minor infractions. Community service is now a sentencing option for judges in many courts.

A few months after I aired the Kurds' situation, the Romanian government allowed them to apply for asylum and granted them housing, as well as dedicated resources to more detainee centers.

National daily became named *7 Plus*, and then *National* again. All of the online archive disappeared, and Voicu left the newspaper that he had founded for a job at the same television station where I had worked. Voicu died at fifty-nine years old, shortly preceded by Horia Tabacu.

I wish I'd found out how my grandfather on Tata's side had died before Maita Maria and Tata passed away. I wanted them to have closure and to know precisely that my grandfather died just two days after he embarked on the train that would bring him and his comrades to Ukraine. On the morning of August 28, 1941, the Fifth Division Infantry attacked Vigoda-Odessa and advanced 2.5 Km South of Vigoda train station. The battalion was decimated, suffered 1601 lives losses, and was buried on a train station's field. My grandfather's name appears on position 1541: Vasile Ioan. Soon after the attack, he was reported *Missing in Action*.

In June 2002, I gave birth to a boy I named after his father.

I have kept these secrets for so long that at times I fear I may have almost forgotten the details. But twenty years after I left my country, the former Minister of Justice Valeriu Stoica, returned my phone call. "I remember you. I remember EVERYTHING."

His message: If you really want to make a change, no one can stop you. It felt good to hear from him.

ABOUT THE AUTHOR

From 1997 to 2001, Maria was the "Diane Sawyer of Romania" (pen name *Dana Achim*.) Before leaving her native country for the United States on a one-way ticket, she was a bestselling author and an investigative reporter for the *National Daily* in Bucharest. The Minister of Justice during that time said Maria could change the world.

Through over 1,000 published investigations and articles and over fifty documentaries and investigations produced for Romania's *Antena 1 TV* station, Maria advocated for human rights and social reform. She was the first reporter to delve into Romania's international adoptions, exposing the scandal of the underground trafficking of children. Her press campaigns forced nationwide reform, ultimately abolishing international adoptions until new laws took effect four years following her departure.

In America, Maria's passion to attain her best has gone beyond journalism and writing. She earned a master's degree in education and taught high school science in Vermont. A recipient of numerous awards, Maria was a 2011 Vermont Teacher of the Year Finalist, the Vermont Academy of Science and Engineering (VASE) Outstanding Science Teacher of the Year for High School in 2014, and the recipient of the Vermont Joseph B. Whitehead Educator of Distinction Award in 2014.

Maria remarried in 2014 and lives with her husband and two children in upstate New York, where she teaches part-time and continues to produce nonfiction inspired by her history.

www.ingramcontent.com/pod-product-compliance
Lightning Source LLC
Chambersburg PA
CBHW020224170426
43201CB00007B/309